MIDSHIPMAN

IN GRAY

SELECTIONS FROM
RECOLLECTIONS
OF A REBEL REEFER

JAMES MORRIS MORGAN

MIDSHIPMAN IN GRAY

SELECTIONS FROM
RECOLLECTIONS
OF A REBEL REEFER

by
James Morris Morgan

Edited and Annotated
R. Thomas Campbell

Burd Street Press

Originally published April 1917 by Houghton Mifflin, Boston

Revised edition © 1997 by R. Thomas Campbell

Photographs are from James Morris Morgan, *Recollections of a Rebel Reefer* (Boston: Houghton Mifflin, 1917).

This Burd Street Press publication
was printed by
Beidel Printing House, Inc.
63 West Burd Street
Shippensburg, PA 17257-0152 USA

In respect for the scholarship contained herein, the acid-free paper used in this book meets the guidelines for permanence and durability of the Committee on Production Guidelines for Book Longevity of the Council on Library Resources.

For a complete list of available publications
please write
Burd Street Press
Division of White Mane Publishing Company, Inc.
P.O. Box 152
Shippensburg, PA 17257-0152 USA

Library of Congress Cataloging-in-Publication Data

Morgan, James Morris, 1845–1928.
    [Recollections of a Rebel reefer. Selections]
    Midshipman in gray : selections from Recollections of a Rebel
reefer / by James Morris Morgan ; edited and annotated by R. Thomas
Campbell.
        p.   cm.
    Includes index.
    ISBN 1-57249-061-6 (alk. paper)
    1. Morgan, James Morris, 1845–1928. 2. Georgia (Confederate
cruiser) 3. Midshipmen--Confederate States of America--Biography.
4. United States--History--Civil War, 1861–1865--Personal
narratives, Confederate. 5. United States--History--Civil War,
1861–1865--Naval operations. 6. Confederate States of America.
Navy--Biography. I. Campbell, R. Thomas, 1937–   . II. Title.
E599.G45M67   1997
973.7'58--dc21   97-23402
                                                                 CIP

TO
MY BELOVED WIFE
FRANCIS F. MORGAN
BUT FOR WHOSE DEVOTION AND TENDER NURSING OF ME
THROUGH WEARY YEARS OF ILL HEALTH THESE
"RECOLLECTIONS"
WOULD NEVER HAVE BEEN
WRITTEN

Contents

President Jefferson Davis and Judah P. Benjamin—Tender services and sword to the Confederacy—Declined with thanks—The "Marseillaise."

Introduction

James Morris Morgan was a product child of the old South. Born on March 10, 1845, in New Orleans, and reared on the sprawling plantations that bordered the great Mississippi River, Morgan grew to adolescence with a deep sentimental attachment to the misty bayous of his native Louisiana. This was his country, his home, his people, and he would never forget from whence he came. Jimmy Morgan, (even to this day his family refers to him as "Jimmy") was the son of Thomas Gibbes Morgan and Sarah Hunt Fowler. Jimmy had four sisters and three brothers, and the family was extremely close.

At the tender age of fifteen, Morgan was appointed a midshipman of cadets at the U.S. Naval Academy at Annapolis, Maryland. With the war clouds forming over the nation, however, it was not long before the young lad found himself on a train for Montgomery, Alabama, capital of the newly formed Confederate States of America. Assigned to the gunboat CSS *McRae* at New Orleans, Morgan had ample opportunities to visit with the family prior to Farragut's attack on the Crescent City. His sister, Sarah, writing in her diary, remembered one of these visits:

April 12th (1862) *Day before yesterday, just about this time of evening, as I came from the graveyard, Jimmy unexpectedly came in. Ever since the 12th of February he has been waiting on the Yankee's pleasure in the Mississippi, at all places below Columbus, and having been under fire for thirteen days at Tiptonville, Island No. 10 having surrendered Monday night, and Commodore Hollins thinking it high time to take possession of the ironclad* ram at *New Orleans, and give them a small party below the forts, he carried off his little aide from the McRae Tuesday morning, and left him here Thursday evening, to our infinite delight, for we felt as though we would never again see our dear little Jimmy. He has grown so tall and stout that it is really astonishing, considering the short time he has been away. As to handsome!—well! perhaps that is only a weakness of the family!*

What a dear little rascal he is! Such affectionate, winning ways! Such a baby to mother and his sisters, such a noble little man to all the world besides![1]

Jimmy is everything that a boy should be, and fit for nothing in the world but an officer. He is such a brave devil-may-care, generous boy; likes fun, frolic and danger so well that he would make a jolly old tar. As it is, he is a perfect duck of a Midshipman. Yesterday to our great distress, he jumped up from dinner, and declared he must go to the city on the very next boat. Commodore Hollins would need him, he must be at his post, etc., and in twenty minutes he was off, the rascal, before we could believe he had been here at all.[2]

Jimmy Morgan escaped injury and capture at the Battle of New Orleans, and later, after being befriended by the famous financier, George Alfred Trenholm, sailed for Europe. In England he was assigned to the newly commissioned commerce raider CSS *Georgia*, under the command of William L. Maury. Morgan spent over a year on the *Georgia*, and when her cruise was finished, he returned to the Confederacy to take up his studies at the Confederate Naval Academy. As a Passed Midshipman he was part of the student body that was detailed to escort the Davis family during their flight from Richmond at the close of the war.

Later, as the world was exploding into another Great War, Morgan, at the urging of his children, agreed to write his "recollections" of those momentous years of his life. We are extremely fortunate that he did.

The editor wishes to thank Mrs. Morgan P. Goldbarth of Austin, Texas, Morgan's great granddaughter, for the invaluable information and insight into "Jimmy" Morgan which she provided.

Here then, to the end of the War Between the States, is Jimmy Morgan's "Recollections of a Rebel Reefer."[3]

R. Thomas Campbell,
May 1997

Preface

Said a writer in *Blackwood's Magazine* many years ago: "None but kings and egoists are fit to inscribe the record of their lives. The king knows himself to be the first of his world, and what to the king is knowledge is to the egoist a confident belief. Pride, then, personal and overwhelming, is essential to the perfect autobiography; and if the pride be simple enough, we may perhaps dispose with the other great quality—self-knowledge. For though it obscure reality, pride can create a phantom at once improving and consistent. *Nequidquam sapit qui sibi non sapit*, wrote Cicero."

The following account of some of my experiences in life will have at least the merit of simplicity, and, the story being about myself, I ask indulgence for its unavoidable egotism.

It has been said that "adventures come only to him who seeks them," but I am doubtful of the correctness of this adage, for I can truthfully say that I had as little to do with the shaping of my course in life as has an empty bottle thrown overboard in mid-ocean. I spent the most important years of a boy's life, those between fifteen and nineteen, so far as education and the formation of character are concerned, tied to a sword and in the midst of a most cruel war, and when peace came I was wafted hither and thither, the sport of the fickle winds varying fortune; and, having "sailed 'neath alien skies and trod the desert path," naturally I imagine that I have met with some adventures out of the usual run of the average schoolboy's experiences, and if I have written some of them down, it has been with the laudable desire of amusing other people rather than personal vanity or desire for notoriety.

The novelty is another excuse for this volume. The shelves of libraries are filled with "Recollections," and "Reminiscences," and "Services Afloat," written by admirals, but whoever before saw the memoirs of a "Reefer," unless it was those of "Mr. Midshipman Easy," and he, being a mythical person, of course did not write them himself. I make no apology for its many faults and shortcomings, for were it told in a scholarly manner and in the rounded periods and faultless language of a Macaulay, it would not be the story of a midshipman who had few opportunities of acquiring an education, and neglected the few which came in his way, as the story will make apparent to the dullest landlubber.

If I have omitted to mention one or two affairs of honor in which I took part, either as principal or second, I trust that my doing so will not be regarded as evidence that I have any doubt as to the correctness of my attitude on those occasions. I do not mention that because I have passed the threescore years and ten and do not wish to offend the sensibilities of the living, or to reawaken old feuds in a State where one of my daughters and my grandchildren live.

If I mention an unfortunate shooting affair which occurred in Columbia, South Carolina, it is because the bloody tragedy became a matter of record in the courts. Other personal encounters are recounted because they had an amusing side to them.

J. M. M.

One

"Billy Bowlegs"—The Choctaws—Blowing up and burning of the steamboat *Princess*—Charloe and Katish—Throwing the Lasso—Buck-jumpers.

Born in the city of New Orleans, Louisiana, in 1845—the youngest of nine children—my parents indulged me as only the youngest of a large family or an only child is spoiled, and they were very ably assisted by my elder brothers and sisters. My old black nurse, Katish, played no unimportant role in the coddling process.

According to the family legends I commenced my adventures at an early age. When I could barely toddle I strayed away from the house and was found stranded in a gutter and brought home in a most sorry plight. In this day, when it is considered the proper thing to boast of one's lowly beginnings, that story ought at least to have secured me a seat in the halls of Congress, but it didn't. Another thriller told me of the adventures of my babyhood was that once, when I was playing near a pond at Pascagoula, a huge alligator was seen slowly creeping toward me when my French governess rushed to the rescue and bravely bore me out of danger. She was ever afterwards regarded as a heroine.

When I was five years of age, my father, Judge Thomas Gibbes Morgan, with his family returned to Baton Rouge, where he had lived prior to his having been appointed Collector of the Port of New Orleans. Baton Rouge at that time was a pretty little town of some three thousand inhabitants. It is situated on the first high ground as one

1

ascends the river from the Gulf of Mexico. The bluff is at least thirty feet high, and before I commenced my travels I thought that it must be the tallest hill in the world.

At that time there was a United States arsenal and quite a large garrison there, mostly composed of heroes who had two or three years before that time conquered Mexico. I loved the soldiers, and one of the officers, Lieutenant Drum, afterwards adjutant-general of the United States Army for many years, loved my eldest sister, so we got on famously together.

General Zachary Taylor had a cottage in the garrison grounds, and his famous old war-horse "Whitey" had the freedom of the beautiful grassy lawns, and the greatest delight of my life was to be placed on the gentle old charger's back, without saddle or bridle, and sit there while "Old Whitey" grazed, not paying as much attention to me as he would have bestowed upon a fly. From that time until I was fourteen, my life was principally spent on horseback. I mean by horseback, the backs of those savage little ponies we called "mustangs" which existed in herds in a wild state in that part of the country in those days. They belonged to the man who could first lasso and put his brand upon them. These ponies were past-masters in the art of bucking, and from their backs I have probably hit the ground in a greater variety of ways than any other man now living, but as my steeds had never been put through a course of the *haut école* before I mounted them, my horsemanship should not be judged by the number of croppers I have come in my time.

There are certain events in a child's life which make an impression that time itself cannot efface. One of these is so vivid that, after a lapse of sixty-five years, I can shut my eyes and again see a crowd of men and women standing on the river-bank wildly gesticulating and vowing that they would be revenged upon a band of Seminole Indians who were being transported from Florida to the Indian Territory. Their chief, the fatuously cruel "Billy Bowlegs," was with them, and so violent were the people on shore in their threats that the captain of the steamboat did not dare to approach the shore. He was wise, as many in that excitable crowd, myself among the number, had had relatives cruelly tortured and murdered by these same Indians in the Seminole War. My uncle, Bedford Morgan, was one of their victims, having been scalped, and his body so horribly mutilated that it was only recognized by the fact that his faithful dog stood guard over it.

In those days there were still Indians in Louisiana. A band of "Choctaws" lived on the Amite River, a few miles back of Baton Rouge, who used to bring into the town, for sale or barter, their bead and basket-work and blow-guns made out of cane poles. The arrows of these blow-guns were made of split cane with a tuft of thistle at one end and we boys delighted in the ownership of these long and apparently harm-less weapons. I say apparently harmless, but in the hands of an Indian they were very deadly to birds and squirrels. The Indians were won-derful shots with them and at twenty or thirty paces could hit a small silver five-cent piece; always provided they were promised the coin if they hit it.

I have a vivid recollection of a tragedy which happened in those days which often troubles the dreams of my old age. I was an eye-wit-ness of the blowing-up and destruction by fire of the *Princess*, the finest steamboat on the Mississippi in those days. The night before the disas-ter my father and mother had kissed me good-bye and gone on board of an old dismantled steamboat, which answered the purposes of a wharf, to await the arrival of the *Princess*, as they intended to take pas-sage on her for New Orleans. Early the next morning I went down to the river to find out if they had yet left. The *Princess* had just drawn out into the stream, and as I stood watching her as she glided down the river, a great column of white smoke suddenly went up from her and she burst into flames. She was loaded with cotton. As though by magic the inhabitants of the town gathered at the riverside, and in the crowd I spied my brother-in-law, Charles La Noue, in a buggy. He called to me; I jumped in alongside him and we dashed down the river road in the direction of the burning boat. The road was rough and the horse was fast. The high levee on our right shut out the view of the river, so we could only see the great column of smoke. On our left were the endless fields of sugar cane, with an occasional glimpse of a planter's house set in a grove of pecan trees.

At last, in a great state of excitement, we arrived at the plantation of Mr. Conrad. "Brother Charlie" jumped out of the vehicle and ran toward the house while I made the horse fast to a tree. I then mounted the levee from where I could see floating cotton bales with people on them; men in skiffs, from both sides of the river, were rescuing the poor terror-stricken creatures and bringing them ashore. From the levee I rushed into the park in front of Mr. Conrad's residence, and there saw a sight which can never be effaced from my memory. Mr. Conrad had had sheets laid on the ground amidst the trees and barrels of flour were broken open and the contents poured over the sheets. As fast as the burned and scalded people were pulled out of the river they were seized by the slaves, and while screaming and shrieking with pain and fright, they were forcibly thrown down on the sheets and rolled in the flour. The clothes had been burned off of many of them. Some, in their agony, could not lie still, and, with the white sheets wrapped round them, looking like ghosts, they danced a weird hornpipe while filling the air with their screams. Terrified by the awful and uncanny scene, I hid behind a huge tree so that I should not see it, but no tree could prevent me from hearing those awful cries and curses which echo in my ears even now.

Suddenly, to my horror, one of the white specters, wrapped in a sheet, his disfigured face plastered over with flour, staggered toward my hiding-place, and before I could run away from the hideous object it extended its arms toward me and quietly said, "Don't be afraid, Jimmie. It is me, Mr. Cheatham, I am dying—hold my hand!" And he sank upon the turf beside me. Although dreadfully frightened, I managed between sobs to ask the question uppermost in my mind: "Can you tell me where I can find my father and mother?" The ghostlike man only replied with a cry which seemed to wrench his soul from his body. He shivered for an instant, and then lay still. A slave passing by pointed to the body and casually remarked, "He done dead."

A Creole Negro woman then came running toward me; she was stout and almost out of breath, but was still able to shout out to me in her native *patois*: "Mo cherche pour toi partout; M'sieur La Noue dit que to vinit toute suite!" When I found "Brother Charlie," he was ministering to the maimed, but found time to tell me that my parents had taken another boat which had stopped at Baton Rouge in the night and thereby had saved their lives. I returned at once to my home, where I was comforted in the strong arms of Katish, my old black nurse.

Katish was a character whose fame was known far and wide through the little town. She was a strapping big woman who weighed over two hundred pounds, but as active as a young girl. She had been my mother's maid before my mother was married, and afterwards had nursed and bossed all of her children. I being the youngest was, of course, her special pet. She ran the establishment to suit my father's and mother's comfort and convenience and ruled the children and the slaves to suit herself; but we all loved her, and no other hand could soothe a fevered child's pillow as could the black hand of Katish. When we were ill she never seemed to sleep, but sat by our bedsides until we were well. The nastiest medicine (and there were nasty medicines in those days) lost much of its terrors when administered by Katish.

Charloe, Katish's husband, was a dried-up, weazened little man of a shiny black complexion; he always insisted that his stature had been stunted when he was a jockey by the horse-trainers putting him on too light a diet and burying him up to his neck in the manure-box for too long a time when it was necessary to reduce his weight sufficiently to ride two-year-old colts. He had been a celebrated jockey in his day when he rode for his then owner, Mr. Duplantier, a planter who amused himself with a racehorse stable. Charloe was my hero, he was a perfect black "Admirable Crichton." It is true that he could neither read nor write, nor did he know a note of music, but many a so-called educated white man envied him (and) his accomplishments. He spoke French, Spanish, and English fluently, and played the violin like a virtuoso. His elegant manners were above criticism. He made beautiful rings and bangles out of tortoise-shell with only his pocket-knife, a round stick, and a pot of hot water for his tools. He was also adept at making fancy ropes for bridle reins and girths out of horsehair.

In 1846 Charloe went to Mexico with Dr. Hamey, an army surgeon, and brother of General Hamey, and remained there until the army came home. Of course if he had wanted his freedom he could have remained in that country where some of the highest aristocrats have a touch of the tar brush in their veins.

Charloe was very much of a gentleman of leisure. He paid his master a certain sum of money every month and spent his time riding around the country. He was the veterinarian of the town and was very successful in curing horses of all sorts of disease, and probably knew too much about spavined horses and how to fix them up so they would be attractive to the innocent and ignorant would-be purchaser. Besides this he made lots of money training horses for gentlemen, and also devoted much of his leisure to catching and breaking wild horses, which he sold for good money after he had handled them for a short time and put some style into their gaits. He was a wonder with the lasso and rarely if ever missed catching a horse, and in this sport he was most ably assisted by his horse "Ben," who knew almost as much as Charloe did about the business.

The slaves had a means of communicating with distant plantations which was always a mystery to their owners. During the Civil War, my mother and three of my sisters were refugees in a little Mississippi village, and were without money and in danger of starvation, as they could not communicate with my elder brother in New Orleans or with friends in Baton Rouge. But hostile armies and picket lines were not obstacles of much importance to Katish when she wanted to get word to Charloe of the condition of the family—Charloe being in Baton Rouge, within the Union lines, and more than a hundred miles away. Charloe immediately mounted his horse, and without much difficulty, managed to pass through both the Federal and Confederate lines, and carried to my mother quite a large sum of real money which he gave to her, and which greatly relieved the distress of the family, especially as my sister, Mrs. La Noue, had a family of little children who were crying for bread. It must he remembered that Charloe was of course a freedman as long as he remained within the Union lines, but knew that he again became a slave when he entered the territory held by the Confederates.

Until I was thirteen years of age I was the constant companion of Charloe. When I was a baby, mounted on his horse, he would carry me around with him, and I do not remember the time when I first rode a horse by myself. My father was a lawyer with a very large practice, and a very busy man; and my mother was in very delicate health. I was a pupil, or supposed to be one, at Professor Magruder's Academy, the best school in Baton Rouge; but I only attended when it suited my convenience, such as rainy days, or when some interesting game was going on at the school, or when Charloe was not going after the wild horses. Since those days I have hunted the wily fox with the "Pytchley" in England, and with Alfred and Burnett, Rhett and Frank Trenholm and Colonel Tom Taylor in South Carolina, but in my opinion fox-hunting is tame sport in comparison with the chase after wild horses.

Under Charloe's tuition I learned to throw the lasso, and if it was an easy chance, he always allowed me to throw first; but I had no fear of the result, for if I missed I knew that I would hear the swish of Charloe's rope which with deadly accuracy would land its loop over the head of the poor terrified beast which had never before felt the power of man. I remember vividly once, when we had turned a herd of horses from a swamp for which they were headed, how they dashed into a canebrake, the cane poles being from ten to fifteen feet high, and almost as close together as the fingers on one's hand. The wild horses smashed their way through and we followed closely at their heels holding the nooses of our lassos in one hand and our reins in the other while our heads were busily engaged in dodging the muscadine vines which hung in festoons from the great trees which grew among the canes. Suddenly we came crashing into an old clearing. Charloe was just ahead of me and this was his opportunity. Instantly his lasso commenced to describe graceful circles over his head, and having selected his victim the loop shot out of his hand and straight as an arrow sailed away. The loop expanded and like a hawk ready to strike, it hovered for an instant over the frightened animal's head. It was impossible for the poor creature to dodge it, and it settled around his neck. Now came "Ben's" part in the performance, and he knew as much about the game as his rider did. He was going at breakneck speed, but the instant the noose left Charloe's hand, stiff-legged, he planted both front feet in the soft ground and as soon as he had stopped his momentum, he reared up and swung himself around. Ben knew that the end of that lasso was made fast to the pommel of his saddle and unless he took the strain down his spinal column he would be jerked onto his nose. As it was, it was the other horse that turned a somersault as the rope checked his wild career, and before he could regain his feet, Charloe was on the ground and had deftly tied them. He was then quickly blindfolded and a bridle without bit, but with a tight-fitting halter to keep him from biting—it was called a "bosal"—and prevented the animal from opening his jaws—was fitted to him. Then his feet were untied and he was made to stand up, still blindfolded. My saddle was then cinched with a hair girth onto him, and I mounted. Charloe then suddenly jerked the cloth from the pony's eyes, and the fun commenced. The animal was dazed for a moment, and then he reached his head around and tried to bite my foot. Finding it impossible to do so, he lowered his head until it was between his forelegs, at the same time arching his back, and leaped straight up into the air landing on the ground stiff-legged, and followed this performance up with a series of bucks both forward, backward, and sideways, until I thought he never would have done. I had to stay there until he gave up, for if once he had got rid of me he would have become a confirmed bucker, and would have tried to get rid of his rider in that way ever afterwards. These mustang ponies had innately every conceivable horse vice such as bucking, biting, pawing, and kicking, besides being endowed with a good memory. When the pony was exhausted he gave up, and I, also weary, was glad to dismount. When the ordeal was over, Charloe simply said, "Bien, tres bien." "Praise from Sir Hubert was praise indeed," and I felt immediately pleased at Charloe's approval of my horsemanship. Scenes like this constituted my school of equitation, so it was not extraordinary that years afterwards I succeeded in astonishing the Bedouins in Egypt with some of my feats.

Two

Unlucky in love—The home of a Louisiana aristocrat—Hospitality and lengthy visits—The sugar-house—Appointed a midshipman—The only Southern man who could not whip ten Yankees—Religious mania—Fortress Monroe—Mexican pulque.

I had other pleasures besides chasing wild horses. I used to delight in going to beautiful Lynwood, the plantation of General Carter in the parish of East Felicians, and some twenty miles from Baton Rouge. Howell Carter, one the general's sons, was near my own age and we were great friends, and Howell had a beautiful sister whom I adored: the fact that she was a young lady in society made no difference to me. She acknowledged that I was her sweetheart and it was heaven for me to stand by the piano while she sang for me; and besides, my favorite brother, Gibbes, some ten years my senior, approved of my choice and complimented my good taste. One day Gibbes and Lydia Carter got married, and it took me a long time to recover from the effects of their treachery. Gibbes was the last man I would have suspected of being my rival.

I also used to spend a great deal of time at the Hope Estate Plantation, about four miles below Baton Rouge. Colonel Philip Hicky, its owner, was the most elegant and the grandest old gentleman I ever knew. He was a man of great wealth and unbounded hospitality. He was tall, slim, and straight, and his manner was most courtly. His welcome to a guest, whether self-invited or not, made the recipient feel very much at home as well as good all over. He was a patriarch of the olden time, and lived with his children, grandchildren, and great-grandchildren around him. The old plantation house seemed to be made of India rubber. There was always room for a few more. I have sat at his table when with his family and guests more than thirty people sat down to dinner, and this was not an unusual occasion, but a thing that happened nearly every day, as his home was convenient to the town and all of his acquaintances knew they would receive a warm welcome if they took a ride and dropped in to dinner. I knew a lady who paid a visit to Hope Estate which lasted for more than fifteen years, and of a gentleman who paid a call one morning when he was a very young man and never left until his hair was white, and the old colonel had been dead for some years.

One of my father's brothers and one of my mother's brothers had married daughters of Colonel Hicky, and their children and the other grandchildren ranged in years from young gentlemen and ladies old enough to go into society, to boys and girls of my own age. There was a herd of horses which roamed about the great pasture and every child had his mount—the young ladies and gentlemen of the family disdained mustang ponies, and possessed highly bred Kentucky saddlers. The great event of the year at Hope Estate was when the sugar-making season arrived. Then all was life and bustle: the fires were lighted and the open kettles of cane juice began to boil while the slaves feeding cane to the carrier which carried it to the great iron rollers would burst into song. The sugar-house was some distance from the residence and when night came the young people and their guests would mount their horses and proceed there to eat colon (taffy) and drink vin de cane (sugar-cane juice) into which some of the older people would put a little spirits if they felt so disposed. With the glare of the furnaces and of the torches around the carrier, it was a pretty picture and of course the young people danced—they always did in the South in those days when two or three boys and girls got together. Toward midnight a start for home was in order. We boys always got off ahead of the older people. The narrow road lay between fields of tall waving and rustling cane calculated in the night to make highly imaginative young people feel creepy. As we approached a certain bridge over a small draining canal, every boy knew what was coming and sat closer to his saddle as he took a fresh and stronger grip with his knees. As the leader's horse's feet touched the bridge his rider would give a whoop and cry, "Runaway nigger!" and in would go the spurs and there would be a wild race for the house, each boy pretending to be frightened to death, although we all knew that such a thing as a "runaway nigger" had never been seen in that part of the country. Slaves there were treated like human beings, and the threat to sell one would tame the most refractory Negro on the place.

Some of the sugar planters in the neighborhood of Baton Rouge were mean enough to object to the town boys devastating their sugar-cane fields. It certainly was marvelous to see how many stalks of cane a small boy could devour. There was a Mr. Hail who owned a large plantation which commenced at the town limits, and on the line he planted early and told the boys that that particular sugar-cane was for them, but such is the contrariness of boys that we never touched it, preferring to raid the fields of planters who promised to do all kinds of things to us if they caught us on their grounds.

It was amidst such scenes as I have tried to describe that my life was spent until I arrived at the age of fourteen, when one day Mr. Edouard Bouligny, a member of Congress, offered me an appointment as a midshipman. I naturally became wild with excitement, for as I had never seen blue water, I longed for a life on the ocean wave. The only unpleasant prospect was that it was impressed upon me that I would have to attend school regularly and study hard to prepare myself for the examination for admission into the United States Naval Academy. Besides my backwardness in my school work another difficulty which was suggested was my size, as I was small for my age; but it turned out that in those days smallness of stature was not taken into consideration if a boy could stand the examinations. So I turned over a new leaf and attended school and studied conscientiously until one day a difference of opinion arose between Mr. Parsons, a six-foot Yankee teacher, and myself. I felt a sudden desire to lick him, and to want and to have, with me, in those days were synonymous terms, so I sailed in with the intention of gratifying my longing. Gee! What that Yankee school-teacher did not do to me is not worth relating. Fortunately, for my self-respect, I had not then heard the expression which became so popular in the South a year or two later, "One Southern man can whip ten Yankees"—but I decided that Magruder's Academy was no place for a gentleman and an officer, *in futuro*, so I severed my connection with it on the spot.

My elder brother, Judge Morgan, then took a hand in the game and came to Baton Rouge from New Orleans and carried me off to a school managed by a Mr. McNair, and situated in a forest of gigantic yellow pine trees, the nearest inhabited place being the little village of Areire, about sixty miles from New Orleans. One would imagine that this was the ideal place for undisturbed study, but it was not. It was the most melancholy place I was ever in, especially when night came. The sighing and moaning of the big pine trees when the wind blew, and the deathly stillness, only broken by the sad notes of the whippoorwills, when it, was calm, were enough to have given any one the creeps—especially a boy who had never before been away from home.

Everything at the school went on like clockwork, and the hundred or more boys seemed contented until one day a very popular boy returned from his home, where he had been to attend a funeral, and where he had also "got religion" (of the virulent Mississippi type) at a camp-meeting. He at once proceeded to inaugurate prayer meetings. There was a huge pine tree a little way from the schoolhouse and the ground at its base was thickly carpeted by pine needles. They were convenient, clean, and soft, and one could kneel upon them with comfort. At first only two or three boys, religiously inclined, joined him; but soon the number increased so rapidly that other trees had to be requisitioned, and then rivalry commenced as to which of the little congregations could exhibit the best prayer-maker. Finally, with one exception (myself), every boy in the school was taken with religious mania which spread amongst the assistant teachers. Mr. McNair at first tried to moderate the enthusiasm, but soon fell a victim to the contagion. Every boy wanted to lead in prayer, and quarrels soon arose as to who could offer up the most eloquent one. Study hours and recitations were alike forgotten—even the meals were postponed until some boy could finish telling the good Lord his woes. In the morning we would assemble in the schoolroom at the usual hour, and of course, the routine of the day would commence by Mr. McNair reading a chapter of the Bible and offering up a prayer; then, instead of proceeding with the lessons, one boy after another would rise in his place and recount his religious experience. There was a remarkable resemblance in these experiences which consisted chiefly in the boys telling their audience what fearful sinners their parents and elder brother and sisters were, and how pure, perfect, and holy they themselves had become since, single-handed, they had come off victorious in a fierce conflict with the Devil, captured glory, and become one of the elect. This sort of thing went on all day and far into the night. Of course it could not go on forever, and the news soon spread far and wide that McNair's whole school had gone crazy.

Parents came from every direction. The storm was about to burst and break up the school. I was the first to be struck by the lightning. I was sitting at my desk listening to one of the very best of the young exhorters, who was eloquently describing the imaginary crimes of which his fond mother was guilty, and unfolding his plan of campaign by which he hoped to save her from the claws of the Devil and reform her at the same time, when a hand the size of a small ham seized me by the back of the neck and awoke me from my trance. I jumped to my feet and squirmed around to find myself in front of the gigantic form of my brother, Judge Philip Hicky Morgan, his handsome face purple with rage. "You come with me, sir!" he fairly bellowed, and I never got out of any place so quickly before that I can remember of.

Accompanied by Judge Morgan's wife and her little children, I was put on board of a steamship at New Orleans bound for New York, and from there sent to Rutland, Vermont, where it was proposed to put me at school, but with vivid memories of the thrashing Mr. Parsons had given me, I did not intend to take any more chances with a Yankee school-teacher, so I flatly refused to go. In despair, my sister-in-law sent me to my eldest sister, the wife of Lieutenant Drum, he being then the adjutant at Fortress Monroe.

The gayety of "Old Point Comfort" and the dancing morn, noon, and night at the hotel, combined with the brilliant uniforms of the officers and the military drills and parades, suited my taste exactly, and I thought I had at last found the life I wanted to live. But Lieutenant Drum had different views. He put me through an examination and found me woefully wanting, and without so much as consulting me, he determined that I should not fail at Annapolis. He elected himself chief school-teacher, bought the necessary books, and insisted that I should spend a certain number of hours every day at my studies while he superintended them. One day it was hot and uncomfortable, and a contrary problem would not come out right and I was cross. Lieutenant Drum was a stubborn man and insisted that I should keep at it. I lost my temper and threw the book at him and for my pains got an awfully good thrashing. Think of it! The war had not yet commenced and here within a year I had twice been thoroughly licked by two Yankees. Thank Heaven, I had not as yet met the other eight that were to make up the ten I was shortly afterwards expected to whip.

While I was at Fortress Monroe the sloop-of-war *Plymouth*, the Annapolis practice ship, arrived with the midshipmen on board. They had just returned from their annual cruise and I went fairly wild about them, especially as some of them condescended to notice me after they learned that I had prospects of becoming one of their number. I almost felt grateful to Lieutenant Drum for that thrashing which had had a remarkable effect in developing my genius for mathematics.

Shortly after the *Plymouth* left, the steam sloop-of-war *Brooklyn*, commanded by Commander, afterwards Admiral David G. Farragut, arrived. She was just about to start on what was known as the "Cheriqui Expedition" for the purpose of finding a new route for a canal across the Isthmus of Panama. The army officers in the fort entertained the officers of the ship and the officers of the *Brooklyn* returned the compliment by giving a reception on board. My sister insisted on my accompanying her, but I did not want to go. The midshipmen on the *Plymouth* had told me a lot about naval commanders and lieutenants, and I already regarded them as the natural enemies of midshipmen. However, I was told that Commander Farragut had his son Loyal, a boy of about my own age, on board, and I was finally persuaded to go. My sister introduced me to Commander Farragut, and the great man, when he was told that I had an appointment to Annapolis, unbent somewhat and asked me what I intended to bring my sister when I returned from my first cruise. Now, as ill luck would have it, my sister greatly admired lapislazuli stones and I blurted out, "I am going to bring her a set of lapsus linguae, sir!" There was a roar of laughter amidst which I made my escape. I knew I had made a bad break, but what it was exactly I did not understand. All the same I felt awfully mortified. Years afterwards I had the honor of meeting the great admiral and to my astonishment and confusion he asked me if I had ever procured that set of lapsus linguae for my sister.

While at Fortress Monroe I saw an interesting test of a piece of ordnance, the "Sawyer" gun, the first rifled cannon invented in the United States. The gun was mounted outside of the Fort on the beach. The officers had little confidence in it, and every precaution was taken to avoid accidents. Lieutenant Drum and I stood by a shed some fifty yards away. The gun was fired and exploded—one half of the breech going up into the air; coming down it struck the weatherboarding just over our heads and fortunately glanced inside instead of outside the shed where we were standing.

The Honorable Jacob Thompson, of Mississippi, who was Secretary of the Interior in Mr. Buchanan's Cabinet, came to Old Point one day and Colonel Dimmick, who was in command, called on him at the Hygeia Hotel. Mr. Thompson was not in. Mr. Thompson returned the visit, when, unfortunately, the colonel was out driving. Neither man had ever seen the other. Colonel Dimmick then sent his adjutant to tender a review to the Secretary for the next morning. The Secretary was so late in appearing on the parade ground that the colonel, losing patience, detailed an officer to meet Mr. Thompson when he should arrive, saying that as soon as Mr. Thompson was in position, he, the colonel, would lead the regiment past.

The Fourth Artillery, which garrisoned the Fort, possessed a drum major of whom they were very proud. He was nearly seven feet tall, and with his great bearskin bonnet he looked like one of the giants one reads about in fairy tales, and his strut and the deftness with which he twirled his gilt baton were inimitable. The dignified commanding officer was rather small in stature and not at all an imposing figure in comparison with his drum major. As Mr. Thompson took up his position, the band commenced to play and the regiment moved like clockwork behind it. Arriving in front of the secretary, the drum major sent his baton into the air, and catching it as it descended, he made it whirl several times and suddenly landed it under his left arm, his right hand simultaneously, like that of a mechanical man, going to his forehead in salute. Mr. Thompson lifted his hat and then fairly swept the ground with it. After the band came little Colonel Dimmick, who with graceful precision saluted with his sword, but by that time the secretary had recovered his equilibrium from his low bow to the drum major, and with his arms folded across his swelled chest, gazed indifferently at the commanding officer and took no further notice of him. After the review he was introduced to the colonel, and remarked, "I always thought the captain walked at the head of his troops!"

There was in the Fourth Artillery a number of officers who were veterans of the Mexican War. One of them had but one arm. It seems that in those days they did not retire an officer on account of the lose of an arm if he was capable of attending to his duties. One evening a dreadful *contretemps* happened. It was at the wedding festivities of the colonel's daughter. The wedding ceremony was over and the guests thronged into the banquet hall, when Lieutenant Drum produced three bottles of Mexican pulque. The bottles were carefully corked and sealed, and the lieutenant had himself filled them and brought them home after the evacuation of Mexico some thirteen years previously. The younger officers were told that only Mexican veterans could appreciate pulque, and therefore they were not to be permitted to taste of the nectar, as there was so little of it. Three of the veterans procured three corkscrews and simultaneously pulled the corks. Suddenly people began to sniff as though they had smelt something. They had—there was a *suave qui peut* from the supper-room and the remainder of the function had to be carried on in the grounds outside the house. Mr. Drum and his brother veterans had forgotten that pulque could only be drunk when fresh from the plant, and that in a few hours after it was gathered, it became putrid. Any one who has ever passed down a street in the City of Mexico, where pulque shops exist, and smelt the foul odors that burden the air can sympathize with the merry-makers at the wedding.

Three

Annapolis—"Old Ironsides"—The habit of command—show remarkable leniency toward the midshipman's hereditary enemies, the
commandant and lieutenants—The "Brood of the Constitution"—
"Bill Pip," our first hero—Other heroes—Skating on thin ice—The
bilged—Secession.

In September, 1860, I went to Annapolis and presented myself
before the Board of Examiners for admittance. The dignity and solemnity of the officers who, arrayed in their uniforms with their swords
beside them, sat at a long table, caused me to have a slight attack of
stage fright; but the ordeal was soon over and I was allowed to go out
in the fresh air in utter ignorance as to whether I had passed successfully or not. My mind, however, was soon relieved by Lieutenant Scott,
who passing by said to me, "Youngster, you are all right."

The historical frigate *Constitution* ("Old Ironsides") had recently
been fitted out as a schoolship and lay at anchor in the Severn River. I
was directed to go on board of her and found on her deck a number of
other boys as green as myself. Things went very easily at first, as we
had nothing to do besides loafing about the decks and wondering at
the strangeness of our surroundings. We had no wants, unless it was a
longing for the cute little jackets with the brass buttons and the beautiful gold anchors on the lapels of the turned-down collars. The captain
and the lieutenants were just too sweet for anything, answering our
fool questions as though their one object in life was to please us. But

we were ungrateful and took much more interest in the boatswain's mates, and the old gray-haired sailors who kept the ship clean and spun yarns. The sailors first initiated us in the mysteries of getting our hammocks ready and how to swing them on the berth deck, and also how to lash them up in the morning when we "turned out" preparatory to stowing them snugly in the hammock nettings. Everything was going on pleasantly until one day, to our great delight, our uniforms arrived; they were so pretty that it seemed a pity they should make such a difference in our happy lives, but such was the fact. We had no sooner got into our regulation togs, than a great change in the demeanor of everybody else seemed to take place. Those affable and chummy lieutenants who an hour before had treated us almost as equals, even condescending to joke with us, now stood on their dignity, and if they spoke at all it was to give an order or a reproof. The old sailors gravely saluted us as they passed, but they would not stop for a little conversation. I wondered what we had done to deserve such treatment, but I was not long in finding out. With the uniform I had come under naval discipline; and it was extraordinary how these soft spoken lieutenants licked us into shape. I, who had never obeyed anybody, within less than a week would jump as though I was shot when one of them would give me an order. The routine of the ship had commenced in earnest—reveille, dress (and woe betide him who had lost a button or whose shoestring was not properly tied), lash the hammocks, carry them up to the spar deck and stow them neatly in the nettings; breakfast; recitation; drill at the great guns; recitation; infantry drill; recitation; cutlass exercise; recitation; dinner; recitation; boat drill, or loosing, reefing or furling sail. After supper were the study hours until nine o'clock, and then, after slinging our hammocks, discipline was suspended and we were allowed half an hour to skylark and have a little roughhouse which would always be interrupted, as taps sounded, by the hoarse voice of the master-at-arms bellowing, "Silence, fore and aft, gentlemen!"

My young sisters at home were constantly, at this time, writing me letters filled with good advice and begging me to control my temper and to be kind to those nice navy officers, samples of whom they had met only at cotillions, and little did they dream how those so gentle and elegant gentlemen could on occasion roar like bulls of Bashan and scare a midshipman out of seven years' growth. They also implored me not to get frisky and try to lasso the commandant of midshipmen. To those who knew the late Rear Admiral C. R. P. Rodgers, that embodiment of dignity and elegance, I need not say that I followed my sisters' advice.

The drill I most enjoyed was when we were exercised aloft making and furling sail. The masts of the old frigate were very tall, and when the officer of the deck through his speaking-trumpet would give the order, "All hands make sail!" we would rush to our stations and stand close to the rails anxious and impatient as young race-horses at the starting barrier. At the order, "Aloft, t'gallant and royal yardmen!" "Aloft, topmen!" "Aloft lower yardmen!" we would spring into the shrouds, and hardly touching the ratlines with our twinkling feet, a perfect stream of midshipmen would dash up to the highest yards decreasing in numbers on the shrouds as they reached their stations. Then they would step on to the foot ropes and crowd as closely as possible to the mast until the order was given to "lay out and loose!" when they would go out on the yardarms and cast off the gaskets. Then would come the orders in rapid succession, "Let fall!" "Sheet home!" "Lay in!" "Lay down from aloft!"—when as though by magic the bare poles would be hidden by her snow-white canvas from her trucks to her deck, and the midshipmen, helter-skelter, would come jumping from ratline to ratline until they reached the deck, while some of the more venturesome would leap to a backstay and slide down with fearful velocity.

They were a gay and reckless set of boys, but the "Brood of the Constitution" will be remembered as long as history is written. It is true that at that time we only had one hero amongst us—that we knew of—but others developed later. Our hero at the time was a red-headed, freckle-faced, loose-jointed, slab-sided, tall, and lanky youth from the muleiest regions of Missouri. He first appeared on the deck of the *Constitution* dressed in coarse and baggy clothes set off by a huge green cravat tied in a monstrous bow-knot. He gazed around the deck in a supercilious sort of way, walked over to a hatchway, and leaned against a windsail that was ventilating the berth deck, with the result that he almost instantaneously found himself three decks below where he thought he was. We thought he had been killed, but his long arms, which he had thrown around the windsail, saved him, as he had only slid the distance rather rapidly. Coming on deck he informed us that he had "slid down three stories." He introduced himself by saying that his name was William Pipkin, but that they always called him "Bill Pip" at home for short, and that he would be just as well pleased if we called him that, as he was more accustomed to it. Needless to say, we accommodated him. He took a plug of tobacco out of his pocket, cut off a big hunk which he placed in his mouth, and then generously offered the exquisite and elegant officer of the deck, Lieutenant Robert Wainwright Scott, a chew, which was declined with a savage glare that would have caused heart failure in any of the rest of us, but which did not faze "Bill Pip." Shortly after he had got into a uniform some ladies, among them the wives of some of the officers, visited the ship and remained aboard rather late. It was getting dark when they made a move to go ashore, and one of them expressed herself as being a little nervous about the long walk after reaching the shore. The gallant Lieutenant Upshur, who was the executive officer of the ship, said that he was sure any one of a number of midshipmen who were standing near would be delighted to accompany them, and unfortunately, for him, he called "Bill Pip," who was the tallest of the lot, and said, "Mr. Pipkin, I am sure you will be glad to escort these ladies." To the lieutenant's horror and amazement, the lanky boy replied, "I am very sorry, Mr. Upshur, but the last thing my mother said to me when I left home was, 'Bill Pip, you keep away from the women!'" But who can foretell what a boy will turn out to be? "Bill Pip" resigned at the outbreak of the Civil War and went South. He did not like the navy and refused an appointment in that of the Confederacy. He enlisted in the army as a private, but the navy still pursued him. He was one of a number of artillerymen detailed to fill the complement of the *Arkansas's* crew and was in that vessel when she ran through the ironclad fleet above Vicksburg and the wooden sloops-of-war of Admiral Farragut's fleet below that city. "Bill Pip" by his own gallantry and merits rose to the rank of full colonel in the army, and after the war went into business, amassed a fortune, and died a millionaire!

Although we were unaware of the fact at the time there were other heroes on that historical deck where Bainbridge, Hull, and Charles Stewart, to say nothing of "Bill Pip," had won fame, and when the two big hawsers were stretched from the forecastle to the sacred quarter-deck, which we looked upon as holy ground, and the boatswain and his mates took charge of the class to teach us how to tie sailor knots, the old white-headed captain of the maintop, if he had looked down upon those two lines of midshipmen who with short lengths of rope yarn and ratline were being taught the difference between a square knot and a "granny," would have seen, among others who afterwards won fame, fifteen boys who were to become rear admirals—Charles E. Clark, who brought the *Oregon* around the continent at the outbreak of the Spanish War; Francis A. Cook, who was to command Commodore Schley's flagship, the *Brooklyn*; Robley D. Evans ("Fighting Bob"), who was to command the *Iowa*; and Harry Taylor, of the *Indiana*. These were the heaviest ships of Admiral Sampson's fleet when they destroyed the Spanish squadron at Santiago. He would also have seen standing there Gridley, who was to command Admiral Dewey's flagship, the *Olympia*; Frank Wildes, of the *Baltimore*, and jolly Joe Coghlan, of the *Raleigh*, the three biggest ships of our fleet when they won the victory at Manila. He could also have seen Sigsbee, who commanded the unfortunate *Maine* when she was destroyed in the harbor of Havana;

Colby M. Chester, who was to command a small squadron which was to make it possible for our army to take possession of Puerto Rico; Crowninshield, who was to be chief of the Bureau of Navigation during the Spanish War; and Dick Leary, who fired the last shot in that campaign. Nearly all of the Northern boys were to serve during the latter part of the Civil War and participate in the assaults on Fort Fisher and Fort Morgan.

Among the Southerners O. A. Brown was to serve on the Confederate cruiser *Shenandoah*, the ship that went on destroying whalers for months after the war was over in blissful ignorance of the fact that the Southern Confederacy had ceased to exist. George Bryan, who was to be in the C.S. cruiser *Florida*; Berrien who was to be in the C.S.S. *Chickamauga*; and Long, who was to be both in the *Merrimac* in her fights in Hampton Roads and in the *Albemarle* when she fought a flotilla of gunboats in Albemarle Sound; handsome Wyndham Mayo, who after brilliant service in the Confederacy behaved with such conspicuous bravery and showed so much ability when a passenger steamer which he commanded after the war was burned in Chesapeake Bay. And then there were also Gardner and Goodwyn, who were promoted for gallantry to lieutenancies when they took part in a small boat expedition which boarded and carried the U.S. gunboats *Resolute* and *Satellite* in the Rappahanock River. Besides these there were many others who gallantly served in the gunboats and naval batteries of the Confederacy. The "Brood of the Constitution" surely contained a lot of good fighting material.

Lieutenant Commander George W. Rodgers was the captain of the *Constitution*. He was the idol of the midshipmen. He was afterwards killed at an assault on Fort Sumter when in command of the U.S. monitor *Katskill*. He was a strict disciplinarian with very gentle manners; all the same, the most refractory midshipman did not care to be haled before him on any charge whatsoever. On Saturday nights we frequently had dances—which we called "hops"—on board the frigate, and many of the belles of Annapolis, Baltimore, and Washington used to attend them just as they do in this day and generation. The berth deck would be decorated with flags and the Academy band furnished the music.

Occasionally we had a little excitement on board of "Old Ironsides." One day "Fighting Bob" Evans, not known by that sobriquet in those days, gave us a thriller. Two boys, one big and the other small, had an altercation. Bob had nothing to do with it, but *con amore* proposed to the big boy that he would help the little one lick him. The little boy, like a goose, said that he did not want anybody to help him, that he would cut his antagonist with a knife if he was touched. An officer passing by heard the remark, and thinking that it was Evans who made it, promptly put him under arrest and marched him to the captain's cabin, and preferred the charge against him. Under the midshipmen's code, poor Bob could not squeal on his comrade.

Captain Rodgers arose from his seat. His wrath was majestic— "And so, sir!" he said to Evans, "you propose to raise a mutiny on board of my ship. I will let you know, sir, that a midshipman has hung to a yardarm for mutiny before this, and you dare try to raise one and I will hang you!" And turning to the officer said, "Confine him below." To one ignorant of the annals of the service this hanging business would have sounded like an empty threat, but it must be remembered that the hanging of Midshipman Spencer, son of the Secretary of War, on board of the brig *Summers* was at that time an affair of comparatively recent date, and worse than that, the captain of the *Summers*, Alexander Slidell McKensie, was a "Rodgers," and Bob did not know but what the hanging of midshipmen ran in the blood.

The wardroom of the old frigate was away down below the waterline and the after staterooms were as dark as Erebus. Bob was confined in the darkest of them. He stood it for about twenty minutes and then requested that he should be allowed to write a letter. Permission being granted, he was taken into the light, and pen, ink, and paper furnished him, and this, according to the story which filtered down to us midshipmen, was the letter he wrote to his uncle, a lawyer in Washington:—

My Dear Uncle:—

I have committed mutiny and they are going to hang me: If you want to see me again come quickly to your affectionate nephew.
Robley D. Evans.

Poor little Bob, he was only fourteen years of age and of very small stature for his years.

The winter of 1860–61 was a very cold one to me. I had once seen a snow flurry at home, but I had never before seen a large body of water like the Severn River frozen over. The Northern boys were delighted, and at once begged permission to go skating. Seeing them gracefully skimming over the ice like so many swallows was fascinating to me, and I could not resist the desire to join them; so procuring a pair of skates, with many doubts, I too went upon the ice. We had gone ashore and walked some distance up the river to a place the higher authorities thought safe, and the master-at-arms patrolled the river-bank to afford assistance in case of need. I had proceeded only a short distance from the shore when suddenly both feet went skyward and the back of my head hit the hard ice and the force of my fall let me crash through it. The depth of the water was over my head, and I was weighted with a heavy regulation overcoat, but I could swim and dive almost as well as the average alligator of my native bayous. I came up under solid ice and then went down again, and was fortunate enough to find the hole I had come through. I tried to climb up on the ice, but it would break as fast as I put my weight on it. Slowly but surely I thus broke my way toward the shore and soon found myself in water that barely reached up to my armpits. Seeing me standing on hard bottom, the master-at-arms suddenly determined to do the great life-saving act and came crashing through the ice and seized me by the arm. I was escorted to the ship in disgrace, and reprimanded by the officer in charge for having gone on the ice without informing any one that I did not know how to skate. The master-at-arms, who had seen my life-and-death struggle from the river-bank, and who had done nothing to help me until I was safely standing on the bottom, and there was no further danger in coming to my assistance than getting the legs of his trousers damp, was showered with compliments and congratulated as a life-saver by the higher officers (who had not seen the incident), much to the amusement of the midshipmen who had been on the ice, many of whom had really risked their lives in their endeavors to get near me.

In February, the time for our first dreaded examination arrived and there was intense excitement in our little floating world. Some forty-odd of our class "bilged," which in midshipman parlance means that they were found deficient in their studies, the result of which was that they received polite letters from the Secretary of the Navy informing them that if they would send him their resignations he would be pleased to accept them at once. These acceptances arrived promptly, and through some misunderstanding, were handed to the unfortunate boys before arrangements for their departure had been completed, and of course there ensued a most extraordinary state of affairs. Here were some forty-odd young civilians suddenly freed from the yoke of naval discipline and detained on board a man-of-war where every movement was regulated by orders. Naturally it was not long before pandemonium broke loose. As long as the "bilged" saw the officers around, the training they had received in the last few months kept them in order; but when night came and two bells (nine o'clock) were struck and the hammocks were slung, the usual rough play on the berth deck became almost a riot.

To separate the goats from the sheep the "bilged" were directed to sling their hammocks as far forward as possible instead of on their customary hooks. When taps sounded and the gruff voice of the master-at-arms bellowed his usual warning of "Gentlemen! Silence, fore and aft!" the almost sacred order was received with derisive shouts of laughter from forward. The petty officer repeated the order, which we all well knew emanated from higher authority. There was an ominous silence as the master-at-arms retired up the hatchway. Then suddenly, by some ingenious device of the "goats" at the order, "Let fall!" a whole row of hammocks occupied by "sheep" came down with a crash, emptying their contents, midshipmen, blankets, and mattresses in indescribable confusion on to the deck. Man is so near akin to monkeys that, as Rochefoucauld said, "We even take a certain amount of pleasure in the very misfortunes of our friends," and all the boys who had escaped the disaster burst into roars of laughter which were quickly hushed by the arrival of a lieutenant on the scene. The hammocks were reslung and for a few minutes after the officer's disappearance from the scene there was silence again. We were just dozing off when the sound of a giggle coming from forward made us sit up and take notice. The order to keep silence was again given and received with laughter. This brought Lieutenant, now Admiral, John H. Upshur, the executive officer, on the scene. He ordered silence again and a "goat" answered him with a "tee-hee." The lieutenant walked a little way farther forward, stooping as he went to avoid the hammocks overhead, and repeated his command, which was received with a chorus of "ha-ha's." When the young demons had enticed him as far forward as they wanted him, they commenced to roll thirty-two-pound round shot down that inclined deck. The lieutenant manfully stood his ground for a moment, but the improvised ten-pin balls came faster than he could skip over them, and he had to take refuge on the hatchway steps. "Beat to quarters!" he fairly roared, and to the accompaniment of the "long roll" of the drums, we jumped into our clothes and tumbled up on deck, where we took our stations at the guns; but not for long, for we were marched down to the main deck and there made to toe a seam and stand at "attention." Such was the habit of discipline that the "goats," forgetting that they were free, accompanied us.

The suave and elegant lieutenant in charge ordered a wardroom boy to bring him a table, a chair, a newspaper, and a hot cup of coffee, and made himself comfortable. After what seemed to me an interminable time the deadly silence was broken by the officer saying that if the gentlemen who had made the disturbance would step forward he would gladly let the rest of us "turn in." He just said that for form's sake, as no one knew better than he did that the traditions of the Naval Academy did not allow a midshipman to "squeal" under any circumstances—and the hours dragged along. At last, becoming desperate, some of the fighting men of the class asked permission to leave the ranks, which was granted, as the lieutenant had been a midshipman himself and knew what was coming as well as the boys did. These fellows went to the guilty parties and intimated to them that there would be some black eyes to carry home if they did not confess and let the rest of us have some rest. The hint acted like a charm, and one after another of the newly made civilians stepped forward. It was then so nearly time for reveille that it was hardly worthwhile for us to go to sleep again, but we had the satisfaction of seeing a very seedy-looking set of civilians go over the side the next morning as they bade farewell forever to a naval career.

Occasionally we were taken ashore for infantry drill with the battalion composed of the "oldsters" who lived in the old Academy buildings. The Professor of Infantry Tactics was Major Lockwood, a gallant officer who afterwards became a brigadier-general in the Union Army. Major Lockwood, unfortunately, stammered and once the battalion got facetious with him. He had instructed them that they must never make a motion to obey an order until they heard the last sound of the command. He was in front of the battalion holding the hilt of his sword in his right hand and the end of the blade in his left. He gave the order to march all right, and then he gave the order to charge while he was walking backward intending to halt them when they got near him, but a fit of stammering came over him and he could only say "Ha-Ha-Ha-!" and before he could finish the word the midshipmen had run over him and also over the sea-wall and into the water, guns, uniforms, and all. Of course for the moment there was a great deal of hilarity, but unfortunately those intelligent navy officers know an antidote for every prank a midshipman can conceive.

By the end of 1860 a dark cloud had settled over our spirits and we no longer spent our few moments of leisure in skylarking, but instead discussed the burning question of secession. We did not know anything about its merits, but conceived the idea that each State was to compose a separate nation. Harry Taylor, afterwards rear admiral, who was from the District of Columbia, said that he was going with New York because that State had more commerce than any other one, and necessarily would have the biggest navy. He was promptly called down by being informed that no one would be allowed to join any State except the one he was born in,—and he was further humiliated by a much-traveled boy who asserted that he had been in Washington and that the District of Columbia had only one little steamboat out of which to make a navy and that one ran between Washington and Acquia Creek and that she was rotten. Personally, I was insulted by being informed that Louisiana had been purchased by the money of the other States just as a man buys a farm, and that therefore she had no right to secede. This was said in retort after I had made the boast that by rights many of the States belonged to Louisiana. So the wrangle went on day after day until the news came that South Carolina had in reality seceded and the boys from that State promptly resigned and went home. Then followed the news of the firing on Fort Sumter. The rest of the lads from the South resigned as rapidly as they could get permission from home to do so—I among the rest.[1]

I passed over the side of the old *Constitution* and out of the United States Navy with a big lump in my throat which I vainly endeavored to swallow, for I had many very dear friends among the Northern boys— in fact, affectionate friendships, some interrupted by death, but a few others which have lasted for more than half a century. To my surprise my captain, George Rodgers, accompanied me ashore and to the railway station, telling me, as I walked beside him, that the trouble would end in a few weeks and that I had made a great mistake, but that even then it was not too late if I would ask to withdraw my resignation.

As we passed through the old gate opening into the town, the gate which I was not to pass through again until my head was white, fifty years afterwards, and as we walked along the street, Captain Rodgers kindly took my hand in his, and then for the first time I realized that I was no longer in the navy, but only a common and very unhappy little boy. But the Confederacy was calling me and I marched firmly on. That call seemed much louder at Annapolis than it did after I reached my native land.

Four

Out of the United States Navy—Complete disguise—Captain Maynadier, U.S.A.—Passing through the Union and Confederate lines—Senator Wigfall and President Andrew Johnson—Montgomery, Alabama—President Jefferson Davis and Judah P. Benjamin—Tender services and sword to the Confederacy—Declined with thanks—The "Marseillaise."

At that time I was very small for my age (fifteen)—so small, in fact, that I was dubbed "Little" Morgan, which nickname has stuck to me to this day despite my five feet nine and a quarter inches in height and over two hundred pounds weight. With as much dignity as my size at the time would permit of my assuming, I took my seat in the car and started for Washington. Then I commenced to size up the situation. I had only twelve dollars, all the pay that was due me when I resigned, and there was a thousand miles for me to travel to reach my home, but what worried me most was the fear that the authorities would arrest me if they knew that I proposed to offer my services to the Southern Confederacy. I had no civilian "togs," but I had taken the gold anchors off my collar, on which they had left dark imprints, and put blue velvet covers, fastened by elastics, over the brass buttons of my jacket. There were only nine buttons on a side, so of course they were not conspicuous. This, with the glazed cover of my cap to hide the silver anchor which adorned its front, constituted my disguise, which I felt sure would be sufficient to enable me to slip through the enemy's capital without recognition. I was just beginning to feel comfortable when a motherly-looking old lady in the opposite seat disturbed my equanimity by asking me in a loud voice if I was "one of those little Naval Academy boys who were going South?" That woman surely had the making of a Sherlock Holmes in her.

I had not an idea as to what I would have to do to reach home after I arrived in Washington, so, to throw the minions of Abraham Lincoln further off my trail I went straight to the house of Captain Henry Maynadier, U.S.A., an ardent Union man who had married one of my first cousins. I told him that I wanted to get home and had no money, and then, washing my hands of all responsibility, left the rest for him to do. He did it. He obtained a permit for himself and me to pass through the lines, and, hiring a hack, we started on our adventure.

The Union pickets held the Long Bridge; half a mile below on the Alexandria Road were posted the Confederate sentries. Of course, with the permit we had no difficulty in crossing the bridge, but before we had proceeded very far on the road a man with a gun jumped out of the bushes and ordered us to halt. The fellow was an Irishman who had formerly done chores at Captain Maynadier's house in Washington, and of course he instantly recognized him, at the same time crying out gleefully, "Begorra! we'll whip those dirty nigger-loving Yanks now that you are coming with us!"

The captain said a few pleasant words and told him that I was going South and asked him to see that I did not miss my way to Alexandria where I was to catch the train. He also told me to jump out quickly and ordered the driver to turn around. I had hardly reached the ground when the driver put whip to his horses and the astounded picket, recovering from his astonishment, raised his gun. I begged him not to shoot, assuring him that Captain Maynadier was coming South later. He did—with Sherman! This adventure occurred in the latter part of April. In November of the same year Captain Maynadier and I were shooting at each other at Island Number 10 on the Mississippi River.

Arriving at the railway station in Alexandria, I found a great crowd wildly cheering ex-Senator Wigfall, who was a volunteer aide on General Beauregard's staff, and who had received the sword of Major Anderson when Fort Sumter surrendered. Wigfall stood on the rear platform of a car, bowing his appreciation of the enthusiasm. I found an unoccupied seat on the train, and was making myself comfortable when a big, broad-shouldered, stumpy man waddled up to where I sat and said, "Sonny, as you are so small and I am so large, I think we will make a good fit for this narrow seat;" and without further ado he seated himself beside me, first asking me to move so he could have the place by the window.

The train started amid wild cheers for Wigfall, the hero of the hour, and at every station where we stopped crowds were gathered demanding a speech from the great man. The stout fellow with the short legs who was seated beside me apparently took no interest in the proceedings, and seemed engrossed by his own thoughts. It was some-time after dark when we arrived at Lynchburg, Virginia, where the largest crowd we had yet seen was waiting for the train. Many of the men bore torches, but they were not cheering for Wigfall; they seemed to be in an ugly humor about something. Suddenly there were cries of "Hang the traitor!" "Here is a rope!" "Bring him out!" as the mad-dened mob fairly swirled about the car.

A man burst through the door and rushed up the aisle to where I was seated, and leaning over me, said to my neighbor: "Are you Andy Johnson?"

"I am, Mr. Johnson!" replied the stout gentleman.

"Well," said the stranger, "I want to pull your nose!" and he made a grab for Mr. Johnson's face.

The latter brushed the man's hand aside, at the same time jump-ing to his feet.

There followed a scuffle for a few seconds, and poor little me, being between the combatants, got much the worst of it: I was most unpleasantly jostled.

The crime for which they wanted to lynch Mr. Johnson was the fact that he was reported to be on his way to Tennessee for the purpose of preventing that State from seceding. Mr. Wigfall came up to Mr. Johnson and asked him to go out on the platform with him. Wigfall at once addressed the mob and urged them to give Mr. Johnson a hear-ing, which they did. The latter commenced his speech by saying, "I am a Union man!" and he talked to them until the train moved off, hold-ing their attention as though they were spellbound. His last words were, "I am a Union man!"—and the last cry we heard from the crowd was, "Hang him!"

Relating the foregoing incident to Mr. George A. Trenholm, then Secretary of the Confederate Treasury, I expressed the opinion that it was one of the greatest exhibitions of courage I had ever witnessed, but Mr. Trenholm cast a damper on my enthusiasm by saying, "My son, I have known Mr. Johnson since we were young men. He rode into prominence on the shoulders of just such a mob as you saw at Lynchburg, and no man knows how to handle such a crowd better than Mr. Johnson. Had he weakened they probably would have hung him." It was the same Andrew Johnson, afterwards President of the United States, who granted Mr. Trenholm amnesty and a pardon in 1866.

Continuing my journey I at last arrived at Montgomery, Alabama, then capital of the Confederate States. My fears that the war would be over before I got there were somewhat allayed—for I had been told positively that it would not last six weeks before the South would finish it victoriously. I found the new capital in a ferment of excitement, nobody seemed to know exactly what it was about, but it was the fashion to be excited. From every house containing a piano the soul-stirring strains of the "Marseillaise" floated out of the open windows. At the hotel where I stopped, champagne flowed like water. The big parlor was crowded with men dressed in uniforms designed to please the wearer, so they looked like a gathering for a fancy-dress ball. On the chairs and window sills were bottles of wine and glasses, while at the piano sat a burly German who, of course, crashed out the everlasting "Marseillaise" while his enthusiastic audience sang it. A more ridiculous sight than a lot of native-born Americans, not understanding a word of French, beating their breasts as they howled what they flattered themselves were the words of the song, it was never before my bad fortune to witness. But there was really good reason for all the excitement: had not twelve millions of people all gone crazy on the same day?

I put my head out of a window so that I could get a little fresh air. There was a moment's halt in the music while someone made a war speech. The tired and sweating German musician took advantage of the respite to get a little air also, and as he stood beside me I heard him mutter: "Dom the Marseillaise!"

The morning after my arrival I went to the capitol to offer my services, and the sword I intended to buy, to the Government. There were numbers of employees rushing about the building in a great state of excitement, but with nothing to do. None of them could tell me where I could find the Secretary of the Navy. At last I ran across an intelligent official who informed me that "there warn't no such person." It appeared to be the custom of the attaches, when in doubt, to refer the stranger to Mr. Judah P. Benjamin, the "Pooh Bah" of the Confederate Government, then Secretary of State. He informed me that there was not as yet any Confederate Navy, and further humiliated me by calling me "Sonny." However, he was very kind and took me into the private office of President Jefferson Davis. Talk about "the blow that killed father"—it was nothing in comparison to the jolt I then and there received. Mr. Davis was kindness personified, and told me to go home and tell my parents that as soon as the Government established a naval school I should have one of the first appointments. I left the presence of the great man crestfallen and convinced that the Confederacy was doomed. I had come to fight, not to go to school. Had I not just left the greatest naval school in the world to avoid getting an education? And here the best they could offer me was a place in some makeshift academy that was to be erected in the dim future. I felt that I had been deceived and badly treated, and I mentally comforted myself with the assurance that I knew more about drill and tactics than the whole mob of civilian generals and colonels who thronged the capitol's corridors. But Mr. Davis did not know this.

I was a full-blown pessimist by the time I reached my hotel where I was greeted by the sounds of the everlasting "Enfants de la patrie" being hiccuped as usual in the parlor; and for the rest of the day I iterated and reiterated the German's prayer, "Dom the Marseillaise!"

The only way to get from Montgomery to Mobile was by steamboat; and all the boats had been seized by the Government for the transportation of troops. After much urging the captain of one of the transports, as a favor, allowed me to pay for my passage to Mobile on condition that I would sleep on the deck, if I could find a place, and supply my own provisions. The boat would start when he received orders, but he did not know when that would be. A two days' wait followed, during which I stayed on the boat so as to be sure that I would not be left and consequently lose the price of my passage. That was important, as my finances were running low. Confederate money had not yet made its appearance and gold was already being hoarded. I had already lost quite a sum in exchanging one State's money for another, as even the paper money issued in one county did not pass at par in the next (if accepted at all), but everybody was jubilant over the fact that the Confederate Congress had appropriated *fifteen millions* of dollars to carry the war on to a successful termination.

Finally, after endless delay, a swarm of volunteers took possession of the boat and we were off. The transport carried no guns, but she was armed with an instrument of torture, called a "calliope," or steam piano, and as she backed out into the river it broke loose, shrieking an imitation of the "Marseillaise," which, with few intermissions, was kept up during the two days and nights it took us to reach Mobile. When the calliope did stop, it was very soothing to hear the Negro deck-hands break into song with their tuneful melodies.

The volunteers were composed of fresh, youthful-looking men, and almost every one of them was accompanied by a "body-servant," as Negro valets were called in the South. They were also accompanied by a great number of baskets of champagne and boxes of brandy. Few aristocrats in those days ever drank whiskey, which was supposed to be a vulgar tipple. They also had huge hampers containing roasted turkeys, chickens, hams, and all sorts of good things with which they were very generous. Every private also had from one to three trunks containing his necessary wardrobe. I saw some of these same young men in the muddy trenches in front of Richmond in 1865, when they were clothed, partially, in rags and were gnawing on ears of hard corn, and would have gladly exchanged half a dozen Negroes or a couple of hundred acres of land for a square meal or a decent bed to sleep on.

Five

Arrive in New Orleans—Brother Harry killed next morning in a duel—Homecoming in Baton Rouge.

At Mobile I had to take another boat for New Orleans which, passing through the Mississippi Sound and Lake Ponchartrain, at last landed me in a country where I felt at home. l never realized before how sweetly the Creole accent sounded. I was met by my brother Harry, who had recently returned from Europe where he had been for the purpose of taking a post-graduate course in his medical studies. Harry was in high spirits because he had received an appointment as an assistant surgeon in the Confederate Army. He told me all the family news and how my brother Gibbes was a lieutenant in the Seventh Louisiana Regiment and had just left for Virginia, and that my brother George was a lieutenant in the First Louisiana and had gone to Pensacola, Florida. It appeared to me that the Confederacy wanted the whole family—with the exception of myself.

Arriving at my brother Judge Morgan's house I was so glad to see the family that for the time being I forgot about the ingratitude the Southern Confederacy had shown me. That evening there was a dinner party at the house and among the guests were Mr. Bouligny, recently member of Congress, and probably the most famous duelist in the State; also Mr. Hériat, editor of "The Bee," the newspaper that never apologized. Mr. Hériat was its fighting editor. Judge Morgan was the only Union man at his table, and as the conversation naturally turned upon the war, he was the target for all the shafts of wit and humor. One of the guests described a ludicrous sight he had witnessed that morning when a youth, well known to my brother, while doing sentry duty in front of a public park, had ordered the gigantic judge to halt as he was on his way to hold court, and how the judge had brushed sentry and gun aside and almost frightened the poor boy out of his wits by saying, "I have a great mind to send you to jail for a month!"

The judge related his experiences at a mass meeting held the night before at the Clay statue on Canal Street. He was one of the speakers and the crowd knew his sentiments and had made their preparations. He told them that if they would fight the abolitionists within the Union he would fight with them, but warned them that if they fired a shot at the Stars and Stripes in less than five years their slaves would be their political masters. This opinion was indeed prophetic, but just then a straw man about fifteen feet long with a placard, on which was written in great letters, "P. H. Morgan—Traitor," pinned to it was set on fire and hoisted on a telegraph pole.

When bedtime came, Harry, who had always made a pet of me, said that I must sleep with him, and the judge told him to go to bed and get some rest, as he wished to speak with me privately. When Harry had gone my elder brother told me I must be very careful and not disturb Harry in the night, as he had to get up very early; in fact he was going to fight a duel shortly after daylight. I instantly made up my mind that I was going to see that duel, and I never doubted for a moment but what my gallant brother would come off victor.

I was awakened before day by a noise and Harry's jumping out of bed and hastily dressing. I, too, hurried on my clothes and followed him downstairs. There was a carriage waiting in front of the house in which were seated Messrs. Bouligny and Hériat. It was still very dark, and as Harry entered the carriage I climbed upon the box and took my seat alongside of the driver. We proceeded to the Oaks, a favorite place for duels, and when I was discovered, Mr. Bouligny told me that under the "code" no blood relative was allowed to be within two hundred yards of the combatants, so I was sent off to stand some distance away.

Mr. James Sparks was my brother's antagonist. One of his seconds was William Howell, a brother of Mrs. Jefferson Davis. The weapons—which my brother chose—were double-barrel shotguns loaded with ball, and the distance at which they fought was twenty paces. They were placed in position and Mr. Bouligny gave the word. Both guns, it seemed to me, went off simultaneously and Mr. Sparks staggered. All four seconds ran to him, and I fairly flew to see what had happened. My brother Harry during this time was standing and had not taken down his gun from his shoulder. Mr. Sparks's head had been grazed and when I had satisfied myself that he was not hurt I turned to look at my brother who to my horror was lying on his back with his gun across his breast. I said, "Mr. Bouligny, look at Harry!" The surgeon was already kneeling by him. The bullet had struck a bone in his right arm, and glancing, had entered his body passing through his lungs and penetrating to his left side.

One of Mr. Spark's younger brothers was a classmate of mine at the Naval Academy and served gallantly in the Confederate Navy afterwards. Mr. James Sparks, who killed my brother, served through the long four years, and after the war was over he was found dead near poor Harry's grave.

The next day Judge Morgan and I took dear Harry's remains to Baton Rouge. The steamboat left New Orleans late in the afternoon, and all that night we sat by the coffin which was placed on the lower deck. Each of us was wrapped in his own sad thoughts, so the long weary hours before we arrived at Baton Rouge seemed endless. Not that either of us was anxious to hasten our arrival, for we knew only too well that we had a sad ordeal to go through when we met our dear father, who would be bent with sorrow; and a mother whose heart would be broken. God help me—this was to be the home-coming to which I had looked forward with such delight.

Volunteers—Lonely—Captain Booth, late U.S.A., finds use for me—Pensacola—"Give them a little more grape, Captain Bragg."

I found little change in the appearance of Baton Rouge except that the once peaceful streets of the pretty little town now resounded with the tramp of soldiers who were gathering at the garrison there from all parts of the State. Having nothing to do, I frequented the garrison where were assembled many of my old schoolmates. The military ideas of these soldiers were very crude—very few, if any, of them knew the manual of arms, and they insisted on calling their colonels and captains, "Billy," "Tommy," and "John." As for the uniforms (?) they would have put to shame an opéra-bouffe army. I remember particularly the "Delta Rifles" of Baton Rouge whose dress was much admired by the ladies, but which greatly tickled my risibles. It was composed of some green gauze-like-looking fabric, the tunic of which, like the sleeves, was trimmed with long fringe which reached below their knees, and these men expected to go to Virginia and possibly spend a winter amidst its snows.

The soldiers at that time elected their own officers, and many men of ability declined commissions, so that popular comrades who were not financially well fixed could enjoy the emoluments appertaining to the ranks of captains and lieutenants. But the Southern soldier was no fool, and it was not very long before he discovered that the "Billy" and "Tommy" captains were not the kind of men they wished to entrust their well-being and lives to.

33

The volunteers were in great dread that the war would be over before they had a chance to get into it. All was bustle and excitement around me, and I alone seemed to have nothing to do. My favorite pony was in the stable, but I had lost all pleasure in riding him—even Charloe no longer chased wild horses. Cousinard, the club-footed town constable, had killed my bull terrier while I was at Annapolis, so I had no sympathetic companion to keep me company. The boys I had formerly played with seemed to have disappeared as though by magic. A cavalry regiment appeared on the scene and among the privates I saw my old playmate and dear friend, Howell Carter, mounted on a fine big horse with a saber as long as himself tied to him. Howell was only about a year older than I, but he was big for his age. The authorities seemed to draw the line only at little runts like myself. Everyone was either going to the war or had gone. I seemed to be the only one for whom there was no place. I was very disconsolate, until one day Captain Booth, an old regular army officer who commanded the arsenal, asked my father to lend me to him, as he wanted me immediately for very important service. My father expressed surprise that one so young should be selected for any mission of importance, but Captain Booth reminded him that I had had an Annapolis training, and it was absolutely necessary for him to have someone who knew how to implicitly obey orders without asking any questions. My father consenting, I was told to put a change of clothes into a carpet-sack and go down to the wharf boat within an hour and there await further orders. Captain Booth soon joined me. An army wagon made its appearance on the river-bank and four soldiers lifted from it a large and very heavy trunk which they brought aboard the wharf boat. Captain Booth then took me aside and told me what the trunk contained and handed me written instructions and an order addressed to all army officers and civilian officials to facilitate and expedite my journey in every possible manner. The order was signed by the hero of my childish imagination, General Bragg, of "Give them a little more grape, Captain Bragg," fame.[1] Captain Booth and the soldiers remained with me till a steamboat bound for New Orleans arrived, when the soldiers put the trunk on board, and Captain Booth, wishing me God speed, away I went feeling very important.

Arriving at New Orleans, I had my trunk put upon a truck, and as my orders were not to part company with it under any circumstances, I sat on it and directed the driver to proceed to Judge Morgan's house on Camp Street. I had one of the many rough rides of my life over the cobblestones with which the streets of the city of that day were paved. A Negro butler opened the door of the house for me and informed me that the family were away, but that my brother was in town and of course would sleep there. With the assistance of the butler, the two truckmen, and myself, we managed to carry the trunk into the hall on the lower floor, and I made an arrangement with the men to come for it at six o'clock in the morning to carry it to the station of the little railway, some five or six miles long, which connected the city with Lake Ponchartrain at the point where the boat for Mobile lay. Feeling safe I then went upstairs and went to bed.

I awoke early in the morning just as the truckmen arrived in front of the house and one can imagine my horror and distress when I found that my precious trunk had disappeared in the night. I was a ruined man, and felt certain that my career was blasted forevermore.

The house was a big one with a wide hall running through its center, and my brother's bedroom was on the lower floor and opened into the hall. I was standing there dazed when he suddenly made his appearance and commenced to scold me for my carelessness. To my amazement he told me that he knew perfectly well what the trunk contained, adding that he had a little more care for my reputation than I seemed to possess, and that he had performed the marvelous feat of dragging that trunk into his bedroom and had actually pushed it under his tall four-poster when he came home late in the night, as otherwise burglars might have carried it away. Others possibly knew as well as he did what its contents were. I was astonished by his remarks, but as I had orders not to discuss the contents of the trunk with anyone I kept silence.

Greatly relieved in my mind I started for Mobile, and on arrival there showed General Bragg's order to the quartermaster officer, who had my trunk carried to another boat which took me to Blakely, across the bay, where I was to take the stage-coach for Pensacola. At Blakely my serious troubles began. The stage agent swore that under no circumstances should so heavy a trunk be placed in the boot of the old-fashioned stage-coach. He would allow me to take passage on the crowded stage, but as for the trunk, "Nix!" There was a company of infantry stationed at Blakely, and I showed General Bragg's order to the captain; and on his threat to seize the stage and have one of his men take charge of it, I was allowed to proceed, for about ten miles, to a place where we changed mules. There the stage-driver said the trunk was fairly killing his team and he would not haul it another mile; it could come on sometime in the dim future by wagon. My protests were in vain, as several of the passengers volunteered to assist him in dumping it on the ground. Fairly desperate, I showed them the order of the commanding officer of the district and made them quite an oration, telling them that the contents of the trunk were of the greatest importance to General Bragg, who had been telegraphed that I would arrive on that stage, but that I would not accompany them without my baggage; and I wound up by asserting that if I was not on that stage when it arrived in Pensacola General Bragg would hang the last one of them for treason.

My imposing-looking official document and-the fear of a military court martial was too much for the nerves of the passengers, but did not raze the stage-driver. But when the passengers refused to continue the journey unless the trunk went also, he relented. He took his revenge, however, by making us walk most of the forty weary miles; because the road was so sandy.

Arriving at Pensacola, the passengers were very glad that they had insisted on the driver bringing my trunk, for there waiting for me was Colonel, afterwards General, Boggs, chief of staff, and several other officers, and a detail of soldiers with an army wagon, and they fairly overwhelmed me with compliments. The colonel said that General Bragg wanted to see me, and we went at once to Fort Barrancus where his headquarters were. The general told me he never was so glad to see anybody before, and that I was to remain at his quarters as his guest until I returned to Baton Rouge. The next day the Confederate batteries opened fire on Fort Pickens.

After the Civil War was over, Judge Morgan, who, as I have before said, was a Union man, was amusing his guests one day at dinner by recounting the many acts of folly of which he considered the defunct Confederacy guilty, and as an illustration pointed at me and said, "Do yon see how young that boy looks now? Well, you can well imagine how he looked at the age of fifteen when I tell you that he was small for his age. The Southern troops stationed at Pensacola early in the war became dissatisfied at not receiving any pay. The newspapers were full of stories about their being mutinous on account of the Government's neglect, when the authorities, becoming frightened, to pacify the men secretly sent that child with a trunk full of silver dollars to be distributed among them, and the mere baby carelessly left it in the hall of my house where any one might have carried it off; but fortunately, for him, he had a big brother who almost pulled his arms out of their sockets to draw it to a place of safety under his own bed. And a worse frightened boy than he was when he could not find his trunk load of money you would rarely see."

There was great laughter at my expense, and when it had somewhat subsided; I asked my brother if he knew what he had slept over that night? "Silver, of course," he replied. "Well," I said, "that memorable night you slept over about three hundred pounds of powder contained in primers and fuses, and there were also in the trunk two live shells that Captain Booth wanted Colonel Boggs to try in a particular gun at Pensacola. They were good shells, too, for I saw both of them explode in Fort Pickens."

"Great Heavens!" exclaimed the judge; "and I examined the fastening with a lighted candle to see if they were secure before I went to bed!"

When I arrived at Pensacola with the trunk, General Bragg had only three primers to a gun and that was the reason he and his staff were so glad to see me.

When I returned to New Orleans I was informed that two steamers were being fitted out for the newly organized Confederate Navy and I crossed the river to see them where they lay at Algiers. I found several old friends who had been first classmen at Annapolis on board of them. One of these ships was a fruiterer called the *Habana*, and the other was a former Mexican pirate, called the *Marquis de la Habana*. The *Habana* became the famous *Sumter* and the other's name was changed to *McRae*. The latter vessel had already had quite an exciting career. A few months previously, in company with a consort, she had appeared off Vera Cruz. She refused to show her colors and the U.S. sloop-of-war *Saratoga* undertook to make her do so. She belonged to General Miramort, who was heading a Mexican revolution. She and her consort opened fire, but were soon reduced to submission by the American ship, but not before some twenty-odd men had been killed or wounded. A prize was put on board of her, and Lieutenant R. T. Chapman was ordered to take her to New Orleans and turn her over to the United States marshal and make the charge against her of "Belonging to an unrecognized revolutionary government and being a pirate on the high seas." Lieutenant Chapman, a few months after he had made this charge, found himself on board of the *Sumter*, under Captain Semmes, which vessel belonged to an unrecognized revolutionary government and was branded as "a pirate on the high seas" by the United States Government.[2]

Seven

The sloop-of-war *McRae* arrives at Baton Rouge—Receives warrant as a midshipman and ordered to the *McRae*—Fail to get through the blockade—Attack on Federal fleet at the Head of the Passes—Heroes until a newspaper "Mahan" discovered that we ought to have towed the whole Federal fleet up to New Orleans in triumph.

The summer dragged its slow length into July. My brothers Gibbes and George were by this time in Virginia, one in Blanchard's brigade and the other with General "Dick" Taylor's brigade, also in "Stonewall" Jackson's division. Everybody, with the exception of the loud-mouthed orators, seemed to have gone to the war. The spellbinders now had only aged men and cripples for audiences, but they could always invoke a feeble cheer by dramatically exclaiming, "One Southern man can whip ten Northerners." This bold statement did not arouse any enthusiasm in my breast, as I doubted its correctness. I had already tackled two Yanks with rather worse than indifferent success. I had eight more coming to me for my share, and as I knew a lot of little fellows from New England, with whom I had skylarked at Annapolis, without showing myself possessed of any marked physical superiority over them individually, I felt justified in my doubts about being able to manhandle the eight combined.

At last there came a great excitement for the town, and the inhabitants, many of whom had never seen an oceangoing steamship, rushed to the riverside and there beheld the bark-rigged Confederate States sloop-of-war *McRae*, of seven guns, which had come up the river to receive her ammunition from the arsenal. She was a beautiful sight as she lay at anchor in the stream with her tall, graceful masts and her yards squared in man-of-war fashion, looking so trim and neat.[1]

I went aboard as soon as possible to see the midshipmen, of course, and was most heartily welcomed. As soon as the captain and lieutenants learned that I had been at Annapolis, they too were very kind to me, agreeing with me that it was a shame I was not in the service. Before the week was ended I went on board again, and reported to Captain Thomas B. Huger for duty.[2] How that delightful moment was brought about is best told by a letter from my father to my elder brother which was given to me by one of my nieces fifty years afterwards:

> *Baton Rouge, La., July 17, 1861.*
>
> *My Dear Son:*
> *The mail has arrived without bringing any letter from Virginia or from you. This has disappointed me much, as Charles La Noue tells me he saw in the "True Delta" of Sunday, a letter advertised for you coming from the First Regiment, Louisiana Volunteers. I presume it must have escaped your attention.*
> *It is now nearly a month since I have heard from George, and I am becoming anxious.*
> *On yesterday Jimmie's warrant as midshipman arrived, at which he is highly delighted, especially as Captain Huge, on yesterday, before the arrival of the mail, requested me to telegraph the Department that there was room for him on the McRae and that he desired to have him. The little scamp seems to take the fancy of all the officers he falls in with; those on the McRae seem to be very clever, and the midshipmen are all acquaintances of his. . . .*
> *Ever yours,*
> *Thomas Gibbes Morgan.*
>
> *Hon. P. H. Morgan*
> *New Orleans, La.*

When that telegram arrived ordering me to report to Captain Huger for duty on the *McRae*, my joy knew no bounds, and rushing to my room it took me about ten seconds to remove those velvet covers from the brass buttons on my jacket, and in less than three minutes more I was in that uniform and had torn off the glazed cover of my cap and displayed my silver anchor. In those days all the naval officers wore the blue uniforms of the United States Navy which they had brought South with them, and they kicked like steers when they were afterwards compelled to don the gray, contemptuously demanding to know, "Who had ever seen a gray sailor, no matter what nationality he served?"

MIDSHIPMAN JAMES MORRIS MORGAN, C.S.N.
At the age of fifteen

I was in mortal dread that the McRae would sail before I could get to her (she in fact only lay there for ten days longer), but it took me only about ten minutes to get to the river where I commenced frantically to signal for a boat. I must have been kept waiting for fifteen minutes; to me it seemed an eternity.

Reporting, I was assigned to my watch and station, and in less than an hour was sent ashore, on duty, in charge of the first cutter, and how my small heart swelled with pride and how my fellow townsmen's eyes opened with amazement as they heard "little Jimmie Morgan" giving orders to the sailors and their ever ready, "Aye, aye, sir!" in reply.

Having got our ammunition on board, at last we started for New Orleans to fill up with coal, and then steamed for the mouths of the river, or rather to the "Head of the Passes," to await an opportunity to run the blockade. Captain Semmes with the Sumter had succeeded in doing it—why should not we? But it was not to be. The passes were much better guarded than when the Sumter escaped. Several times we got ready to attempt the feat at night, but on each occasion the pilots raised objections, saying that the McRae drew too much water for them to take the responsibility, or that they were not pilots for the bar of the pass selected. Strange to say, most, if not all, the pilots, were Northern men. So we spent weeks laying at the Head of the Passes, or between there and Forts Jackson and St. Philip, waiting our chance until our coal supply was exhausted and then we returned to New Orleans to refill our bunkers.

The "Crescent City" was gay in those days, as the people had not yet realized what a serious thing war was, or what it was to live in a captured city, an experience that was to be theirs before many months had passed. There were balls and dinners ashore, and the ship was constantly filled with visitors.

In the olden times little midshipmen were punished by being "mastheaded," which consisted in the youngster having to climb up to the cap of the foretopmast and stand there with barely space enough for his two little feet, and he had to hold on to the stays to keep from falling. Unfortunately I was frequently detected in some deviltry, and as a consequence, passed much of my leisure time aloft. I am doubtful if I ever quite forgave our gallant second lieutenant, Mr. Eggleston, for saying to me on one occasion, after I had presented the first lieutenant's compliments and requested him to masthead me, "Well, sir, you surely ought to know the way up there by this time!"—I always suspected that he meant to be sarcastic.

Captain Huger was a very handsome man; he was also a widower, his late wife having been a sister of General Meade, U.S.A., of Gettysburg fame. The captain was at the time of which I write engaged to one of the most beautiful girls in New Orleans, so it was not strange that when lying off the city he always found it convenient to anchor the *McRae* in front of Jackson Square because the Pontalba buildings faced the park, and in one of them, near the old Cathedral of St. Louis, his sweetheart dwelt. I knew all about the courtship because I carried so many notes from the captain, and the young lady made such a pet of me.

When the month of October arrived, it brought with it some excitement. Three towboats and a river tug each armed with a smoothbore thirty-two pounder had been added to the Confederate fleet on the Mississippi. There was also a tugboat, called the *Enoch Train*, belonging to private parties, who had covered her over with a wooden turtleback over which they had placed railway iron "T" rails, dovetailed, for an armor. The patriotic owners wanted to make a contract with the Confederate Government (for a huge sum) for every Federal vessel they would sink.

The United States fleet, consisting of the steam sloop-of-war *Richmond* of twenty-six nine-inch guns, the *Preble* and *Vincennes*, sailing sloops-of-war of twenty-two guns each, and the *Waterwitch*, a steamer carrying five guns one of which was a rifle, had taken possession of the Head of the Passes of the Mississippi and put an end to any possible blockade-running.

Commodore Hollins had now assumed command of the naval defenses of the Mississippi River.[3] He was no longer young, having been a midshipman on the U.S. frigate *President* when he was captured by a British fleet in the War of 1812. He was also the man who had (in the U.S. sloop-of-war *Cyane*) bombarded Greytown in Nicaragua. He now determined to attempt to drive the United States fleet out of the river and to do this he decided to seize the ram, now called the *Manassas*, which was anchored in the stream.[4] To a polite request that she should be turned over to us came the reply that we "did not have men enough to take her." The *McRae* was ranged up alongside of her and a boat was lowered. Lieutenant Warley ordered me to accompany him.[5] On arriving alongside of the ram we found her crew lined up on the turtleback, swearing that they would kill the first man who attempted to board her. There was a ladder reaching to the water from the top of her armor to the waterline. Lieutenant Warley, pistol in hand, ordered me to keep the men in the boat until he gave the order for them to join him. Running up the ladder, his face set in grim determination, he caused a sudden panic among the heroic (?) crew of longshoremen who incontinently took to their heels and like so many prairie dogs disappeared down their hole of a hatchway with Mr. Warley after them. He drove them back on deck and then drove them ashore, some of them jumping overboard and swimming for it. With the addition of two fire rafts our fleet was now complete and we proceeded to the forts, where we anchored awaiting an opportunity to attack the enemy. This chance arrived on the night of the 12th of October, when we weighed anchor and proceeded down the river, the *Manassas*, under the command of Warley, leading, followed by the fire rafts in tow of tugs, the *McRae*, the *Ivy*, the *Tuscarora*, the *Calhoun*, and the *Jackson*.[6] The *Calhoun*, a towboat, with a walking-beam engine, was considered too vulnerable in her boilers and machinery, so she was ordered to keep out of it. The *Jackson*, a high-pressure paddlewheel towboat of great power, made so much noise from her escape pipes that she could be heard ten miles away, so she was ordered to stay as far behind as possible. It must have been about three o'clock in the morning when we saw a rocket go up which was the signal agreed upon that the *Manassas* had rammed something. Instantly the heavy broadsides of the United States ships blazed forth as they shot holes through the darkness, or, as we hoped, through one another. Our fire rafts also burst into flame and were floating down upon them. It was a magnificent spectacle to those of us who were a mile away.

When daylight came, all firing ceased, and to our amazement we saw the Federal fleet fleeing down the Southwest Pass, and the *Manassas* (which we had never expected to see again), lying a helpless wreck in the marsh, against which she had drifted. She had rammed the *Richmond* and torn off of that vessel's bow a couple of planks, but as the *Richmond* had a coaling schooner alongside, the speed of the ram had been checked by the hawser of the collier which was made fast to the bow of the warship. The cable had slipped over the bow of the *Manassas* and mowed off her little smokestacks even with the turtleback, rendering her helpless. The *Richmond* had frantically worked her broadside, but the ram lay so low in the water that all the projectiles passed over her. This was fortunate, as the dense smoke which filled the *Manassas* had forced her crew to take refuge on her deck. The little ram was too light for the work, and too weak in power. She had been a good tug, but the weight of her armor had completely deadened her speed, and while she did very well going downstream she could not make more than one or two knots an hour against the current.

"It is a poor cock that won't chase a fleeing rooster." Emboldened by the sight of the retreating enemy we gave chase. On arriving at the mouth of the river the *Preble* and *Waterwitch* passed over the shallow bar safely, but the big *Richmond* and the *Vincennes* grounded, the latter with her stern pointing upstream. The *Richmond* when she struck the bottom was swung around by the current and presented her formidable broadside to us. Outside, in the Gulf, about three miles away, was the fiftygun sailing frigate *Santee* under a cloud of canvas, sailing back and forth like a caged lion, unable to get into the fray on account of her great draft, but she made as glorious a picture as ever delighted the eye of a sailor.

U.S. SLOOP-OF-WAR *RICHMOND*, OF FARRAGUT'S FLEET

C.S. RAM *MANASSAS*, WHICH RAMMED THE *RICHMOND*

We opened fire with our nine-inch pivot gun on the *Richmond*, but from a very respectful distance, as otherwise we might have spoiled her pretty paint. She replied at first with single guns, and afterwards with broadsides, many of the projectiles passing over us. The *Waterwitch* from outside used a rifled gun, but her shots also, fortunately for us, went high.

The towboat *Ivy*, commanded by Lieutenant Fry (the man who was some years later captured in the blockade-runner *Virginius* and so cruelly put to death by the Spaniards at Santiago, Cuba), made a dash for the helpless *Vincennes*, and, taking up a position under her stem, commenced to throw thirty-two-pound shells, from her one little smooth-bore gun, into the sloop-of-war's cabin windows. Suddenly, to our, amazement, we witnessed a sight the like of which was never before seen in the United States Navy. The boats of the *Vincennes* were lowered and her crew, after putting a fuse to her magazine, abandoned her, and took refuge on the *Richmond*!

The shots from the *Richmond*, in her efforts to protect the *Vincennes*'s boats, almost drowned the little *Ivy* with spray and she was recalled.

A most extraordinary thing had occurred on the abandoned ship. Her cartridges were in red flannel bags, as was the custom at that time, and they were packed in metal cylinders about the size of barrels. One of these had been emptied and the fuse end was placed at its bottom and the powder cartridges replaced. The fuse led out of the magazine and up the hatchway on to the upper deck and down into the magazine, up the side of the cylinder, and down through the spaces between the cartridges to the bottom without exploding a cartridge!

Commodore Hollins, knowing that the *Richmond*, alone, could whip the Gulf of Mexico full of such vessels as he commanded, if she could only get at them, withdrew from action and proceeded up the river, taking possession of three schooners on the way which the Federal fleet had left behind them in their hurry to get away.

Arriving at the fort we anchored and I was sent up to New Orleans as a bearer of dispatches. The news of the fight had preceded me, and we found a great crowd on the levee when the steamboat made her landing. For the only time in my life I experienced the delights of having myself made into a hero. When it became known to the crowd that I had been in the fight, they cheered and seemed wild with excitement, but unfortunately for our glory the enthusiasm wore off when a "newspaper admiral" came out in an editorial denouncing Commodore Hollins, stating that his conduct was most reprehensible in that he had not brought to the city, as prizes, the whole Federal fleet. I suppose the frigate *Santee*, which drew so much water it would have required a rather large truck to have carried her over the bar, ought to have been brought also!

I had the permission of my captain to visit my home in Baton Rouge after mailing the commodore's dispatches, and when I arrived there I found my father dying. I went into his room and he made a sign that he wanted to speak to me. Bending over him I placed my ear close to his mouth and he whispered, "Good-night; God bless you, my son." Those were his last words.

Eight

The *McRae* made flagship of the Mississippi flotilla—Commodore Hollins appointed aide-de-camp to the commodore—Island No. 10— New Madrid—The Swamp Fox of Missouri—Masked batteries— Wanted to challenge a major—U.S. ironclads pass Island No. 10— Stung—New Madrid and Island No. 10 evacuated—"Savez" Read administers a lesson in discipline to the volunteers—Gunboats pretty badly cut up by shore batteries—Go back to New Orleans—Fort Jackson under heavy bombardment from Porter's mortar fleet—Commodore Hollins relieved from his command—Farragut passes the forts— Death of Captain Huger and sinking of the *McRae*.

Here is a coronach for Confederate soldiers evidently written by an "unreconstructed rebel." It appears on a headstone in the Methodist Cemetery, St. Louis:—

> Here lize a stranger braiv,
> Who died while fightin' the Suthern Confederacy to save
> Piece to his dust.
> Braive Suthern friend
> From iland 10
> You reached a Glory us end.
> We plase these flowrs above the stranger's hed,
> In honer of the shiverlus ded.
> Sweet spirit rest in Heven
> Ther'l be know Yankis there.

47

When I returned to the *McRae*, I found great changes had occurred during my two weeks' absence. All idea of running the blockade and going to sea as a cruiser had been abandoned, and judging from my later experience in a "commerce destroyer" it was well that the intention had been abandoned, for with her limited coal capacity, and her want of speed owing to the small power and uncertain humor of her gear engines, it is doubtful if she would have lasted a month in that business.

I now found her much changed in outward appearance. The tall and graceful spars, with the exception of the lower masts, had disappeared. With the exception of Captain Huger, Sailing Master Read ("Savez"),[1] and Midshipman Blanc,[2] all of the line officers, whom I loved so dearly, were detached. Lieutenant Warley was to command permanently the *Manassas*; Lieutenant Eggleston[3] and Midshipman Marmaduke[4] were to join the *Merrimac* at Norfolk; Lieutenant Dunnington[5] was to command the gunboat *Ponchartrain*; Midshipman Sardine Graham Stone[6] was to go to the cruiser *Florida*; and Midshipman Comstock[7] was to go to the gunboat *Selma*, on board of which he was cut in two by a shell at the Battle of Mobile Bay; and I was appointed aide-de-camp to Commodore Hollins, whose flagship the *McRae* was to be.

Three river steamboats had been converted into men-of-war by having their luxurious cabins removed and their boilers protected by iron rails. They each carried four guns—three forward and one aft—and there had also been built (from designs by a locomotive roundhouse architect, I suppose) the most wonderful contraption that ever was seen afloat, called the *Livingston*. She carried six guns, three forward and three abaft the paddleboxes, and she was almost circular in shape. She was so slow that her crew facetiously complained that when she was going downstream at full speed they could not sleep on account of the noise made by the drift logs catching up with her and bumping against her stern. These boats, with the *Ivy* and the tug *Tuscarora*, constituted our fleet.

Information reached us that a number of real ironclads which the Federal Government was building at St. Louis and on the Ohio River were completed and were about to come down the river.

The Confederates hastily fortified Island Number 10, a few miles above New Madrid, Missouri, and at the latter place had built two forts (Bankhead and Thompson). Our fleet was ordered to make all haste up the river to assist them in preventing the Federal fleet from coming down.

On the way up the river our first disaster happened, when on a dark and foggy night we rammed the plantation of Mr. Jefferson Davis,

C.S.S. *McRAE*, COMMODORE HOLLINS'S FLAGSHIP
Coaling at Baton Rouge, 1861

President of the Confederacy. For this heroic performance, it is needless to say, none of us were promoted, and we lay ingloriously stuck in the mud until we were pulled off by a towboat. Disaster number two came when we were passing Helena, Arkansas, —the *Tuscarora* caught fire and was destroyed.

Day after day, with our insufficient power and great draft, we struggled against the mighty current of the Mississippi, occasionally bumping into a mud bank and lying helpless there until we were pulled off. At the cities of Vicksburg and Memphis we received ovations. The dear people were very enthusiastic, and knowing nothing about naval warfare, they felt sure we could whip the combined fleets of the universe.

When we finally arrived at Island Number 10, we found a lively bombardment going on. It was, however, decided that we should drop down to New Madrid to assist in the defense of that city.

The winter of 1861–62 was a very cold and bleak one in that part of the country, and for several weeks the monotony of our lives was broken only by the sound of the distant booming of the guns at Island Number 10.

The *McRae* had been laid alongside the river-bank at the head of the main street of the town and the muzzles of her guns were just above the levee, thus giving us the whole state of Missouri for a breastwork.

Everything seemed to be very peaceful until one day a solitary horseman made his appearance galloping at full speed. He stopped when he arrived opposite the *McRae*, and shouted from the shore that he wanted to see Commodore Hollins. The commodore, who was standing on the deck, asked him what he wanted, and the excited cavalier shouted back: "I am General Jeff Thompson, the swamp fox of Missouri. There are a hundred thousand Yankees after me and they have captured one of my guns, and if you don't get out of this pretty quick they will be on board of your old steamboat in less than fifteen minutes!" Just then another man, apparently riding in a sulky, between the shafts of which was hitched a moth-eaten mule, appeared on the scene. On closer inspection it was discovered that he was sitting astride of a small brass cannon which was mounted on a pair of buggy wheels. This piece of ordnance was scarcely three feet long. The general gazed on it admiringly, and for our information said: "That is a one-pounder—I invented it myself. The Yanks have got its mate, and if you don't get out of this they will hammer you to pieces with it." By this time there was great commotion in the two forts— seeing which General Jeff Thompson, nodding his head at the commodore, said, "So long!" and galloped away. That was the last we saw of him in that campaign.

As the gallant "swamp fox" disappeared in the distance, the gun's crew of his one-gun battery resignedly observed, "I can't keep up with Jeff;" and brought down his thong on the mule's bony back, and the poor beast leisurely walked away.

Above New Madrid a bayou emptied itself into the river. It meandered through a swamp for miles into the interior and was supposed to be impassable by troops, but General Pope and his thirty thousand men had accomplished the feat and taken New Madrid in the rear. His army was marching boldly up to our lines, and had they kept on they would have taken the place at once; but when the *McRae's* big nine-inch Dahlgren gun opened on them at long range, they stopped and proceeded to lay siege to it. It was evidently intended that they would take the place by regular approaches and the dirt commenced to fly while the artillery kept up a desultory fire.

The Confederate forts were situated at each end of the town and the flotilla of gunboats lay between them. Unfortunately the *McRae's* battery was the only one mounted at a sufficient height above the river-bank to fire over it while at the same time using it for a breastwork; the other boats had to lie out in the stream where they were very much exposed to the enemy's fire.

Some three thousand raw recruits formed the garrisons and manned the trenches which connected the forts. The forts had been built with regard to commanding the river and were very weak on the land side.

Day by day the Union troops drew nearer and the firing increased in fury. Commodore Hollins sent me frequently with communications to General Bankhead, who commanded our land forces.[8] One day, when the firing was particularly furious, I was sent with one of these missives and found General Bankhead on the firing line. Shells were bursting frequently in unpleasant proximity to where he was standing with his field-glasses pressed to his eyes. Just behind him stood several officers. I saluted the General and handed him the envelope. He told me to wait until he could send back an answer. As I joined the group of officers I distinctly heard a major say, "What a damned shame to send a child into a place like this!" The other officers must have noticed that my dignity was offended, for they spoke very kindly, but I could not get over the insult—it stuck in my gorge. I was so mad I could hardly speak. Returning to the ship I at once consulted my friend, the first lieutenant, who was now Mr. Read ("Savez"), on the propriety of sending the major a challenge, but "Savez" soothed my wounded feelings by telling me that "the commodore would not approve of such action and anyhow I need not mind what the major said, as he was nothing but a damned soldier, and a volunteer at that, and of course did not know any better."

The enemy got to the river-bank below us and a new danger menaced us. They prevented our transports from coming up the stream. The levees were breastworks ready-made, and day after day our gunboats had to go down to clear them out. We would be drifting down the apparently peaceful river, when suddenly a row of tall cottonwood saplings would make us a graceful bow and fall into the stream as a dozen or more field pieces poured a galling broadside into us. Of course, with our heavy guns we would soon chase them away, but only to have them reappear a mile above or below in a little while, and then the same thing had to be gone through again. Later they brought up some heavy guns and then we had some really good tussles with them. Our troops were forced back until they were under cover of the forts, leaving the space between, which was the abandoned town, to be protected by the guns of the *McRae*. I was standing by the commodore on the poop deck watching the firing when we saw a light battery enter the other end of the main street. Our nine-inch gun was trained on them, and when it was fired the shell struck the head of the column and burst in about the middle of the company. To see horses, men, and guns cavorting in the air was a most appalling sight. Flushed with success the officer in charge of the gun reloaded and tried another shot, when the gun exploded, the muzzle falling between the ship's side and the river-bank, while one half of the great breech fell on the deck beside its carriage. The other half went away up into the air and coming down struck the rail between the commodore and myself and cut the side of the ship, fortunately glancing out instead of inside. The commodore coolly remarked, "Youngster, you came near getting your toes mashed!"

We had a rough little steam launch, about twenty-five feet in length, which acted as a tender to the *McRae*, and our gunboats were makeshift ones, they were not provided either with signals or any place to fly them from. I used this launch to convey to them the flag officer's orders. The commodore suspected that the enemy were fortifying the point above us which, if done, would have cut us off from communication with Island Number 10 which was making a heroic defense and preventing the Union ironclads from coming down and annihilating our little mosquito fleet. So he sent me on a reconnaissance, cautioning me to be careful and not approach too close to the point until I was satisfied there was no battery there.

The launch had no deck and consequently her little boiler and engine were all exposed to the weather. Her crew consisted of a fireman from the *McRae* and a sailor to steer her. I proceeded to the point keeping well out in the stream, but saw nothing suspicious. Being of a curious turn of mind I wanted to see what was around the river bend, so kept on. As we turned the point my helmsman exclaimed, "The *Tom Benton!*" The *Tom Benton* was the largest Union ironclad on the river and all ironclads were "*Tom Bentons*" to us. Sure enough, across the next bend we saw a column of black smoke, evidently issuing from the funnel of a steamer and we turned tail and ran for the *McRae* with all speed possible. As we passed the point, which I had previously satisfied myself was absolutely harmless, the small cottonwood trees fell into the river and a battery opened on us, one of the shells exploding as it struck the water, drenching us. But our noble craft kept on her way, the engineer by this time having tied down the safety-valve. Arriving within hailing distance of the flagship, I sang out, "*Tom Benton* coming down, sir!" Commodore Hollins being on deck shouted back, "Come aboard, sir!"—My *chief* engineer gasped out, "For God's sake, don't stop, sir; she will blow up!" We ran around the *McRae* while the officer of the deck, and it seemed to me everybody else, was shouting, "Come aboard!" The safety-valve by this time had been unlashed and she was blowing off steam, while the whirling engine was also using up as much of the surplus as possible as around and around we went, while the commodore was stamping on the deck and fairly frothing at the mouth. At last—it seemed to me an age—the engineer pronounced it safe to stop, and we went alongside the flagship. As I stepped on to the quarter-deck, Commodore Hollins demanded to know why I had disobeyed his instructions and gone around the point. Hesitatingly I answered, "I thought, sir—" But I got no further, as the commodore interrupted me with "You thought, sir! You dared to think, sir! I will have you understand I am the only man in this fleet who is allowed to think!" I was so badly scared that probably that awful interview with the commodore was the reason I was never afterwards so thoughtless.

The Federal ironclad, not knowing our weakness, after she had run by the Island Number 10 batteries in the night, was quietly waiting at her anchors for her consorts to do likewise before attacking us.

The houses of New Madrid interfered with our fire. They were just as their owners had left them when they fled in such haste that they had not time to move their furniture or belongings, and it had up to this time seemed a pity to destroy them, but now they had been riddled by shells and were very much in the way. The commodore sent for me one night and ordered me to take a detail of men and go ashore and set fire to the town. I begged him not to send me and told him the history of the place, and how in 1787 the King of Spain had given my great grandfather, Colonel George Morgan, formerly of the Revolutionary Army, a grant of land comprising, according to Gayarre, in his history of Louisiana, some seventeen millions of acres, and how my ancestor had rounded the city of New Madrid on it, and that it would be dreadful for me to have to destroy it. The old commodore simply remarked that it would be a singular coincidence and that it was all the more appropriate that I should destroy my ancestor's town.

I went ashore with a number of men all provided with matches and fat-pine torches. The wind was blowing toward the river and we sneaked along in the darkness until we arrived at the last houses in the suburbs. I then remembered that in my frequent visits to the army headquarters I had noticed a barn that was filled with straw situated some two hundred yards beyond the last house in an open field. I knew that the enemy's pickets were very near and did not like to send one of my men to set it on fire, so I gave them instructions to wait until I myself touched it off or the pickets commenced to shoot and then to set fire to everything within reach as rapidly as possible. I knew little of the effects of lights and shadows. I made my way out to the barn all right and found the straw bulging out of a window well within my reach. I struck a match and applied it to the straw with the result that a mass of flame instantly leaped many feet above the roof, and the minie bullets commenced to sing like so many big mosquitoes around my ears. I fled toward my comrades. I don't think I ever ran so fast in my life as I did on that occasion. I was fairly flying when I felt a sting in the upper part of my left arm, and I also distinctly remembered that I exclaimed, "Thank God, it is not in one of my legs!" The only effect of the shot was to increase my speed, if that was possible: the bullet had only grazed my arm. A line of houses were in flames by the time I rejoined my men. The wind fanned the flames and the light exposed us to the fire of the enemy, but we succeeded in reaching the ship without the loss of a man. I had undone the work of my ancestor, and I was not particularly proud of the job.

A few days after this adventure things at New Madrid came to a head. We were cut off from Island Number 10 by the ironclad, and the batteries below cut us off from communication with the lower river. We commanded only the little stretch along which our gunboats lay. Our soldiers were completely demoralized and it was decided to evacuate New Madrid. At midnight the gunboats were brought alongside the bank, gangplanks were put out, and we had not long to wait before the terrified troops, every man for himself, rushed aboard the smaller gunboats in the greatest disorder. They at once rushed to the side farthest from the enemy, and in doing so almost capsized the top heavy and cranky little *Ivy*.

But it was a different thing with the *McRae*, where they found a sentry at the gangway who ordered them to halt. They raged and swore and openly threatened to rush the sentry, but at that moment the gentle "Savez" Read appeared on the scene and told the men that if they came on board it would have to be in an orderly manner as soldiers, and not as a mob. At this the men commenced to threaten him, but he only asked them where their officers were, and was told that they did not care a rap where they were, but that they were coming aboard. By this time Read had gone ashore and was standing amongst them. He quietly asked them to be silent for a moment, and then inquired who was their head man. A big fellow, with much profanity said he "had as much to say as any other man." Instantly Read's sabre flashed out of its scabbard and came down on the head of the mutineer, felling him to the ground, as in a thunderous voice the usually mild "Savez" roared, "Fall in!"—and the mob ranged themselves in line like so many lambs and were marched quietly across the gangplank and on to the ship.[9]

We carried the frightened creatures across the river to the Tennessee side and put them ashore at Point Pleasant, some two or three miles below New Madrid, and near Tiptonville. That was the last we saw of them.

The garrison of Island Number 10 also escaped, but some five hundred of them were afterwards captured.[10] I mention this fact because these men composed the ten thousand prisoners General Pope telegraphed Washington that he had taken in his great victory. All the Northern newspapers published this dispatch at the time and made such a hero of Pope that he was shortly afterwards placed in command of the Army of the Potomac, with what result history records. My brother-in-law, the late Brigadier-General R. C. Drum, who was adjutant-general of the United States Army for many years, told me that he had frequently seen that dispatch in the archives of his office, but some years after he was retired, General Pope denied that such a paper existed and dared the newspaper reporters to produce it. They were allowed to search the archives, but it was not to be found.

We lay for several days at anchor near Tiptonville, expecting every moment that the Federal ironclads would come down and attack us, but they did not put in an appearance before we left. Nevertheless, we received a very unpleasant surprise one morning while we were at breakfast when the cottonwood trees on the opposite side of the river suddenly tumbled down and a long line of guns opened fire on us. We got up our anchors as quickly as possible and went into action, with the result that our flotilla suffered considerably. The first disaster happened, when a shell burst in the pantry of the *Livingston* and smashed all of Commander Pinckney's beautiful chinaware of which he was very proud. The *General Polk* then received several shells in her hull on the water line and was run ashore to keep her from sinking, and the other boats were cut up considerably, but running close in to the masked batteries the grape and canister from our big guns caused the enemy to limber up and disappear. Commodore Hollins said, "The campaign had taught him one thing and that was that gunboats were not fitted for chasing cavalry."

It was at Tiptonville that Commodore Hollins received a message from the senior naval officer at New Orleans begging him to bring his gunboats as quickly as possible, as it was certain that Admiral Farragut would soon try to dash by Forts Jackson and St. Philip. No one knew the danger better than the old commodore did. Ordering his flagship to follow, he went on board of the fast *Ivy* accompanied by his small aide, and we started at full speed for New Orleans.

At Fort Pillow we stopped so that the commodore could send a telegram to the Secretary of the Navy asking him to order all the gunboats to follow him. I also carried a communication to General Villapigue, the commander of Fort Pillow, telling him of the fall of Island Number 10 and New Madrid, and advising him to prepare for an attack by the enemy's ironclads. We also stopped at Baton Rouge, where I took ashore more telegrams for the Navy Department at Richmond, for the capital had been removed to that city by this time. The authorities at Richmond, like swivel-chair naval strategists all over the world, differed entirely with the naval officers as to what was best to be done with the gunboats and never sent them any instructions at all.

Arriving at New Orleans, Commodore Hollins made his headquarters at the old St. Charles Hotel, and I was immediately sent down to the forts with a communication for General Duncan, who was in command, in which the commodore asked the general where he would like the gunboats placed for the coming fight and suggesting the head of the reach above the forts as the most effective position for them to take up.[11]

I found on my arrival that Fort Jackson was undergoing a most terrific bombardment from Commander Porter's mortar fleet which was hidden behind the trees around the bend below. The air was full of shells and the fort was full of smoke from their explosions.

Accompanying Commander Kennon, captain of the *Governor Moore*, we crossed the bridge over the moat which was the only means of access to the old-fashioned brick fortress. As we walked a shell fell into the moat and gave us a dirty shower bath, at the same time disturbing several large alligators who lashed the water furiously with their tails. Entering through the sallyport we saw no one but a solitary sentry, as the whole garrison was gathered in the casemates to protect them from the mortar fire. The fort was filled with debris. However, we had a very pleasant dinner with General Duncan, after which I returned to New Orleans.

I found the commodore busy with the preparations of the *Louisiana*, a most marvelous craft shaped like a huge square box. From her midship section aft she divided into two hulls and between them were placed two paddlewheels, one large and one small, the smaller one being placed in front of the big ones, so as to insure the latter's working in a mill-race when both were turning at the same time. On her sides were iron rails for an armor. At her trial trip it was found that it was with difficulty she kept up with the current when going downstream, and when pointed upstream she was carried down at the rate of two or three knots an hour. Towed back to the wharf, two engines from little tugs were placed aboard, one in each of her sterns. This increased power was not perceptible, and as she would not steer, she was towed down the river and moored to the bank where she served as an additional fort.[12]

The other ironclad was a magnificent vessel. She had real plates for her armor and they were of great thickness. She had great power, having triple screws, and her battery was to consist of eighteen of the heaviest guns. Had she been completed in time, she would have been like a bull in a china shop among Admiral Farragut's light wooden sloops-of-war. But the great admiral knew as much about her as we did and had no intention of postponing his attack until she was finished.[13]

Our gunboats from up the river had not arrived—they never did—but instead were run into the various tributaries of the lower Mississippi and destroyed by their own crews. I cannot say that they would have stopped Admiral Farragut's fleet, but their eighteen guns would have made it more interesting for him when he passed the forts.

All was work and hurry preparing for the great fight when one morning I went into the commodore's room and found the old gentleman seated by his work-table holding a telegram in one hand while his head was bowed in evident distress. When he became aware of my presence he raised his head and proffering the telegram said, "Read this." If the message had been sent to a cabin boy it would have been sufficiently curt to have wounded his feelings. It read: "Report in Richmond in person and give an account of your conduct"—signed, "S. R. Mallory, Secretary of the Navy." On arriving at Richmond a court of inquiry on his conduct was held, and as New Orleans had fallen, of course he was acquitted.

Admiral Farragut's victory is a matter of history. The *McRae* was in the thick of the fight. Her sides were riddled and the heavy projectiles knocked her guns off the carriages and rolled them along the deck crunching the dead and wounded. Her deck was a perfect shambles. Captain Huger was struck in the groin by a grapeshot and afterwards his temple was laid open by a canister bullet. When taken below he pleaded with Mr. Read, saying, "Mr. Read, don't surrender my little ship. I have always promised myself that I would fight her until she was under the water!" And right gallantly did "Savez" Read keep his word to his stricken captain, for when day broke the *McRae* was the only thing afloat with the Confederate flag flying. Admiral Farragut, with his flagship the *Hartford*, was by this time at the Quarantine Station, about four miles above the forts. Read sent the only boat he had that would float over to the *Hartford* to tell Admiral Farragut the condition of his vessel and the difficulty he was having to keep her afloat—that he did not have a gun left on a carriage, and no one to care for his dying captain or the many other wounded. Admiral Farragut asked why he did not haul his flag down and was told of the promise to the captain. Admiral Farragut then sent word to Read to bring the *McRae* alongside the *Hartford*, and then gave him permission to proceed to New Orleans, saying that he would tell him there what disposition he would make of the ship. When she arrived at New Orleans the *McRae* was leaking like a sieve; the exhausted remnant of the crew refused to continue at the pumps, and as the last-wounded men were taken out of the ship—down she went.[14]

Admiral Dewey, the admiral of the United States Navy, was a shipmate of Read's on board of the frigate *Powhatan* when the war broke out, and at the battle of New Orleans was the executive officer of the frigate *Mississippi* which was afterwards sunk at Port Hudson. The admiral told me that Read had not acted fairly about the sinking of the *McRae* and escaping himself, as he had cut the sea-pipes to hasten her foundering. But the *McRae* did not go down with her flag flying, for just as her spanker gaff was about to disappear beneath the muddy waters of the Mississippi, a boat from one of the Federal men-of-war (already arrived opposite the city) dashed up to the sinking ship and removed the flag from its proud position at the peak.

Commodore Hollins I saw once again after the war was over—it was at Charleston, South Carolina in 1867. This fine old gentlemen and able seaman, who had commanded fleets in the United States Navy as well as in the Confederacy, and who had been the honored guest of royalty, was then in command of a miserable little coaster trading between Baltimore and Charleston. He died a few years afterwards while holding the position of "crier" of a minor court in Baltimore. A like fate was the lot of many of the officers who resigned from the old navy to serve the Confederacy.

Nine

Farragut's fleet at New Orleans—Mob threatens to kill his officers who demand the surrender of the city—Farragut threatens to destroy the city if a hair of their heads is hurt—Pierre Soule's hypnotic forefinger saves the critical situation—I take to the swamp—The "Irreconcilable Home Guard"—Reach General Lovell's camp at Amite—Reach Norfolk in time for evacuation—Richmond—The battle between the U.S. Ironclads *Galena, Monitor,* and *Naugatuck* and Drewry's Bluff batteries—Battle of Seven Pines (Fair Oaks)—Seven Days' Battle.

Admiral Farragut's fleet was anchored in line in front of New Orleans. He sent Captain Bailey and his flag lieutenant on shore to demand the surrender of the city. The mayor received them at the Mint, a public building situated on Esplanade Street, near the river. I saw a great crowd gather in front of the place of meeting and heard the threats made that they were going to kill the Federal officers when they came out. The mob little knew that the sailors of the fleet were standing with lanyards in hand and that the great guns were trained on the city as well as on themselves. They were also ignorant of the fact that Admiral Farragut had sworn, if a hair on the heads of his officers was hurt, he would not leave two stones on top of each other in the city of New Orleans.

The mob, which was composed of men who had funked going to the front, seemed determined to bring destruction on themselves as well as on the innocent women and children of the place. How to get the Federal officers out of the building after the meeting, and thus avoid disaster, was the question which agitated the city officials when Mr. Soulé, formerly a United States Senator, and also United States Minister to Spain, came to their rescue. He was the possessor of wonderful eloquence and a hypnotic forefinger. He told the mayor that he believed he could hold the attention of the mob while the naval officers were passed out of a back door. He appeared on the portico and was received with cheers. He raised his arm and that magic forefinger commenced to tremble and there was instant silence. I thought the finger would never stop trembling, but it was evident that as long as it did so it fascinated the attention of the crowd. I don't remember what he said, but I do recollect that he commenced his speech with the words, "Sons of Louisiana," when at last he broke the silence with his wonderful and sonorous voice, which had a strong French accent. Long before he had finished talking the United States officers were safely back on board of the *Hartford*. New Orleans never paid her debt to Mr. Soulé. It is appalling to think of the havoc a few hundred bushels of grapeshot scattered amongst that mob would have wrought, to say nothing of the destruction of the old city.

Leaving the Mint, Mr. Soulé proceeded to the telegraph office and wired the provost marshal at Vicksburg to arrest the Tift brothers, the contractors who had built the formidable ironclad *Mississippi*, charging them with treason for having destroyed that vessel and ordering them to be confined in prison. This order was carried out, although at the time Mr. Soulé occupied no office either civil or military under the Confederacy, and despite the fact that Captain St. Clair was on board of the same steamboat with the Tifts when it arrived at Vicksburg and assured the provost marshal that the *Mississippi* had been burned by his, St. Clair's, orders when he found it impossible to tow her up the river on account of her size, as he wished to prevent her falling into the hands of the enemy.

I had neither ambition nor desire to take a trip North or to spend an indefinite time in a Northern prison, so with all speed I hiked me unto the country behind the city, where I found a train waiting on a siding, and with neither money nor ticket and without invitation I boarded it without the least idea of where I was going—and I did not care much so long as my destination was outside of the limits of the city where I was born.

I found the train crowded with a lot of prosperous and ponderous old gentlemen who were members of the "Home Guard," clothed in every conceivable garb, except that of a soldier—each one of them being hampered by a musket which he did not know how to handle.

They were all swearing by a multitudinous variety of strange gods that death was preferable to existence under the detested Yankee's rule. At the first stop at Manchac Pass it was noticed that their numbers perceptibly decreased, and after passing the second station there was plenty of room in the coaches and some people had even a whole seat to themselves. We arrived at Amite, where I had once been at school, and we detrained. General Lovell, who commanded the troops, had determined to make this place his headquarters and already there was quite a large camp there. The remnant of the "Home Guard" stood the rigors of camp life for a day or two, and then, deciding that the duty of a home guard was to guard his home, silently and singly, without consulting their superiors, they sneaked off to count how many railroad ties there were between Amite and their home comforts. It was afterwards said that the wretched condition of Napoleon's soldiers on the retreat from Moscow was not a circumstance to the plight in which these fat old gentlemen arrived at their comfortable mansions in New Orleans, convinced that the killing of Yankees was work fitted only for butchers.

We spent several days at Amite waiting for transportation farther north. I say "we," because on the train I had met Commander Pegram and a number of naval officers who were to have been attached to the ill-fated *Mississippi*. Among these officers was gallant Clarence Cary, who was to become my lifelong friend, and Frank Dawson, who was eventually to become my brother-in-law. These officers had recently made a sensational dash through the blockade in the *Nashville*, and they were now on their way to Norfolk for further orders.[1] A waif myself, I decided to join their party.

The trains in the Confederacy were not allowed to run faster than ten miles an hour, and the particular train on which we traveled to Virginia broke down every few miles, so I doubt if we even averaged that slow speed. There were so many soldiers on the train that it was difficult to get refreshments at the various little stations, and on this journey I had my first experience in going hungry for more than twenty-four hours at a time, but as I was ill and suffering from old-fashioned chills and fever, which I had contracted on the lower Mississippi, I don't remember that I missed the food greatly.

Arriving at Norfolk I parted with my *compagnons de voyage* and went on board of the *Merrimac* on which I knew two of my old shipmates on the *McRae* were serving-Lieutenant Eggleston and Midshipman Marmaduke. It was only recently that the *Merrimac* had been engaged in her great fights in Hampton Roads.[2] I gazed with admiration on the shot-holes in her armor and felt sure that she could whip anything afloat, and I believe her officers and crew thought so too. I little dreamed that before many hours she was to be ingloriously destroyed by her own crew on account of her drawing too much water to go up the James River.

Mr. Eggleston advised me to go at once and report to Captain Sidney Smith Lee, the elder brother of General Robert E. Lee, who was in command of the naval station, and ask him for orders. As I passed through the streets on my way I saw many batteries of artillery and regiments of infantry hurrying in one direction and accompanied by trains of wagons. When I came into the presence of Captain Lee, before I had a chance to say a word he demanded to know what I was doing there. When I told him that I was a fugitive from New Orleans, his whole manner changed and he said, "You appear to be ill, sir." I replied, "Chills and fever, sir." And the next moment he said, "You must leave here at once; this place is being evacuated!" I asked him where I should go, and he replied, "Any place so that you get out of here." And then turning to a clerk he told him to make out an order for transportation for me to Richmond.

On my way to and at the station, I saw many queer sights. There were orderly commands marching out of the place and disorganized mobs of men in uniform who were free from all restraint and discipline. At one place a gang of men were trying to put a heavy piece of artillery on a light spring wagon drawn by one horse! I don't think they succeeded in doing it, but I did not wait to see the result of their labors. At the station there was a crowd of civilians, and piles of household goods; also many pretty and jolly girls who seemed to regard the matter as a picnic devised to amuse them. Government mules were being driven by in droves scattering the crowd in every direction. There were crates containing pigs and chickens blocking the way, and everything seemed to be in inconceivable confusion—infantrymen with arms, and infants in arms, jostling each other. One poor old stout woman carrying her baby was anxiously searching for her baggage and only found somebody else's lost four-year-old boy who clung to her skirts with such a grip that she could not shake him off. Everybody was in a hurry to get to some place, but few seemed to know what the name of the place was.

After a most uncomfortable journey I arrived in Richmond. I had noticed in Norfolk that people looked at me askance, if not with real enmity expressed in their glances in my direction, but that was nothing in comparison to the gruff way I was treated in Richmond if I dared ask a stranger to direct me on my way. It did not take me long to find out the cause—it was my blue uniform with the United States naval buttons. The gray uniform for naval officers had not reached New Orleans before its fall, but the blue was an unusual sight in Richmond except when it was worn by a Union soldier who was a prisoner. I was told that but for my youth and small stature I might have been roughly handled. However, I soon got rid of the hated blue, as I had a little money due me and had the good fortune to meet Paymaster Semple, a son-in-law of ex-President Tyler, with whom I had been shipmates for a time on board of the *McRae*. He advanced me on my pay and I was soon arrayed in gray like the rest.

I was a very lonely little boy in Richmond for a few days. Louisiana was farther away in those days than it is in these of fast express trains, and somehow I was made to feel as though I was a foreigner. I suppose that was on account of our accent being different from that of other Southerners. It was only a few years ago in Washington when I was introduced to a Southern lady, my only recommendation being that I was a Confederate veteran, that she looked at me doubtfully and said, "Mr. Morgan, I can't believe that you are a Southerner; you neither look nor talk like any Southerner I ever met before." I replied, "Madam, I can assure you that had I been born any farther south than I was, I would have had to come into this world either as a pompino or a soft-shell crab, for the hard ground stops where I was born in the southern part of Louisiana!"

When I received my orders they were to the naval battery at Drewry's Bluff, seven miles below Richmond on the James River—a place of great natural strength. Pits were dug, wooden platforms were built at the bottom of them, and the guns were mounted on navy carriages with all their blocks and tackle such as were used on board of the men-of-war of that day. It was manned by sailors principally from the gallant crew of the *Merrimac*. The river had been barricaded by sinking in the channel the ocean-going steamship *Jamestown* and several steamboats besides crates made of logs and filled with stone, leaving only a narrow passageway for our own boats. It was while there that I witnessed a most magnificent exhibition of coolness and nerve—Commander John Rodgers, U.S.N., had been ordered to test the new ironclad under his command to find out whether she was shot-proof or not. Her name was the *Galena*.

It was about eight o'clock on the morning of the 16th of May, 1862, that we saw a squadron consisting of the *Galena*, the original *Monitor* (the one that fought the *Merrimac*), the ironclad *Naugatuck*, and two wooden gunboats coming up the river, and our drums beat to quarters while we rushed to our stations at the guns. Neither Commander Farrand, who commanded at Drewry's Bluff, nor Commander Rodgers, who commanded the Federal squadron, seemed in any hurry to open fire, so we in the battery waited patiently at our silent guns while the *Galena* came up to within four hundred yards of us accompanied by the *Monitor*, the rest of the squadron remaining below the bend seeking its protection from our plunging fire. The *Monitor* also

U.S. IRONCLAD *GALENA*

C.S. IRONCLAD *CHICORA*, ON WHICH THE AUTHOR SERVED AT CHARLESTON

dropped below, as her flat decks made her particularly vulnerable. The *Galena* quietly and peacefully, as though no enemy was within miles of her, let go her anchor. She then got out a hawser which sailors call a "spring," and made it fast to her anchor chain. Paying out her cable she swung across the stream, which brought her broadside to bear on us. Down the river-bank, hidden by the bushes, were two or three thousand Confederate infantrymen.[3]

Commander Rodgers was most leisurely in his movements. At last he fired a shot to get our range; there were no range-finders in those days, and it could only be found by experiment. That gun was the signal for the fun to commence. It was not necessary for us to find the range, as from our great height we had only to fire down on him; our guns were depressed to such an extent that we had to put grommets of rope over our round projectiles to keep them from rolling out of the muzzles. The shot from the *Galena* was our signal to open fire, and for three hours we were at it hammer and tongs. The *Galena* was perforated twenty-two times without counting the shots which struck her without going through her armor. The riflemen on the river-bank fairly rained bullets at her portholes, one of which became jammed, and when a sailor put his arm outside in an attempt to free it, the limb fell into the river amputated by musket balls. The wooden gunboats around the bend also suffered the loss of several men.

Although we were supposed to be safe in our covered gun pits perched so high on the bluff, all had not been cakes and ale with us. Several men had been killed and wounded, among them my classmate at Annapolis, Midshipman Carroll, of Maryland, had been literally cut in two by a shell.

When Commander Rodgers had satisfied himself that the *Galena* was not shot-proof, he weighed his anchor as deliberately as though he was about to leave a friendly port, and dropped slowly and in a most dignified way down the river. He had lost many men in killed and wounded. Commander Rodgers, in his report to the Secretary of the Navy, says: "The result of our experiment with the *Galena* I enclose. We demonstrated that she is not shot-proof; balls came through and many men were killed with fragments of her own iron.... The *Galena* should be repaired before sending her to sea."

Sailors are a generous lot and admire gallantry whether shown by friend or foe, and the men in the gun pits at Drewry's Bluff gave hearty cheers for the *Galena* as she drew out of action.

Historians seem to be ignorant concerning the importance of this fight. At the time there was nothing between Richmond and the Federal squadron but the guns of Drewry's Bluff. A passage had purposely been left through the obstructions in the river for our own boats and it was sufficiently wide and deep for the Federal vessels to have passed through. McClellan's army was within a few miles of the capital, and if Commander Rodgers' squadron had not been stopped by the naval battery there was nothing else to prevent them from going on to Richmond.

General Joe Johnston's army was now at Richmond, and I obtained a short leave to go to the city to see my brother George who was a captain and acting quartermaster in Blanchard's Louisiana brigade. I accompanied him to the front and found many friends among the Louisiana boys. There was with the brigade a light battery, in which there were many young men from Baton Rouge, and one day, while a number of us were sitting at the foot of a large tree, in fancied security, and watching a captive balloon belonging to the enemy, bullets began to rattle against the trunk of the tree, and we got away from there as quickly as possible. Horses were rapidly hitched to the caissons, the guns were limbered up, and the battery dashed off to another part of the field. The picket firing by that time had increased until it had become a constant rattle sounding somewhat like the roll of hundreds of snare drums.

Blanchard's brigade was in Huger's division on the extreme right of our army. I made my way to the camp of the First Louisiana, which I found under arms. Their part in the Battle of Seven Pines, or Fair Oaks, as the Federals called it, had begun. The regiment advanced and I followed on behind until suddenly I saw an officer riding up to where General Blanchard and his staff were seated on their horses. Before he reached them his horse suddenly reared and in that instant I recognized my brother. The horse fell dead, and when I came up I found he was lying on one of George's legs and that George could not extricate himself. It was a big undertaking for me, but I managed to move the fore shoulder of that horse far enough to free my brother. He was quite severely hurt and had to be removed to the rear. That was all I saw of the battle of Seven Pines.[4] Could I have seen what was going on the other side, I should have beheld my dear cousin, Colonel A.S.M. Morgan, being borne off the field shot through both hips, while gallantly leading his regiment, the Second Pennsylvania.

I accompanied my brother to Richmond where he was carried to the most fashionable hostelry in the city, the old Spotswood Hotel, and I remained there for several days with him. The doors of the bedrooms on the corridors were mostly kept open and it seemed to me that a game of poker was going on in every room. The lobby of the hotel was crowded with officers, most of whom carried an arm in a sling. The cause of this was the wearing of the flaring gold chevrons on their sleeves to indicate their rank. They made beautiful targets for the sharpshooters; but not for long, as later in the war even generals wore only three small stars on their coat-collars.

Passing through the lobby one morning I met an old acquaintance, a Louisiana Zouave, dressed in red Turkish trousers with a short blue jacket elaborately trimmed with yellow braid—of course he too had an arm in a sling. He stopped me and asked if I had seen the "zoozoo" fight—he was very enthusiastic and very excitable. "Oh!" said he, in broken English, "You ought to see ze zoozoo fight. Colonel Copin he draw his long sabre and say, 'Charge!' We charge and we charge right on top ze Yankee breastwork; Yankee drop down and say 'quatta!' 'quatta!' I say, 'No quatta fer Bootla (Butler): I stick he wid de bayonette!'" Those Acadians imagined that they were only engaged in a holy crusade against the tyrant of New Orleans.

My brother George thought that a little trip to the hills would benefit my health, and as he had heard that "Stonewall" Jackson's division was, at Gordonsville, he furnished me with the means to go there where I would be with my brother Gibbes, then a captain in the Seventh Louisiana Regiment. I found him flushed with victory, having just returned from the marvelous Shenandoah Valley campaign in which Jackson had fought so many battles in so few weeks, and he seemed very proud to belong to Jackson's "foot cavalry." To my great delight I found my brother's young and beautiful wife with him. It was no uncommon thing at that time for the wives of officers to follow their husbands so as to be near the battlefields. Unfortunately for me, my pleasure at being with my favorite brother and his wife was of short duration, as in a few hours after my arrival in Gordonsville, Jackson's "foot cavalry" moved on, and I returned to Richmond.

On my arrival in Richmond I saw several thousand Union prisoners, guarded by Confederates, seated on the ground, resting themselves. Few if any of them could speak English and the most accomplished linguists among them could only say, "I fights mit Sigel."

At Drewry's Bluff we lived in tents and were very comfortable. Parties composed of ladies and gentlemen would frequently visit the Bluff and they made it quite gay; besides, by this time, quite a large number of midshipmen were stationed there and they made it lively for their superior officers as well as for themselves. I had while there an interesting experience in steering the boat from which Commander Matthew F. Maury buoyed the places in the river where he afterwards had placed what were probably the first floating mines used in war. We called them "spar torpedoes" as the mines were attached to an anchored and floating spar.[5]

I shall never forget a very unpleasant hour in connection with these mines. Colonel Page, a former officer of the navy, who looked to be about seven feet high, wanted to go from Drewry's Bluff to Chaffin's Bluff, a fortification that he commanded, on the opposite side of the river and about a mile below. I was ordered to take charge of the boat that was to take him to his post because it was supposed I knew where the mines were. It was a dark night, but we got on all right for some distance. Suddenly the side of the boat grated against something and the boat slightly careened. Colonel Page, whose sobriquet in the navy was "Ramrod" on account of his erect bearing, and who was well known in the service as a very strict disciplinarian, exclaimed, "What is that?—I thought you knew where the torpedoes were." "Yes, sir," I replied, "that is one of them." There was silence in the boat until we reached the little wharf at Chaffin's Bluff, and when Colonel Page disembarked he expressed his opinion of me and my professional accomplishments in language which left nothing for the imagination to work on. Had the boat been a little heavier we should all have gone to heaven by the most direct route.

"Stonewall" Jackson's army came down from the Valley and joined General Lee. I went over to the camp of the Seventh Louisiana to see my brother Gibbes, and while I did not participate in any of the battles of the "Seven Days," I saw some of the fighting. One day McClellan sent an ammunition train, with a fuse attached to it, down the railroad tracks—of course it was running "wild." Jackson's division, thinking that it carried reinforcements, rushed for the railroad intending to fire into it as it passed, but while they were some distance away the train exploded destroying many windows in Richmond, several miles away. For two or three days after the explosion a Negro boy who waited on my brother and the officers of his company was not to be found. This boy had always bragged that in action he was to the front, and continually boasted about the number of Yankees he had killed. When he finally turned up and was asked the meaning of his long absence, he replied: "Mass' Gibbes, I stood their shot and shell and bullets, but when it came to shootin' a whole train of cars at one poor nigger I tell you de truf, sah, I done lit out right dar and den!"

At this time I had been detached from Drewry's Bluff and was on board of the gunboat *Beaufort* a small river tug about forty feet long and carrying one small gun on her forecastle; her complement consisted of two officers and eight men—she was crowded.[6] This little boat had covered herself all over with glory when the *Merrimac* sank the frigates *Congress* and *Cumberland*. The *Beaufort* was then commanded by Lieutenant William H. Parker, and it was to the *Beaufort* that the *Congress* surrendered. She was now commanded by Lieutenant Sharp,[7] who had many other duties to attend to at the ordnance works and elsewhere, so that he was very little on board his ship.

We were lying alongside the river-bank at Rockett's (the lower end of Richmond) one day, when my brother Gibbes made me a visit.[8]

We were cozily chatting about home when a quartermaster poked his head in at the little cabin door and, saluting, said, "Jurgenson has come aboard, sir." I replied, "Very good, quartermaster." The man then said, "Jurgenson is drunk and noisy, sir." I said, "Tell Jurgenson to turn into his bunk and keep quiet." There was an awful din going on forward and the quartermaster came back and reported that the man would not keep quiet. "All right," I said, "tell the master-at-arms to put him in double irons and gag and buck him unless he stops his racket." The quartermaster saluted and again withdrew. Gibbes looked at me with amazement and asked me if it was possible that a little boy like myself had authority to order such severe punishment. I told him that I was not a little boy on that boat, but for the moment I was her commanding officer. He then expressed doubts as to whether the master-at-arms would obey the order and wanted me to go outside with him and see. I declined, on the ground that it might look as though I doubted if my orders would be carried out, and Gibbes went forward to see for himself. He came back shortly shaking his head and said that he must return to his command, as he wanted to tell the boys what he had seen that day. I tried to make him understand that I had not indulged in any cruelty on my own part, but that in the navy every misdemeanor had its punishment set forth in the Regulations and that I was liable to punishment myself if I did not carry out the orders. I told him that Jurgenson was an old man-of-warsman and knew as well if not better than I what was going to happen if he did not obey the order to keep silence and behave himself. I could not make Gibbes believe that I was very fond of old Jurgenson; that he was one of the best men in the ship, and that he would have lost all respect for me if I had not carried out the discipline of the service; that I was going to have the gag taken out of his mouth as soon as be stopped yelling. It was all of no avail, my gallant volunteer brother left, still shaking his head and repeating, "I must go hack and tell my boys what I have seen this day." That was the last time I ever saw my brother.

Ten

Charleston—Commodore Ingraham—C.S. Ironclad *Chicora*—The looting of my home in Baton Rouge—George Hollins dies of yellow fever—The Honorable George A. Trenholm—Naval officers "never unbutton their coats."—Ordered abroad.

With all my state pride, I must acknowledge that the article of chills and fever handed to me on the James River was superior to the brand on the lower Mississippi, and complicated by chronic dysentery, so sapped my strength that the doctor ordered me to show myself at the Navy Department and ask for orders to some other station. Commodore French Forrest was chief of the Bureau of Orders and Detail, and I really thought he had some sympathy for my condition when he looked me over. He asked me where I would like to be ordered to, and I quickly said that I would be delighted if I was sent to the naval battery at Port Hudson. The commodore then asked if I had relatives near there, and on my assuring him that my mother and sisters were refugees and were staying at the plantation of General Carter, only a few miles distant, he turned to a clerk and said, "Make out an order for Midshipman Morgan to report to Commodore Ingraham at Charleston, South Carolina. I don't believe in having young officers tied to their mother's apron string."—And so to Charleston I went.[1]

Commodore Ingraham, to whom I reported, was the man who some years previously, when in command of the little sloop-of-war *St. Louis* in the port of Smyrna, had bluffed an Austrian frigate and

70

compelled her to surrender Martin Koszta, a naturalized American citizen, whom they held as a prisoner. This act made Ingraham the idol of the people at that time; if repeated in this day (1916), it would cost an officer his commission. Commodore Ingraham also commanded the Confederate gunboats when they drove the Federal blockading fleet away from Charleston.

I was assigned to the *Chicora*,[2] a little ironclad that was being built between two wharves which served as a navy yard. She was not nearly completed, so I was forced to hunt for quarters on shore. Being directed to a miserable boarding-house which was fourth-rate, and consequently supposed to be cheap, I found that the cheapest board to be had was at the rate of forty-five dollars a month, so I did not see exactly how I could manage it, as my shore pay was only forty. However, the generous hotel proprietor, when the situation was explained, consented to let me stay for that sum on condition that I would make up the other five dollars if my friends at home sent me any money. The man was certainly taking a long chance for that extra five dollars. Where were my friends, and where was my home? My mother and sisters were refugees; and as for home the following extract from Mrs. McHattan-Ripley's book "From Flag to Flag" will give some idea of its condition. Mrs. McHattan lived on a plantation about three miles below Baton Rouge and after the battle visited the town. She says:

At last I descended and walked the dusty, littered, shadeless streets from square to square. Seeing the front door of the late Judge Morgan's house thrown wide open, and knowing that his widow and daughters, after asking protection for their property of the commanding general, had left before the battle, I entered. No words can tell the scene that those deserted rooms presented. The grand portraits, heirlooms of that aristocratic family—men of the Revolutionary period, high-bred dames of a long-past generation, in short bodices, puffed sleeves, towering headdresses, and quaint golden chains, ancestors long since dead, not only valuable as likenesses that could not be duplicated, but acknowledged works of art—these portraits hung from the walls, slashed by swords clear across from side to side, stabbed and mutilated in every brutal way! The contents of store-closets had been poured over the floors; molasses and vinegar and everything that defaces and stains had been smeared over the walls and furniture. Upstairs, armoires with mirror-doors had been smashed in with heavy axes or hammers, and the dainty dresses of the young ladies torn and crushed with studied, painstaking malignity, while china, toilet articles, and bits of glass that ornamented the room were thrown upon the beds and broken and ground into a mass of fragments. Desks were wrenched open, and the contents scattered, not only through the house; but out upon the streets, to be wafted in all directions; parts of their private letters as well as letters from the desks of other violated homes, and family records torn from number-less Bibles, were found on the sidewalks of the town, and even on the public roads beyond town limits.

Lieutenant Warley, with whom I had served on the *McRae*, was the only living human being I knew in Charleston, and the great difference in our rank, as well as age, precluded the possibility of my making a companion of him; so, a lonely boy, I roamed the streets of the quaint old city. Evidently the war as yet had had no effect on the style kept up by the old blue-bloods, for I was amazed to see handsome equipages, with coachmen in livery on the box, driving through the town. Little did their owners dream that before very long those same fine horses would be hauling artillery and commissary wagons, and those proud liveried servants would be at work with pick and spade throwing up breastworks!

To my great delight, George Hollins, a son of my dearly loved old commodore, a boy of about my own age with whom I had been ship-mate on the Mississippi River, arrived in town, and the boarding-house man consented to allow him to share my little room at the same rate charged me. George had been in Charleston only a few days when yellow fever became epidemic. It was the latter part of August and the heat was something fearful. I had no fear of the fever, as I had been accustomed to its frequent visits to my old home, but with Hollins, a native of Baltimore, it was different.

One afternoon he came into our room and complained of a headache and a pain in his back. The symptoms were familiar to me, so I persuaded him to go to bed and covered him with the dirty rag of a blanket. I then went quickly downstairs and asked the wife of the proprietor to let me have some hot water for a footbath and also to give me a little mustard. The woman was shocked at my presumption, but consented to give me the hot water; at parting with the mustard she demurred. As I was about to leave her kitchen she demanded to know what I wanted with hot water, and when I told her that my friend had the yellow fever, there was a scene in which she accused me of trying to ruin the reputation of the house and threatened me with dire punishment from her husband.

I made Hollins put his feet in the hot water and then, I went to a near-by druggist, telling him the situation, and asking him if he would credit me for the mustard, explaining that neither Hollins nor myself had any money. The kindly apothecary gave me the mustard and told me I could have any medicines needed, and also advised me to go at once and see Dr. Lebby, who, he was sure, would attend to the case without charge. The doctor came and did all that was possible. Poor George grew rapidly worse; he seemed to cling to me as his only friend, and could not bear to have me leave him for an instant. We slept that night huddled up together in the narrow bed.

The next morning a strange Negro man, very well dressed, and carrying a bunch of flowers in one hand and a bundle in the other, entered the room and proceeded to make himself very much at home. When asked what his business was, he said he was a yellow-fever nurse. I told him that we had no money and could not pay a nurse, at which he burst into a broad grin and said that he did not want any money; that he belonged to Mr. Trenholm who had sent him there.[3] Throughout the day all sorts of delicacies continued to arrive, and to every inquiry as to whom they came from, the reply was, "Mr. Trenholm."

The second night of his illness George was taken with the black vomit, which, as I held him in my arms, saturated my clothes. A shiver passed through his frame and without a word he passed away. Leaving my friend's body in charge of the nurse I went in search of Lieutenant Warley, and he told me not to worry about his funeral, as Mr. Trenholm would make all the arrangements. This Mr. Trenholm, unknown to me, seemed to be my providence, as well as being all-powerful. George Hollins was buried in the beautiful Magnolia Cemetery and immediately after the funeral Mr. Warley told me that I was not to go back to the boarding-house, but was for the present to share his room at the Mills House, a fashionable hotel.

A few days after the funeral I was walking down Broad Street with Mr. Warley and we saw coming toward us a tall and very handsome man with silvery hair. Mr. Warley told me that he was Mr. Trenholm, and that I must thank him for all his kindness to my friend. Mr. Trenholm said that he was only sorry that he could not have done more for the poor boy, and, turning to the lieutenant, said: "Warley, can't you let this young gentleman come and stay at my house? There are some young people there, and we will try and make it pleasant for him."

I thanked Mr. Trenholm and told him that I had recently been sleeping in the same bed with my friend, who had died of the most virulent form of yellow fever, and of course I could not go into anybody's house for some time to come; but the generous gentleman assured me that his family had no fears of the fever and insisted on my accepting his kind invitation. However, I did not think it right to go, and did not accept at that time; a day or two afterwards, however, I again met him with Mr. Warley, and he said, "Warley, I am sorry this young gentleman won't accept my invitation, we would try to make it pleasant for him." Mr. Warley turned to me, saying, "Youngster, you pack your bag and go up to Mr. Trenholm's house."

That settled it and I went, arriving at the great mansion shortly before the dinner hour. I did not, however, take a bag with me. If I had owned one, I would not have had anything to put in it.

HONORABLE GEORGE A. TRENHOLM
Secretary of the Confederate States Treasury

I will not attempt to describe Mr. Trenholm's beautiful home. For more than half a century now it has been pointed out to tourists as one of the show places of Charleston, and it has long since passed into the hands of strangers. I must confess that as I opened the iron gate and walked through the well-kept grounds to the front door I was a little awed by the imposing building, with its great volumes supporting the portico. I could not but feel some misgivings as to the reception I would get, stranger as I was, from the family whom I had never met. Still, I did not dare run away, and so I timidly rang the bell. A slave, much better dressed than myself, and with the manners of a Chesterfield, appeared and showed me into the parlors; it was all very grand, but very lonely, as there was no one there to receive me. I took a seat and made myself comfortable; it had been a long time since I had sat on a luxurious sofa. In a few minutes two young ladies entered the room. Of course I had never seen either of them before, but the idea instantly flashed through my mind that I was going to marry the taller of the two, who advanced toward me and introduced herself as "Miss Trenholm."

Soon there arrived a Frenchman, a Colonel Le Mat, the inventor of the "Grapeshot revolver," a horrible contraption, the cylinder of which revolved around a section of a gun barrel.[4] The cylinder contained ten bullets, and the grapeshot barrel was loaded with buckshot which, when fired, would almost tear the arm off a man with its recoil. Le Mat's English vocabulary was limited, and his only subject of conversation was his invention, so he used me to explain to the young ladies how the infernal machine worked. Now that sounds all very easy, but one must remember that Le Mat was a highly imaginative Gaul and insisted on posing me to illustrate his lecture. This was embarrassing—especially as he considered it polite to begin all over again as each new guest entered the room. At last relief came when Mr. Trenholm came in with a beautiful lady, well past middle age, leaning on his arm; and I was introduced to my hostess, whose kind face and gentle manner put me at my ease at once.

Oh, but it was a good dinner I sat down to that day! After all these years the taste of the good things lingers in my memory and I can almost smell the "aurora," as Boatswain Miller used to call the aroma, of the wonderful old madeira. It was in the month of September and the weather was intensely hot; I had my heavy cloth uniform coat buttoned closely, and only the rim of my celluloid collar showed above. Dinner over, we assembled in the drawing room where we were enjoying music, when suddenly I found myself in a most embarrassing position. Dear, kind Mrs. Trenholm was the cause of it. Despite my protestations that naval officers were never allowed to open their uniform coats, she insisted, as it was so warm, that I should unbutton mine and be comfortable. Unbutton that coat! Never! I would have died first. I had no shirt under that coat; I did not own one.

When bedtime arrived, Mr. Trenholm escorted me to a handsomely furnished room. What a sleep I had that night between those snow-white sheets, and what a surprise there was in the morning when I opened my eyes and saw a manservant putting studs and cuff-buttons in a clean white shirt. On a chair there lay a newly pressed suit of civilian togs. I assured the man that he had made a mistake, but he told me he had orders from his mistress and that all those things and the contents of a trunk he had brought into the room were for me, adding that they had belonged to his young "Mass' Alfred," a boy of about my own age, whose health had broken down in the army and who had been sent abroad. I wanted the servant to leave the room so I could rise. I was too modest to get out of bed in his presence and too diffident to ask him to leave; but at last reflected that everybody must know that I had no shirt, so I jumped up and tumbled into a bath, and when the "body servant" had arrayed me in those fine clothes I hardly knew myself.

After breakfast two horses were brought to the front of the house, one with a lady's saddle was called "Gypsy" and was one of the most beautiful Arabs I ever saw (and I have seen many); the other, a grand chestnut, called "Jonce Hooper," one of the most famous race-horses on the Southern turf when the war commenced. He had been bought by Colonel William Trenholm, my host's eldest son, for a charger, but Colonel Trenholm soon found that the pampered racer was too delicate for rough field work in time of war. Miss Trenholm and I mounted these superb animals and that morning and many mornings afterwards we went for long rides. In the afternoons I would accompany the young ladies in a landau drawn by a superb pair of bays with two men on the box. Just at that time the life of a Confederate midshipman did not seem to be one of great hardship to me; but my life of ease and luxury was fast drawing to an end.

In the evenings the family and their friends used to sit on the big porch where tea, cakes, and ice cream were served, and the gentlemen could smoke if they felt so inclined. One day the distinguished Commodore Matthew F. Maury,[5] who was on his way to Europe to fit out Confederate cruisers, dined at the house, and after dinner, with Mr. Trenholm, had joined the gay party on the piazza. Mr. Trenholm was the head of the firm of Fraser, Trenholm & Co., of Liverpool and Charleston, financial agents of the Confederate Government. Suddenly Mr. Trenholm came over to where I was laughing and talking with a group of young people, and asked me if I would like to go abroad and join a cruiser. I told him that nothing would delight me more, but that those details were for officers who had distinguished themselves, or who had influence, and that as I had not done the one thing and did not possess the other requisite, I could stand no possible chance of being ordered. Mr. Trenholm said that was not the question; he wanted to know if I really wished to go. On being assured that I would give anything to have the chance, he returned to Commodore Maury and resumed his conversation about the peculiarities of the "Gulf Stream."

Imagine my surprise the next morning when, after returning from riding, I was handed a telegram, the contents of which read: "Report to Commodore M. F. Maury for duty abroad. Mr. Trenholm will arrange for your passage." signed, "S. R. Mallory, Secretary of the Navy." It fairly took my breath away!

Eleven

Run through the U.S. blockading fleet—Out of our reckoning—Bermuda—Blockade-runners throw money into the street—Commodore Wilkes's famous ship *San Jacinto* gives us a scare—Halifax—Sail for England in company with some of Her Majesty's Life Guardsmen.

Mr. Trenholm owned many blockade-runners—one of them, the little light-draft steamer *Herald*, was lying in Charleston Harbor loaded with cotton and all ready to make an attempt to run through the blockading fleet. Commodore Maury, accompanied by his little son a boy of twelve years of age, and myself, whom he had designated as his aide-de-camp for the voyage, went on board after bidding good-bye to our kind friends. About ten o'clock at night we got under way and steamed slowly down the harbor, headed for the sea. The moon was about half full, but heavy clouds coming in from the ocean obscured it. We passed between the great towering forts of Moultrie and Sumter and were soon on the bar, when suddenly there was a rift in the clouds, through which the moon shone brightly, and there, right ahead of us, we plainly saw a big sloop-of-war.

There was no use trying to hide. She also had seen us, and the order, "Hard-a-starboard!" which rang out on our boat was nearly drowned by the roar of the warship's great guns. The friendly clouds closed again and obscured the moon, and we rushed back to the protecting guns of the forts without having had our paint scratched. Two or three more days were passed delightfully in Charleston; then there

78

came a drizzling rain and on the night of the 9th of October, 1862, we made another attempt to get through the blockade. All lights were out except the one in the covered binnacle protecting the compass. Not a word was spoken save by the pilot, who gave his orders to the man at the wheel in whispers. Captain Coxetter, who commanded the *Herald*, had previously commanded the privateer *Jeff Davis*, and had no desire to be taken prisoner, as he had been proclaimed by the Federal Government to be a pirate and he was doubtful about the treatment he would receive if he fell into the enemy's hands.[1] He was convinced that the great danger in running the blockade was in his own engine room, so he seated himself on the ladder leading down to it and politely informed the engineer that if the engine stopped before he was clear of the fleet, he, the engineer, would be a dead man. As Coxetter held in his hand a Colt's revolver, this sounded like no idle threat. Presently I heard the whispered word passed along the deck that we were on the bar. This information was immediately followed by a series of bumps as the little ship rose on the seas, which were quite high, and then plunging downward, hit the bottom, causing her to ring like an old tin pan. However, we safely bumped our way across the shallows, and, plunging and tossing in the gale, this little cockleshell, whose rail was scarcely five feet above the sea level, bucked her way toward Bermuda. She was about as much under the water as she was on top of it for most of the voyage.

Bermuda is only six hundred miles from Charleston; a fast ship could do the distance easily in forty-eight hours, but the *Herald* was slow: six or seven knots was her ordinary speed in good weather and eight when she was pushed. She had tumbled about in the sea so much that she had put one of her engines out of commission and it had to be disconnected. We were thus compelled to limp along with one, which of course greatly reduced her speed. On the fifth day the weather moderated and we sighted two schooners. To our surprise Captain Coxetter headed for them and, hailing one, asked for their latitude and longitude. The schooner gave the information, adding that she navigated with a "blue pigeon" (a deep-sea lead), which of course was very reassuring. We limped away and went on groping for Bermuda. Captain Coxetter had spent his life in the coasting trade between Charleston and the Florida ports, and even when he commanded for a few months the privateer *Jeff Davis* he had never been far away from the land. Such was the jealousy, however, of merchant sailors toward officers of the navy that, with one of the most celebrated navigators in the world on board his ship, he had not as yet confided to anybody the fact that he was lost.

On the sixth day, however, he told Commodore Maury that something terrible must have happened, as he had sailed his ship directly over the spot where the Bermuda Islands ought to be! Commodore Maury told him that he could do nothing for him before ten o'clock that night and advised him to slow down. At ten o'clock the great scientist and geographer went on deck and took observations, at times lying flat on his back, sextant in hand, as he made measurements of the stars. When he had finished his calculations he gave the captain a course and told him that by steering it at a certain speed he would sight the light at Port Hamilton by two o'clock in the morning. No one turned into his bunk that night except the commodore and his little son; the rest of us were too anxious. Four bells struck and no light was in sight. Five minutes more passed and still no sign of it; then grumbling commenced, and the passengers generally agreed with the man who expressed the opinion that there was too much d——d science on board, and that we should all be on our way to Fort Lafayette in New York Harbor as soon as day broke. At ten minutes past two the masthead lookout sang out, "Light ho!"—and the learned old commodore's reputation as a navigator was saved.

We ran around the islands and entered the picturesque harbor of St. George shortly after daylight. There were eight or ten other blockade-runners lying in the harbor, and their captains and mates lived at the same little white-washed hotel where the commodore and I stopped, which gave us an opportunity of seeing something of their manner of life when on shore. Their business was risky and the penalty of being caught was severe; they were a reckless lot, and believed in eating, drinking, and being merry, for fear that they would die on the morrow and might miss something. Their orgies reminded me of the stories of the way the pirates in the West Indies spent their time when in their secret havens. The men who commanded many of these blockade-runners had probably never before in their lives received more than fifty to seventy-five dollars a month for their services; now they received ten thousand dollars in gold for a round trip, besides being allowed cargo space to take into the Confederacy, for their own account, goods which could be sold at a fabulous price, and also to bring out a limited number of bales of cotton worth a dollar a pound. In Bermuda these men seemed to suffer from a chronic thirst which could only be assuaged by champagne, and one of their amusements was to sit in the windows with bags of shillings and throw handfuls of the coins to a crowd of loafing Negroes in the street to see them scramble. It is a singular fact that five years after the war not one of these men had a dollar to bless himself with. Another singular fact was that it was not always the speedier craft that was the most successful. The *Kate* (named after Mrs. William Trenholm) ran through the blockading fleets sixty times and she could not steam faster than seven or eight knots. That was the record; next to her came the *Herald*, or the *Antonica* as she was afterwards called.[2]

Commodore Maury was a deeply religious man. He had been lame for many years of his life, but no one ever heard him complain. He had been many years in the navy, but had scarcely ever put his foot on board of a ship without being seasick, and through it all he never allowed it to interfere with his duty. He was the only man I ever saw who could be seasick and amiable at the same time; while suffering from nausea he could actually joke! I remember once entering his stateroom where he was seated with a Bible on his lap and a basin alongside of him. I told him that there was a ship in sight, and between paroxysms he said, "Sometimes we see a ship, and sometimes ship a sea!"

Not knowing of his world-wide celebrity, I was surprised to see the deference paid him by foreigners. We had no sooner settled ourselves at the hotel than the governor sent an aide to tell Lieutenant Maury that he would be pleased to receive him in his private capacity at the Government House. In Europe the commodore was only known as "the great Lieutenant Maury," they entirely ignored any promotions which might have come to him. The commandant of Fort St. George also called on him, but took pains to explain that it was the great scientist to whom he was paying homage, and not the Confederate naval officer. As the commodore's aide I came in for a little of the reflected glory and had the pleasure of accompanying him to a dinner given in his honor on board of H.M.S. *Immortality* at Port Hamilton. She was a beautiful frigate and her officers were very kind to me.

We remained in Bermuda for more than two weeks waiting for the Royal Mail Steamer from St. Thomas, on which we were to take passage for Halifax, Nova Scotia. Simultaneously with her arrival, the U.S. sloops-of-war *Cincinnati* and *Mohican* put in an appearance, but did not enter the harbor, cruising instead just outside the three-mile limit and in the track the British ship *Delta* would have to follow. Instantly the rumor spread that they were going to take Commodore Maury out of the ship as soon as she got outside, color being lent to this rumor by the fact that it was the *San Jacinto* which had only a year before taken the Confederate Commissioners, Mason and Slidell, out of the Royal Mail steamship *Trent*—and I must say that we felt quite uneasy.[3]

On the day of our departure a Mr. Bourne, a gentleman of whom I had never heard before, asked me to accompany him to his office and there counted out a hundred gold sovereigns, sealed them in a canvas bag, and asked me to sign a receipt for them. I assured him that there must be some mistake, but he insisted that I was the right party and that it was Mr. Trenholm's orders that he should give the money to me. Having had free meals and lodging on the blockade-runner, it was the first intimation I had that money would be necessary on so long a journey as the one I was about to undertake.

We sailed out of the harbor, and the two American warships, as soon as we got outside, followed us. As we rounded the headland we saw the *Immortality* and the British sloop-of-war *Desperate* coming from Port Hamilton under a full head of steam and we expected every moment to witness a naval fight; the American ships, however, seemed satisfied with having given us a scare, while the British followed us until we lost sight of them in the night.

The governor of the colony of Nova Scotia, the general commanding the troops, and the admiral of the fleet, all treated "Lieutenant" Maury, as they insisted on calling him, with the most distinguished consideration, inviting him to dinners and receptions, etc., to which, as his aide, I had to accompany the great man. I particularly enjoyed the visit to Admiral Milne's flagship, the *Nile*, of seventy-two guns carried on three decks. The old wooden line-of-battle ship with her lofty spars was a splendid sight, and the like of her will never be seen again. What interested me most on board was the eighteen or twenty midshipmen in her complement, many of them younger and smaller than myself. They all made much of me and frankly envied me on account of my having been in battle and having run the blockade.

The officers of the garrison were also very kind to me and told me a story about their commander, General O'Dougherty, which I have never forgotten. It was about a visit the chief of the O'Dougherty clan paid to the general. Not finding him at home, he left his card on which was simply engraved, "The O'Dougherty." The general returned the visit and wrote on a blank card, "The other O'Dougherty."

After a few pleasant days spent in Halifax the Cunard steamer *Arabia*, plying between Boston and Liverpool, came into port and we took passage on her for Liverpool. The Americans on board resented our presence and of course had nothing to do with us, but a number of young officers of the Scots Fusilier Guards, who were returning home for the fox hunting, were very friendly. They had been hurriedly sent to Canada when war seemed imminent on account of the Trent affair. It was the first time a regiment of the Guards had been out of England since Waterloo, they were very glad to be returning to their beloved "Merry" England. Among these young officers was the Earl of Dunmore, who, a few months before, wishing to see something of the War Between the States, had obtained a leave of absence, passed through the Federal lines and gone to Richmond and thence to Charleston. He had traveled *incog.* under his family name of Murray.

At Charleston he had been entertained by Mr. Trenholm, and that gave us something to talk about. Dunmore was of a very venturesome disposition and instead of returning North on his pass, he decided to enjoy the sensation of running the blockade. The boat he took passage on successfully eluded the Federal fleet off Charleston, but she was captured by an outside cruiser the very next day. The prisoners were of course searched and around the body of "Mr. Murray," under his shirt, was found wrapped a Confederate flag—the flag of the C.S.S. *Nashville*, which had been presented to him by Captain Pegram. Despite his protestations that he was a Britisher traveling for pleasure, he was confined, as "Mr. Murray," in Fort Lafayette. The British Minister, Lord-Lyons, soon heard of his predicament and requested the authorities in Washington to order his release, representing him as being the Earl of Dunmore, a lieutenant in Her Majesty's Life Guards. But the commandant of Fort Lafayette denied that he had any such prisoner and it required quite a correspondence to persuade him that a man by the name of Murray could at the same time be Lord Dunmore.

Another of the Guardsmen was Captain Richard Cooper, who, at the relief of Lucknow, was the first man through the breach in the wall, on which occasion he received a fearful wound across his forehead from a scimitar in the hands of a Sepoy, which had left a vivid red scar. Several of the young Guardsmen had never yet flirted with death; they envied Captain Cooper and would gladly have been the possessors of his ugly scarlet blemish.

The *Arabia* was a paddlewheel full-rigged ship. She appeared to us to be enormous in size, though, as a matter of fact, she was not one tenth as large as the modern Cunard liner. She did not even have a smoking-room, the lovers of the weed, when they wished to indulge in a whiff, having to seek the shelter of the lee side of the smokestack in all sorts of weather. A part of this pleasant voyage was very smooth, but when we struck the "roaring forties" the big ship tumbled about considerably and my commodore was as seasick and amiable as usual.

*T*welve

Liverpool—London—Visit "Hill Morton," near Rugby—Ordered to the C.S.S. *Alexandra*—Snubbed—Ordered to Paris—Ordered to London—Birthday properly celebrated—Damn the Marquis of Westminster and lose my only friend—Meet several Mr. Grigsons.

We arrived in Liverpool safely, and as soon as we could go ashore I accompanied Commodore Maury to No. 10 Rumford Place, the offices of Messrs. Fraser, Trenholm & Co., the financial agents of the Confederacy. There had been no Mr. Fraser in the firm for many years prior to this time, and Mr. Prioleau, a junior partner, was in charge of the Liverpool branch. But it was not to see him that our visit was made. The commodore wanted to see Captain Bulloch, C.S.N., who had recently fitted out the *Alabama* and who was busy superintending the building of other ships intended for Confederate cruisers.[1] Captain Bulloch was very kind to me, particularly after I had told him that I knew Mrs. Bulloch when she was Miss Harriet Cross and lived in Baton Rouge.

Before the commodore finished his interview a clerk came into Captain Bulloch's office and asked if I was Mr. Morgan; he said Mr. Prioleau wanted to see me. Mr. Prioleau was very affable and gave me two letters of introduction, one to a fashionable London tailor and the other to the firm of Dent, the celebrated chronometer makers of that day. He said it was by Mr. Trenholm's orders and that the letters contained instructions as to what those people would give me.

84

The commodore and I stopped overnight at the old Adelphi Hotel. I was by this time accustomed to commodores and I had met a live lord, but the head waiter, the most pompous and dignified human being I had ever encountered, filled my little soul with awe whenever he condescended to come near me. I was hungry, but felt diffident about asking such an important personage to allow me to have anything to eat. I soon found, however, that he was not as dangerous as he looked and that on occasion he could slightly unbend, and as for knowing things, why he knew a great deal better than I did what I wanted for my dinner.

When we reached London I found that a house in Sackville Street had already been engaged for the commodore, who kindly invited me to be his guest. As I have before said, Commodore Maury was much more appreciated in Europe than he was in his native land. All day long there would be in front of the house a string of carriages with coronets on their doors, while their owners were paying their respect to the great "Lieutenant" Maury. The Emperor of Russia sent him an offer of the rank of admiral, with a salary of thirty thousand dollars a year attached to the rank, if he would enter His Majesty's service, and to build him an observatory and a palatial residence in any part of Russia which he should select. Commodore Maury thanked him and told him that it would be impossible to accept his very flattering offer, as he, the commodore, had devoted his life and abilities to the cause of the South.

Having nothing else to do, I hired a cab and presented first my letter of introduction to Dent, the watchmaker, where the polite manager placed before me a whole trayful of gold watches and another of watch chains, and begged me to take my choice. I was a little dazed, but managed to carry off with me a beautiful timepiece. Next I went to the tailor, who measured me in every conceivable way and then assured me, with many bows, that he would expedite my order and keep me waiting as short a time as possible. When that order arrived in Sackville Street I was surprised, indeed. At most I had expected a new sack coat, but here was a great box containing a full-dress suit, a morning or business suit, an afternoon frock coat, a smoking-jacket Heaven only knows what else.

I had not been in London more than a week when my friends the Guardsmen put in an appearance and invited me to visit their various homes. The commodore selected the invitation of Captain Cooper as the first one for me to accept, as he was the oldest officer, and I went to his place called "Hill Morton," near Rugby. I found gathered there Lord Dunmore, Lieutenant the Honorable Charles White, and Lieutenant Ram, of Ramsgate, who had been my fellow passengers on the *Arabia*. That visit is among the most pleasant recollections of my long life. Captain Cooper took me to see Rugby School where I insisted on seeing the exact spot on which "Tom Brown" had fought his memorable fight. "Tom Brown" was a real personage to me in those days, and although the request might have puzzled the Head Master, it was easy for those young Guardsmen to take me to the place and make me thrill with their vivid description of the contest. I afterwards found out that they were all Eton boys and did not know any more about Rugby than I did.

On the days when we did not hunt I was taken on a round of calls on the county families. I never before knew that there were so many lords and ladies in the world, and to my great satisfaction all the aristocrats I met seemed to sympathize with the South in her fight for the right of secession. In the smoking-rooms after dinner I was made to recount the stories of the battles I had been in, and they flattered me so that I began almost to believe that I was something of a hero.

Like all pleasant things my visits to my Guardsmen friends came to an end and I returned to London, where I received orders to proceed to Liverpool and report to Lieutenant J. R. Hamilton, C.S.N., for duty on the *Alexandra*.[2] This was only a *nom de guerre* given her in the hope of hoodwinking the British Government as to the real purposes for which she was being built; but no matter how blind the British might be, Mr. Charles Francis Adams, the American minister, to use a vulgar expression, was "on to her," and knew as well as we did what she was intended for. Only her keel and ribs were in place when I first saw her and I do not think the builders were in any hurry to complete her, but rather devoted their energies to the construction of an iron blockade-runner called the *Phantom* which was being built in the same yard.[3]

It was now the middle of winter. The days were shorter than I ever believed days could be—it was not light before ten in the morning, and dark again by half-past two in the afternoon with the exception of foggy days, and then there was no daylight at all. How I repented ever having abused that bright, burning Louisiana sun. What would I not have given for a few hours of its presence.

My life in Liverpool that winter was a very lonely one, as I was the only Confederate midshipman, at the time, in Europe. I only knew two families in the city—that of Captain Huger's sister, Mrs. Calder, who was very kind to me on account of my having served in the *McRae* under her heroic brother, and the family of Mr. Blacklock, a retired merchant of Charleston, South Carolina. Captain Bulloch and Lieutenant Hamilton lived out of town, as did Mr. Prioleau who resided in a baronial mansion called "Allerton Hall," some miles out. Having naturally, midshipman-like, squandered all the money Mr. Trenholm had so kindly instructed his agent in Bermuda to give me, I was now again dependent on my pay of forty dollars a month and was compelled, for reasons of economy, to live in a little dingy house in a back street, called Upper Newington, a couple of blocks away from the

Adelphi Hotel. Unaccustomed as I was to cold weather, the constant storms and the snow added to the cheerlessness of the situation. The only break in the monotony of my existence came on the days I attended a nautical school, where I was taught navigation, and my fencing and boxing classes. I thought there was going to be a rift in the clouds when Mr. Prioleau invited me to Allerton Hall for Christmas, but there was a fly in the ointment despite the magnificence of the place with its hothouses supplying abundance of flowers and tropical fruits in December. I don't know whether to lay the blame of my trouble on my age or on a young lady, but the facts were these: A young girl, a stepdaughter of a Confederate general who commanded for some time at Charleston, was at school in England and was spending the holidays with the Prioleaus. There was a large number of guests at dinner on Christmas Day, and Mrs. Prioleau designated me to escort the young lady into the bauquet hall. Now the young lady was just my own age, sixteen, when girls most hate boys and look down upon them with supreme contempt, and this young lady thought it beneath her dignity to be seated by a boy—and she took no particular pains to hide her displeasure. On my side I naturally felt hurt, for was I not an officer of the navy and a veteran? At all events, I did not enjoy my dinner, and I ought to have been happy, for Mr. Prioleau had handed me that morning fifty pounds sterling, saying it was a present from my kind friend Mr. Trenholm who wished me a merry Christmas. The first use I made of my wealth was to ask and obtain permission to visit Paris, but even Paris, despite its beauty and objects of interest, is a dull place for a boy of sixteen with no acquaintances and not knowing what to do with himself, so I returned to my dismal life in Liverpool.

In February, 1863, I received an order detaching me from the uncompleted *Alexandra*, and ordering me to proceed to Paris and await orders. After a couple of weeks sojourn in what was to other people the gayest city in the world, I received an order to go to London and await orders at the Westminster Palace Hotel.

I arrived in London on the morning of the 10th of March. It was my birthday, and I must say this for the Britishers, it was the only occasion in any life that I ever saw the day properly celebrated. There were royal processions in the streets during the day, and the city was gay with bunting, while at night the city was illuminated. Such crowds as there were in the streets I could never have imagined before. It was said that despite the fact that the throng was most amiable, forty people were crushed to death by its mere pressure in the narrow streets. I should add incidentally that the Prince of Wales, afterwards His Majesty King Edward the Seventh, and the Princess Alexandra of Denmark were married that day.

Never before had I been so lonely as I was in that great city. The old, dignified, and taciturn waiter who served my meals was the only human being who took any notice of me. He, after a time, appeared to be sorry for me and gave me a table by a window looking out on the street; occasionally he would vouchsafe me a word, for which I was truly grateful; but I was ignorant of the fact that he was a friend of the Marquis of Westminster, and I made a bad break which cost me his friendship. The trouble occurred in this way. I came to breakfast one morning feeling cross and unhappy. I was gazing out of the window when a pedestrian, whose clothes did not look any too fresh, passed by on the sidewalk. My friend the waiter called my attention to the man and in an awed whisper said, "The Marquis of Westminster!" I sulkily remarked, "Oh, damn the Marquis of Westminster!" The waiter flushed and angrily retorted, "But ye can't, ye know; he owns all this part of Lunnon!" After that our relations were too strained to allow of any further social intercourse. But as I was under orders not to make any promiscuous acquaintances, probably it was just as well that he snubbed me when I attempted to resume friendly chats with him. We Confederates in Europe were very secretive and mysterious. The higher officers traveled *incog.* and all that sort of thing. It was interesting to me in after years to read Mr. Charles Francis Adams's letters to his Government, from which I learned that he not only knew our names, but probably had a diagram of every plank and bolt that was being put into our ships.

On the 4th of April, 1863, I received an order to go to a house in Little St. James's Street and inquire for a "Mr. Grigson," who would give me further instructions. When I found the house the door was opened by a pleasant-faced, middle-aged woman who seemed much amused when I asked for "Mr. Grigson." She replied, laughing, "You will find them in there," pointing to a door. From her language I inferred that the mysterious Mr. Grigson was not so singular a man after all; evidently there must be more than one of him. Entering the room indicated I found myself in the presence of Lieutenants Chapman and Evans, who had been on the *Sumter* when she was fitted out in New Orleans two years previously, and Mr. Ingraham, a son of the commodore, who had been a first classman when I was at Annapolis.[4] These gentlemen were also laughing and told me that I had given them a scare, as they were afraid I might be a detective. I asked which one of them might be Mr. Grigson, as I had business of importance to transact with that gentleman? Mr. Chapman answered that they were all Grigsons, but he thought he was a good enough Grigson for my purposes. He handed me an order to report to Commander William L. Maury, and when I asked where I should find that officer, he told me that if I would stay close to him, Chapman, I would surely meet the gentleman very shortly.[5] I was then told to return to the hotel, get my belongings, and return to Little St. James's Street.

*T*hirteen

White Haven—The active tug *Alar*—Meet the *Japan*, which turns out to be the Confederate cruiser *Georgia*—Ushant Island—Break neutrality laws, and away to sea—Hoist Confederate flag but don't use it much—Capture Verde Islands—Narrow escape from U.S.S. *Mohican*—Crew of *Dictator* ship with us—Chasing ships.

Returning to Little St. James's Street I found that Passed Midshipman Walker[1] had joined the party, and about half-past nine that evening we all proceeded to a railway station where we took a train for White Haven, a little seaport about an hour's ride from London. There we went to a small inn, where we met Commander Maury, Dr. Wheeden, and Paymaster Curtis, and were soon joined by others—all strangers to me.[2] We waited at the inn for about a couple of hours; there was little, if any, conversation, as we were all too anxious and were all thinking about the same thing. In those two hours it was to be decided whether our expedition was to be a success or a failure. If Mr. Adams, the American Minister, was going to get in his fine work and balk us, now was his last opportunity.

A little after midnight, two by two, we sauntered down to the quay, where we found at least a hundred people gathered near a little sea-going tug called the *Alar*. It was blowing a gale and a heavy sea was rolling in, which caused the little boat to bump herself viciously against the stone dock, so that but for her ample fenders she must have stove her side in. We hurried on board and Mr. Chapman, taking up a position by the pilot house, said to the crowd on the dock, "Now, men, you know what we want of you; all who want to go with us jump aboard!" About sixty responded to the invitation. The lines were cast off and the *Alar* shot out of the slip as a man on shore proposed three cheers for the *Alabama*, which were lustily responded to by our fellow passengers.

As we cleared the end of the docks the little *Alar* poked her nose into a huge sea and tried to stand erect on her stern, but not being able to accomplish that feat, she fell down into the trough and the next wave passed over her, drenching to the skin every man aboard. She next tried to hold her stern in the air while she stood on her nose, and when the foaming sea reached her pilot house she rolled over on her side as though she was tired and wanted to take a nap; but she was disturbed by another comber picking her up and slamming her down on the other side with such force as to make every rib in her tiny body quiver. There were no secrets in that contracted space. The men aboard were supposed to be the crew of our cruiser, when we found her, and the cargo of the tug consisted of our guns, shipped as hardware in boxes, and our ammunition. We were all huddled up together, and plainly heard the engineer tell the captain that one more sea like the last one which came aboard would put out the fires. For more than three days and nights, cold and wet, with no place to sleep and little to eat, we stumbled and tumbled down the English Channel. When the gale abated at last, we saw on the horizon a trim-looking little brig-rigged steamer idly rolling on the swell of the sea, apparently waiting for something, and we steered for her. She proved to be the British (?) steamer *Japan*; her papers said that she was bound from Glasgow to Nagasaki, with an assorted cargo, but we doubted their accuracy.

Commodore Matthew F. Maury, who had bought and fitted out this ship, just completed at Dunbarton on the Clyde, had outwitted the British Government, but not Mr. Adams, who had warned the authorities of her character. How the British Government could have been held responsible for her escape without stopping their whole commerce is beyond my understanding. The vessel had not the slightest resemblance to a man-of-war; she nominally belonged to a private party, and there was not an ounce of contraband in her cargo, which consisted of provisions, coal, and empty boxes. Her captain himself did not know for what purpose she was intended. His orders were to proceed to a certain latitude and longitude near the island of Ushant on the French coast, where a tug would meet him and give him further instructions from his owner.

When we had approached close enough to the *Japan* to hail, Captain Maury asked her captain to send a boat, as he had a communication for him. Captain Maury then went aboard the brig and what passed between him and her skipper of course I had no means of knowing, but soon the Japan passed us a hawser, as there was some slight trouble with the *Alar's* engines which needed immediate attention. We were taken in tow, and no sooner did the *Japan* start ahead than accident number one occurred. The hawser became entangled in the *Japan's* screw, jamming it. It took several hours to cut it loose, and when this was finally accomplished, we proceeded to Ushant, going around it in search of smooth waters so that we could transfer our guns from the tug to the cruiser that was to be. We dropped anchor after dark in a little cove and commenced operations, despite the angry protests of the French coastguards from the shore. Judging from their language they must have been furious as well as helpless. The men we had brought from White Haven worked most energetically, and by midnight we had our two twenty-four pounders and the two little ten-pounder Whitworth guns on board, as well as the ammunition and the traverses; but unfortunately the sea was rising all the time and the little tug alongside was pitching and rolling so much that it was too dangerous to attempt to get the biggest gun, a thirty-two-pounder Blakeley rifle, out of her. So we got under way again and proceeded to the mainland, not many miles from Brest, a great naval station where we knew a French fleet was assembled. Working like beavers and protected by a headland there, we finally succeeded in shifting the Blakeley gun. We then stood out to sea, where, after we had got safely beyond the three-mile limit, we stopped. Captain Maury called all hands to the mast and read his orders, hoisted the Confederate flag and his pennant, and declared the Confederate States cruiser *Georgia* to be in commission.[3]

His remarks were received with three lusty cheers. He then asked the men who were going with us to step forward and enlist for three years or the war, but alas, a lawyer had been at work, and not a man came forward. The spokesman demanded higher wages on account of the dangers of the service, and when told that the *Georgia* was a man-of-war and the pay was fixed by law, they, to a man, went over the side and boarded the tug. To our surprise nine men of the crew of the late merchantman *Japan* now stepped forward and said they would like to go with us and of course they were accepted at once. With these men as a nucleus for a crew, we cast off the *Alar's* line and never saw or heard of her or the men on board of her again, and never wanted to. We afterwards learned that our presence at Ushant and on the coast of France had been signaled to Brest and that a fast frigate had been sent in all haste to capture us for our breach of French neutrality; but we never saw her.

CAPTAIN W. L. MAURY
Commanding the CSS *Georgia*

It was the 9th of April, 1863, when this little friendless ship of only about five hundred and fifty tons started on her long and hazardous cruise. She was as absolutely unfitted for the work as any vessel could conceivably be: she lay very low in the water and was very long for her beam; her engines were gear engines, that is, a large wheel fitted with lignum-vitae cogs turned the iron cogs on the shaft, and frequently the wooden cogs would break. When they did it was worse than if a shrapnel shell had burst in the engine room, as they flew in every direction, endangering the lives of every one within reach. Her sail power was insufficient, and, owing to her length, it was impossible to put her about under canvas. She was slow under either sail or steam, or both together. Such was the little craft in which we got slowly under way, bound we knew not where. Ushant Island bearing east southeast, distant four and a half miles.

The morning of the 10th of April dawned fair, with light breezes and a comparatively smooth sea, and officers and men set to work fastening to the deck iron traverses for our pivot gun. Then came a most difficult job, shorthanded as we were,—that of mounting the guns on their carriages; and to add to our troubles the sea commenced to rise. With all the most intricate and ingenious tackles our seamanlike first lieutenant could devise, it was an awful strain upon us, as the heavy gun swung back and forth with the roll of the ship. However, by almost superhuman exertions we succeeded in getting the guns into their places on the carriages; then we felt very man-of-warrish indeed.

Day after day, with a pleasant breeze, we steered a course somewhat west of south; meeting but few ships, and those we saw displayed neutral colors when we showed them the British or American ensign. During the whole cruise we saw our Confederate flag only when we were in the act of making a capture or when we were in port. Usually we showed strange sails the Stars and Stripes. On April 25, there being several sails in sight, we got up steam and made chase after them. The merchantmen we approached one after the other showed us neutral colors until we were becoming disheartened, when suddenly, about 4 p.m., we descried on the horizon a big full-rigged ship with long skysail poles,—the sure sign of the Yankee. She appeared unwilling to take any chances with us and cracked on more sail while we pursued her under steam. A little after five o'clock, we hauled down the British colors, hoisted the Confederate flag, and sent a shot bounding over the water just ahead of her, which in the language of the sea, was an order to heave to. In less time than it takes to tell, the main yard of the doomed ship swung around and her sails on the main and mizzen masts were thrown aback as the American flag was broken out and fluttered from her peak. We immediately lowered a boat and our second lieutenant,

Mr. Evans, accompanied by myself, rowed over to the prize which proved to be the splendid ship *Dictator* of between three and four thousand tons, from New York bound to Hong Kong with a cargo of coal. She carried no passengers.

After looking over the ship's papers, we made her crew lower their own boats and forced the captain, his three mates, and the crew of twenty-seven men to get into them with their personal belongings. We then ordered them to pull for the *Georgia*, which they did with no enthusiasm whatever. On arriving alongside the cruiser they were allowed to come over the side one at a time, and were then hurried below and placed in irons. It was not considered advisable to give them time enough to see how weak our force was. The captain was invited by our commander to share the cabin with him, and the first mate was confined in my room, but neither of them had any restraint put on him except that neither was allowed to go forward of the mainmast, or to hold any communication with the men. On board the *Dictator* we found a fine assortment of provisions and sent several boat loads to our own ship. This was necessary as we had now to feed the prize's crew as well as our own.

The *Georgia* lay near the *Dictator* all night, and in the morning we attempted to replenish our coal bunkers from her, but the rising sea made this impossible; and after coming very near swamping our small boats, we gave it up. It seemed hard that we should have to go without the fuel so precious to us while several thousand tons of the very best were within a few cables' lengths of our vessel. However, it might as well have been in the mines of Pennsylvania whence it came for all the good it was to us.

The *Georgia* made signal to burn the prize, and Lieutenant Evans asked me if I would like to try my hand at setting her on fire. There were a large number of broken provisions boxes lying about the deck which I gathered and, placing them against her rail, I lighted a match and applied it. The kindling wood burned beautifully, but when its flames expired there was not a sign of fire on the side of the ship. I was surprised and puzzled, and turned to seek an explanation from my superior officer, who was standing near by fairly convulsed with laughter. He told me not to mind; he would show me how it was done. (He had had previous experience in the gentle art when lieutenant with Captain Semmes on the *Sumter*.) I followed him into the cabin where he pulled out several drawers from under the captain's berth, and, filling them with old newspapers, he applied a match. The effect was almost instantaneous. Flames leaped up and caught the chintz curtains of the berth and the bedclothes, at the same time setting fire to the light woodwork. The sight fascinated me and I stood watching it as though I was dazed, when suddenly I heard the lieutenant's voice call excitedly: "Run, youngster, run, or we will be cut off from the door!" We rushed out, followed by a dense smoke and leaping flames, reaching the gangway just ahead of them, and hastily went over the side and down the ladder into our boat which was waiting for us. By the time we reached the *Georgia*, the prize was one seething mass of flames from her hold to her trucks. It was a strange and weird sight to see the flames leaping up her tarred rigging, while dense volumes of smoke, lighted up by fire from the mass of coal below, rolled up through her hatches.

The *Dictator*, exclusive of her cargo, was valued at eighty-six thousand dollars. By decree of the Confederate Government we were to receive one half of the value of every ship destroyed, and the full amount of the bonds given by vessels carrying neutral cargo. Under the law regulating the distribution of prize money the total amount was divided into twentieths of which the commanding officer got two and the steerage officers got the same, the rest being shared by the wardroom officers and the crew. I being the only midshipman, or steerage officer, on board of the *Georgia* for most of the cruise, the amount of prize money (still due me) which I should have received would have almost equaled the share of the captain.

When we parted company with the burning *Dictator* we had hardly got well under way when the always exciting, "Sail ho!" was heard coming from the masthead lookout followed by the officer of the deck's query, "Where away?" and the answer, "Two points off the port bow, sir!" Away we dashed in chase, only to be disappointed again and again when the chase showed neutral colors. If we had any cause to suspect that they were not what their colors represented them to be we boarded them and examined their papers. Strange sail were plentiful, but no American craft among them. One day we chased a paddle wheel bark-rigged steamer; it seemed rather strange that we should overhaul her so rapidly, but when we got near to her we discovered that her engines were disconnected and that her paddles were being turned by her momentum through the water. We had the British flag proudly flying at our peak, and suddenly we made another discovery; she was a man-of-war! Suddenly she broke out her ensign and there we saw the British Union Jack! The way that British flag came down from our peak and was replaced by the Confederate flag looked like legerdemain. The Englishman then dipped his colors to us—a courtesy that we very much appreciated and which we returned with great satisfaction, as it was the first salute of any kind we had received.

On the 29th of April, at about three bells in the forenoon watch, we found ourselves near the island of San Antonio, one of the Cape Verdes.

C.S. CRUISER *GEORGIA*

With all sail set we bowled along before a stiff northeast trade wind which soon brought us in between San Antonio and the island of St. Vincent, where the high land on either beam acted as a funnel for the trade wind which now increased to a gale. We shot by a promontory and there before our eyes we saw the town and harbor of Porto Grande, and there also we saw lying peacefully at her anchor a sloop-of-war, with the Stars and Stripes fluttering from her peak! Instantly everybody on our ship was in a state of excitement and commotion. The officer of the deck gave the order "Hard-a-port!" quickly followed in rapid succession through his speaking-trumpet by "Main clew garnets and buntlines!"—"Haul taut!"—"Up courses!"—"T'gallant and topsail halyards!"—"Let go!"—"Haul down!"—"Clew up!"—"All hands furl sail!"—and officers and men rushed aloft and, working like Trojans, soon had her under bare poles. Four bells were rung for full speed ahead, and the little ship gallantly breasted the high sea in the face of the half-gale of wind; but neither patent log nor the old-fashioned chip-and-line could be persuaded to show more than four knots speed.

Captain Maury was evidently very anxious and sent for the English chief engineer and asked him if that was the best he could do. The chief said he thought it was. Captain Maury then told him that if the American man-of-war was the *Mohican*, as he thought she was, he had served on board of her and she could make seven knots an hour easily against that sea and wind—and significantly added, "You know that being caught means hanging with us according to Mr. Lincoln's proclamation!"

The chief disappeared below and in a few minutes our improvement in speed was remarkable. We were gratified as well as surprised when we found that we were not being pursued. We afterwards learned that the sloop-of-war, not expecting a visit from us at such an unconventional hour, had let her steam go down and could not get under way until she got it up again. We ran around the island and, finding a cove, anchored near the shore, sending a lieutenant ashore to climb the promontory, from which lofty point of vantage, with the aid of his marine glasses, he plainly saw our would-be captor steaming out to sea in the opposite direction from our snug hiding-place. If she had sighted us it is easy to imagine what would have happened, as she carried ten gun,—all of which were much heavier than our biggest piece of ordnance—and the little *Georgia* had more than twice as many prisoners on board of her as she had crew. In fact, our crew would not have been sufficient in numbers to handle and serve our forward pivot gun.

When night came we weighed anchor and put to sea and the next morning were busily engaged chasing and examining ships. Sometimes we would "bring to" an American, then be disappointed because he had changed his flag, and his papers as a neutral would be all correct. Most neutral vessels feared us, and as soon as they suspected our character would attempt to escape, thus causing us much unnecessary burning of coal. Few of them appeared to be friendly to us, and when asked for news seemed delighted when they had the courage to tell us some rigmarole about great disasters to the Confederate armies which they invented for the occasion. Some few gave us newspapers and kindly told us the truth as to what had happened before they left port in the world from which we were excluded.

It was a fortunate thing for us that we had not been able to land our prisoners in the Cape Verde islands, as we had intended to do. We had treated these unfortunates kindly; they received the same rations our own men did, and one half of them were released from their irons and allowed to roam around the deck in the daytime. They must have become attached to us, for first one man and then another asked to be permitted to talk to our first lieutenant, and when this was granted, would request to be allowed to ship aboard. To our surprise the second and third mates and the twenty-seven seamen joined us and afterwards proved to be among the very best men we had.

The captain of the *Dictator* had shared Captain Maury's cabin and seemed a very nice man, but the first mate was of a very different type. He was quartered in my stateroom, while I had to sleep in a hammock slung out in the steerage. He took his meals with me and was allowed to take his exercise on the poop deck. Of course neither he nor the captain was subjected to the inconvenience of having irons put on them; but Mr. Snow, the first mate, repaid our consideration by writing the story of his capture and "inhuman" treatment by the "pirates" on board the *Georgia*. He placed this romance in a bottle which he corked tightly and sealed with sealing-wax which he borrowed from me; then he threw it out of the air-port in hopes that it would drift ashore. It did. Years after the war was over it was picked up on the coast of Norway, and its lying contents were published to the world.

Fourteen

The Doldrums—Waterspouts—Bahia—Meet the *Alabama*—Changing the Confederate flag—Corsairos—Brazilian ball—Midshipman Anderson makes a pillow out of Captain Semmes—U.S.S. *Niagara* and *Mohican* on our trail—"Does he want his pretty white paint spoiled?"—Refused permission to depart after 4 p.m.—Brazilian battery fires one shot as we pass out.

Chasing ships without making any captures was getting to be a little monotonous. Some of the vessels we halted had captains who were cross and ugly about being detained while we examined their papers, while others seemed to enjoy the adventure of being held up by a "pirate" and showed our boarding officers every hospitality in the way of wines, liquors, and cigars. We passed close to a man-of-war and showed her our true colors, which attention she reciprocated by running up the British flag and dipping it to us. Every time this occurred we would congratulate ourselves, insisting that the mere courtesy constituted a recognition of the Confederate States.

Exactly where we were, the captain and the navigator alone knew. The old sailors told me that we were in the "doldrums"—as they call that portion of the Atlantic Ocean which lies in the equatorial belt extending from about ten degrees north of the Equator to the same distance south of it. This they knew by the baffling winds, squalls from every point of the compass, and "Irishmen's hurricanes," as they call dead calms. Another unfailing sign to them was the numerous

99

great waterspouts whirling around in every direction. To see one of these spouts in process of formation is indeed a wonderful sight—first the whirlwind on the surface of the sea and the eddying of a cloud above, then the formation of the column of water twisting and swaying like the body of some huge serpent as it rises out of the sea, the loud, roaring sound and the great commotion of the water around it until it has ascended to a great height, and then the most extraordinary part of all, when the cloud above sends down a similar column of whirling water and the two, with unerring accuracy, join and complete the awe-inspiring funnel. On one occasion one of these spouts was making so straight for us that we fired one of the guns to burst it, for had it come aboard the little *Georgia* it would have instantly swamped her.

One night—in the morning watch, just before daylight—an old sailor said to me, "We are near land, sir." I asked him how he knew and he told me to feel how wet the deck was with dew; and although the sea was smooth, the stars shining brightly, and the ship becalmed, I found the deck as wet as though water had been poured over it. The old "shellback" then informed me that dew never extended more than thirty miles from land. This was news to me, but I found that the Jack Tar was right.

In the middle of the night of May 13–14, we entered the great Bay of Todos os Santos, or All Saints' Bay, and dropped anchor in front of the Brazilian city of Bahia, a picturesque place situated on a high bluff overlooking the bay. There were many vessels anchored near us, and the practiced eyes of our senior lieutenants pronounced two of them to be men-of-war; but of course their nationality could not be made out in the darkness. We had good reason, had we known, for feeling anxious about them, for it was in this same harbor, a few months after our visit, that the Confederate cruiser *Florida* was lying, as her commander thought, in peaceful security. So much at ease was he that he had given half his crew liberty, which they were enjoying on shore when the U.S.S. *Wachusett*, disregarding Brazilian neutrality, in the middle of the night, rammed, boarded, and captured her, carrying her to Hampton Roads where she was sunk to avoid having to give her up on the demand of Brazil that she be returned to Bahia.[1]

There was little sleep on the *Georgia* the night of our arrival. Day broke and we found ourselves very near the two men-of-war. What was their nationality? It seemed an age before the hour for colors arrived, but when it did, to our great delight, the most rakish-looking of the two warships broke out the Stars and Bars! "It is the *Alabama*!" we gasped, and commenced to dance with delight. The officers hugged one another, each embracing a man of his own rank, except the captain and myself. Like the commander, I was the only one of my rank aboard, so I hugged myself.

The Confederate Government had changed its flag since we had left home, and the Stars and Bars had given way to the white field with a St. Andrew's cross which we fondly believed represented the Southern Cross. The *Alabama* had not yet heard of the change, and we furnished the anomalous and embarrassing spectacle of two warships belonging to the same Government and flying flags which bore no resemblance to each other! Fortunately the new flag was not a difficult one to make, and the *Alabama's* sailors soon had the new colors proudly fluttering from her peak.[2]

Captain Semmes, of the *Alabama*, being the ranking officer, our captain quickly got into his gig and went on board the famous ship to pay his respects. The other man-of-war proved to be a Portuguese sloop, very small, and carrying sixteen little popguns.

As soon as we arrived in neutral waters our prisoners, the captain and the first mate of the *Dictator*, were told that they were free and were sent ashore in the first boat. The American Consul demanded that the rest of the crew of the burnt ship should be delivered up to him, and rather than have trouble with the Brazilian Government, we told the men they could go ashore. This they did, and some of the rascals went to the American Consul and told him a tale of woe and got everything possible out of him. With the prisoners landed from the *Alabama* they had a royal time ashore for several days; but, strange to say, when we got to sea there they all were on our decks! They had smuggled themselves aboard the *Georgia* with the connivance of our crew and had remained hidden until we were outside of Brazilian jurisdiction.

The *Alabama* had recently fought and sunk the U.S.S. *Hatteras* off Galveston, and as soon as possible I went on board the pride of the Confederate Navy to see the midshipmen. There were four of them— Irving Bulloch, an uncle of Theodore Roosevelt; Eugene Maffitt, son of that captain of the *Florida*, who, while ill with the yellow fever, ran her through the blockading fleet off Mobile in broad daylight—taking their broadsides as he passed and finally anchoring his much-cut-up ship under the protecting guns of Fort Morgan. There was also William St. Clair, and my dear friend Edward M. Anderson, who is still living (1916). The holes in the *Alabama's* side and the scars on her deck where the shot from the *Hatteras* had ripped them were still fresh, and I heard the story of the battle at first hand. Of course the midshipmen's account of the fight was the one which interested me most. When one has heard their story, one wonders why Captain Homer Blake, of the *Hatteras*, never received more credit for his gallant fight. He fought his ship until the muzzles of his guns were almost on a level with the sea and she was about to disappear beneath the waves forever.[3]

MIDSHIPMAN "JIMMY" MORGAN
While attached to the cruiser *Georgia*, 1863

Captain Semmes was a fine Spanish scholar, but did not speak Portuguese, the national language of Brazil. As I could speak French fluently he borrowed me from Captain Maury to carry communications to the governor of Bahia, who, like most educated South Americans, spoke French perfectly. The American Consul protested against our being allowed to replenish our coal bunkers from the British bark *Castor* which lay near us. Today (1916) the meeting of colliers and warships at appointed rendezvous is supposed to be an invention of the Germans; but colliers followed, or were supposed to be where the *Alabama* and *Georgia* would need them. I am sorry to say that they were rarely on time, but as they were sailing vessels there was some excuse for them. The *Castor* was under contract to deliver us the coal and the coal was our property, paid for by the Confederate agent in England; on the protest of the United States Consul, however, the governor refused to allow us to coal from her. We then made a "sale" of part of the cargo to a native merchant, had it put ashore, and then "bought" it from him. Of course the native was well paid for his trouble, and the probability is that the officials got their rake-off from the transaction.

Brazil was a slave-owning country at that time, but the natives seemed to fear and avoid us, and as we would pass through the streets we could hear the Negro nurses threaten crying children that they would be carried off by the "corsairos" if they were not good. An English engineer who was building a railroad into the interior was the only person in Bahia who showed us any attention or hospitality. He invited the officers of the *Alabama* and *Georgia* to go on an excursion on his unfinished railroad. The country through which it passed was rich and beautiful, and at the end of the finished line our officers were regaled with all sorts of good things to eat and drink. On returning to Bahia he invited us to a dance to be given at his residence that night, and naturally as many of the officers as could be spared from duty accepted. The ball was quite a swell affair; all the British colony were there, of course, and many Brazilian ladies; they came from curiosity, but nothing could induce them to risk dancing with the "corsairos." This, of course, made us youngsters imagine that we looked rather formidable.

Shortly after midnight we said good-night to our host and hostess and such of the guests as were not afraid to speak to us, and proceeded to the quay where Captain Semmes' gig was waiting for him. The cutters from the *Alabama* and *Georgia*, which were to take the officers to their respective ships, had not yet come for us, and we thought we saw before us a long wait; but Captain Semmes very kindly invited us to crowd into his gig, saying that after she put him aboard of the *Alabama* she would take those of us belonging to the *Georgia* to our ship. On our way to the *Alabama*, Midshipman Anderson, the personal aide, who had had a rather strenuous day of it, fell asleep. He was seated alongside of his commanding officer and his head fell on the captain's shoulder. Lieutenant Armstrong, who was seated opposite him, was about to reach over and awaken Anderson, but Captain Semmes by a gesture stopped him, saying, "Let the boy sleep; he is tired out." Had Anderson been awake he would rather have dropped his head in the ship's furnace than on Captain Semmes' shoulder, for the captain was not a man with whom any one would care to take liberties. As it was, however, Ned had the honor of being the only man who ever made a pillow out of "old Beeswax" as Semmes was called behind his back.

Captain Semmes was an austere and formal man, and, with the exception of Dr. Galt, the surgeon, and Mr. Kell, his first lieutenant, he rarely held any intercourse with officers except officially. He waxed the ends of his mustache (which the sailors called his "st'unsail booms") and he would pace his quarter-deck, alone, twisting and retwisting those long ends. He reminded one of Byron's description of the captain of a man-of-war in "Childe Harold:"—

> "Look on that part which sacred doth remain
> For the lone chieftain, who majestic stalks,
> Silent and feared by all—not oft he talks
> With aught beneath him, if he would preserve
> That strict restraint, which broken, ever balks
> Conquest and fame. . . . "

Captain Semmes was a past-master in the art of dealing with Latin-Americans. When the *Alabama* entered the port of Bahia, the governor sent an aide, attired in mufti, to demand that Captain Semmes show his commission. Captain Semmes fixed his steely eyes on the visitor, and then quietly demanded that the gentleman first show his own, and his authority for making the demand. Naturally the aide-de-camp had not had the forethought to provide himself with either, so he took his departure. As he left the cabin, Captain Semmes kindly suggested that if the gentleman wished to be treated courteously on his next visit, it would be advisable to wear his uniform. Of course the aide shortly came back, properly costumed, and with his commission in his pocket, and also a courteous request that Captain Semmes would call at the palace and show his commission to the governor in person. No man knew better than Captain Semmes that he who attempts to enter into a bowing contest with a Latin-American is lost.

Shortly before we left Bahia a coasting steamer entered the port, bringing the news that the United States ships *Niagara* and *Mohican* were either at Pernambuco, a short run to the north, or else on their way south, in search of us. Whether this information had any influence on our movements or not, of course a midshipman could not be expected to know; but all the same we got ready to depart. The *Niagara* carried twelve eleven-inch pivot guns, which enabled her to fight them all on either side. She was designed by Steers on the lines of the famed yacht *America*, of which also he was the designer; and the *Niagara*, although a steamer, had shown marvelous speed under sail. She had accompanied the British fleet across the Atlantic when the first Atlantic cable had been laid, and it was of her that Admiral Milne spoke when he wrote to the British Admiralty from on board his seventy-two-gun line-of-battle ship that he was in company with a sloop-of-war which carried only twelve guns, but could outrun his line-of-battle ship and whip her when caught. Consequently there was no doubt on the part of any of us that the *Niagara* could clear the South Atlantic Ocean of *Alabamas* and *Georgias*.

When this news concerning the *Niagara* and her consort reached the port we had not finished coaling, and the natives, who had seemed so anxious to be rid of our presence, now appeared to seek for excuses to delay our departure. Having transferred some five hundred pounds of powder from the *Georgia* to the *Alabama*, as the latter ship had used up some of her very short supply in her fight with the *Hatteras*, in the forenoon of May 22, Captain Semmes sent me with a verbal message to the governor informing him that he would sail at half-past four that afternoon. While I was standing respectfully before the governor awaiting his answer, the captain of the little white Portuguese sloop was striding up and down the room with a fierce expression on his face. Finally the governor told me to tell Captain Semmes that the *Alabama* would not be permitted to depart at that hour, as the port regulations did not allow vessels to depart after four o'clock; and the Portuguese captain said to the governor, in French (evidently for my benefit), that if the governor wanted the "corsairs" stopped, he would stop them for him! When I repeated this remark to Captain Semmes, he only smiled and said, "Does he want his pretty white paint spoiled?"

Captain Semmes then sent me back to the governor with a message to the effect that the port regulation applied only to merchant vessels and that the *Alabama* and *Georgia* were men-of-war. At 4 p.m. the *Alabama* fired a gun as a signal to one of her boats to come aboard and at once commenced to weight anchor. We could see from our deck a company of soldiers trotting at the double-quick down to an obsolete water battery, where the old-fashioned rust-eaten cannon were mostly mounted in an extraordinary fashion, their muzzles resting on the parapet and their breeches supported on logs of wood. On board the Portuguese corvette there also seemed to be great excitement, as they beat to quarters with such a racket that every man aboard seemed to be giving orders or directions to someone else. At exactly half-past four the *Alabama* hoisted her boat, weighed anchor, and slowly got under way; then, turning around, and hoisting her flag at the main, she steered for the Portuguese. She passed so close to that vessel that I thought for a moment their yards would crash together, but the Portuguese allowed her to pass by without molestation. It was none of her business anyhow!

When we followed the *Alabama* out, we passed very close to the water battery where the men were standing at their guns, but not a shot was fired until we were at least a mile and a half away, when we saw a puff of smoke and immediately afterwards a shot skipped over the placid waters of the bay, falling half a mile short of us. We wondered how many men in the fort had been killed, for it was a brave and reckless act to fire one of those guns. We did not reply, as we did not know how soon it might be necessary for us again to enter a Brazilian port.

As we passed out of the Bay of Todos os Santos it was wrapped in the golden splendors of the most gorgeous sunset it has ever been my good fortune to behold.

Fifteen

"Tempest in a teapot"—Capture clipper ship *George Griswold* of New York—Burn bark *Good Hope* of Boston—Funeral at sea—Bark *Seaver* goes to assistance of the *Good Hope* and is captured—Transfer prisoners to the *Seaver*.

We followed in the track of the *Alabama* down the Brazilian coast. The weather overhead was fine, but suddenly a terrific tempest broke loose out of our mess teapot, a piece of crockery which had been bought by the joint funds of Passed Midshipman Walker and myself. Mr. Walker had been promoted to the dignity of a quarter-deck watch recently. Unfortunately I was the only line officer he ranked, and he never allowed me to forget the fact. My position on board reminded me of the story of the old sailor who, in spinning a yarn, had told how every man in the navy ranked someone else, but, catching sight of the "powder-monkey," he added: "Except you, Jacky!" whereupon Jacky retorted, "Yes, I does; I rank Dennis,"—Dennis being the name of the pig who enjoyed the enviable position of mascot and pet of the whole ship's crew.

The cause of the hurricane bursting out of the teapot was my ordering the steerage steward to make me some chocolate, which he served in the teapot. The passed midshipman, passing through the steerage, smelled the odor, very peremptorily demanded to know by whose orders chocolate had been put into that teapot, and on being informed that I was the culprit, he told me that he would attend to my

107

case as soon as he came off watch. It was the first dogwatch that he was keeping—I was impatient for it to be over. I went at last out on the deck and walked up and down under the waist boats so that I should be on hand when it was over. At last eight bells sounded, and after being relieved from the deck the passed midshipman came down from the poop and was about to proceed to his quarters when I stopped him and told him that I had stood all I intended to stand. Then I struck him. We fought all over the deck and the men ran aft making a circle around us, urging us on. The officer of the deck came to part us, but the men crowded so that he could not get to us. He then ran into the wardroom, returning accompanied by all the officers, who, with their side arms, drove the men forward and proceeded to separate the combatants. The first lieutenant then marched us into the presence of the captain, who placed us both under close arrest, but not for long; the ship was too short of officers, and while Walker's confinement gave the watch officers extra duty, as the only midshipman on board I had a great deal of unpleasant work which some officer had to attend to during my incarceration, such as boat duty, acting as master's mate of the berth deck, and superintending the issuing of the grog ration, besides my regular watch on the forecastle. So kind influence was used in our behalf,—of course, disinterested,—and our captain, who was a most good-hearted and amiable gentleman, let us off and restored us to duty after a week's confinement and a lecture.

We were beginning to think that the *Alabama* had cleared up all the Yankee merchantmen in that part of the ocean, when one day we spied a ship with the unmistakable long skysail poles and brought her to. She proved to be the American ship *Prince of Wales*, but as she had a neutral cargo aboard we had to bond her. These bonds were given by the master in the name of his owners and stipulated that in consideration of our not burning his vessel, they would be paid six months after the ratification of a treaty of peace between the United States and the Confederate States Governments.[1]

On June 8, at daylight, we found ourselves off the entrance to the harbor of Rio de Janeiro and in plain sight of the famous landmark called the Sugar Loaf. We also saw a splendid big clipper ship making her way toward the port. Putting on a full head of steam and setting all sail that would draw, we started in chase of her. The stranger evidently had no doubt as to our character for she immediately set all of her kites and studding sails and made all possible haste for her haven of refuge, which lay within the charmed marine league from the shore. Some thought that she had made it, but Mr. Ingraham, our youthful navigator, announced that in his opinion she was a few inches outside of it. There was no time to be lost, so we cast loose our guns and after a few shots brought her to. The prize proved to be the clipper ship *George Griswold* of New York, manned by a Negro crew with the exception of her captain and mates. There was great rejoicing on the *Georgia* over this capture, as the *Griswold* was the ship which had carried a cargo of flour and wheat, a gift from the people of the United States, to the starving factory operatives of Lancashire, whose means of earning a livelihood had been interfered with by our war. Some of the bread made from this cargo had been distributed at Birkenhead, opposite Liverpool, by a distinguished committee at the head of which was the celebrated preacher Henry Ward Beecher, who from a stand on which had been placed a model of the *Alabama*, made a speech strongly denouncing the South in general, and the *Alabama* in particular. At the conclusion of his oration the loaves of bread were tossed to the crowd, who, instead of eating it, used it to pelt the unoffending effigy of the *Alabama*. It did not look as though they were so very hungry; but there can be no doubt that this gift of breadstuff changed the sympathies of the working classes of England and converted them into ardent adherents to the cause of the North.

The captain of the *Griswold* had no trouble in proving that she carried a neutral cargo, so we had reluctantly to bond her for her own value of one hundred thousand dollars and let her go. In the mean while, the booming of our guns had evidently been heard in Rio, as Brazilian men-of-war and battleships of other nationalities began to send great columns of black smoke out of their funnels in their haste to get up steam. We thought it advisable to leave the locality, and draw out to sea. Soon we saw the warships coming after us and they followed us all day; shortly after dark, however, we put out our lights,— "dowsed our glims," as the sailors say,—and had the satisfaction of seeing the pursuers "pass in the night."

On June 13, after a long chase, we captured a very fast clipper bark called the *Good Hope* of Boston, bound for Cape Town, whose crew asserted that they had escaped from the *Alabama* the day before and insisted that if the wind had held we could not have caught them. The *Good Hope's* cargo was composed of "Yankee notions" as her mate called it, consisting of every imaginable thing from a portable country villa to a cough lozenge, and including carriages, pianos, parlor organs, sewing machines, furniture, dry goods, etc. On boarding her we were informed that her captain—Gordon by name—had died on the voyage and that his son, a youth of eighteen, who was a member of the crew, had objected so strenuously to his father being buried at sea that in deference to his wishes the carpenter had made a rough, oblong box and partly filled it with brine from the beef casks, and the ship's steward had slashed the body in every way with a carving-knife and into these gaping wounds had stuck slices of ship's pickles, the better to preserve it. The body had then been put into the briny, improvised coffin and the cover tightly nailed down.

It was late in the afternoon when we made the capture and Lieutenant Evans went on board as prize master. We had expected to lay by the *Good Hope* all night with the object of taking provisions out of her in the morning, but Lieutenant Smith, who had the mid-watch on the *Georgia*, allowed the prize to drift out of sight and when daylight came she was not to be seen. Naturally we were very anxious, as Mr. Evans had only five of our men with him and the *Good Hope's* crew numbered over twenty. Shortly after sunrise we were greatly relieved again to catch sight of her and soon we were near enough to commence transferring her provisions to our own ship. When we had got all we wanted, Captain Maury ordered the coffin containing the dead captain to be brought aboard the *Georgia*. This was no easy thing to do in a small boat with the sea running quite high, but the feat was accomplished and it was safely hoisted out of the boat by means of a "whip" sent down from our main yard, and reverently placed on two carpenter's "horses" which awaited it just in front of the entrance to the cabin, where it was covered with the Stars and Stripes, the flag the dead man had sailed under, and which we were told he loved so well in life. Several of our heaviest projectiles were made fast to the foot of the coffin and when all was ready the ship's bell was tolled for divine service, the prisoners were relieved of their irons (the dead captain's son had never had them put on him), and all hands were summoned to bury the dead. The prisoners and our crew mingled together as they gathered around the coffin, at the head of which stood Captain Maury, prayer book in hand, with the son of the dead man standing beside him, while our officers reverently took their places behind. Captain Maury then read the beautiful ritual of the Episcopal Church for the burial of the dead at sea.

I was in charge of the deck while the service was going on. It was a bright sunny Sunday morning, a fresh breeze blowing, and from the burning prize, which had been set on fire when our last boat left her, a great column of smoke, hundreds of feet in height, soared toward the sky. Just over our main truck, all through the service, two white sea birds (the superstitious sailors called them "angel" birds) circled round and round. The solemnity of the occasion was somewhat marred when suddenly the lookout on the foretopmast sang out: "Sail ho!" Not wishing further to disturb the impressive ceremony by asking the usual question of "Where away?" I tiptoed forward and went aloft to see for myself, and beheld a strange craft rising on the horizon very rapidly. She appeared to be coming directly for us; she was close-hauled and it was impossible to tell whether or not a smokestack was hidden by her foresail, especially as United States crusiers used anthracite coal and made little or no smoke.

As the stranger approached, I noticed the unusual whiteness of her sails—a sure sign of a man-of-war; next I noticed a long pennant flying gayly from the top of her main skysail pole—another sure sign; and as she came still nearer she broke out the Stars and Stripes! I waited no longer, but scampered down from aloft, and softly stealing up behind Captain Maury, who was still reading from his prayer book, said in a whisper—"American man-of-war bearing down on us rapidly!" Never a muscle did he move, nor was there the slightest change in his solemn voice until he had finished, and the prisoners had lifted the coffin and committed the body to the care of the deep blue sea. Then he ordered me to beat to quarters and cast loose the guns.

By the time this was done it was discovered that the stranger was not a man-of-war, but an innocent merchantman. What could be her object thus to court her doom when she must have seen the burning *Good Hope* only a few cables' lengths from us? Nearer and nearer she came, while our gunners, lanyards in hand, kept their pieces trained on her. When within about a hundred and fifty yards of us she was suddenly thrown up into the wind, her main sail thrown aback, and, as she hove to, she lowered a whaleboat and her captain came over to the *Georgia*.

We lowered a Jacob's ladder over the side, and the captain of the bark, jumping out of his boat, ran up it like the true sailor he was. As he leaped on to our deck he exclaimed, "This is dreadful! Can I be of any assistance?—How did it happen?" Captain Maury stepped forward and told him the *Good Hope* had been burned by his orders. The man for a moment looked aghast, and then an expression of indignation passed over his features as he asked, "Are you a pirate?" Captain Maury replied, "That is what your people call me." He then took the skipper into his cabin and heard his story.

He had sailed from the United States before the war had begun and had made the long voyage around Cape Horn into the Pacific, where he had wandered about until he had got as far north as the Bering Sea. On his return he had stopped at one of the South Sea islands, overhauled and painted his ship and whitewashed his sails, and had then hoisted a homeward-bound pennant. He was well on his way when, that morning, he had seen a dense column of smoke which he felt sure could come only from some unfortunate ship that had caught fire in the middle of the South Atlantic, and had at once left his course to go to her assistance. The first lieutenant of the *Georgia* went on board of the bark, whose name was the *J. W. Seaver* and searched her, finding many old newspapers, but none of later date than October, 1860. Although her cargo was American, Captain Maury let him go, saying that he would stand a court-martial before he would burn the ship of a man who had come on an errand of mercy to help fellow seamen in distress. We put our prisoners, as many as wanted to go, on board of the *Seaver*; we also put sufficient of the provisions we had taken from the *Good Hope* to last them for the voyage. There were not many of them, as most of the crew expressed a desire to ship with us, and they proved to be among the best men we had.[2]

Sixteen

Barren island of Trinidad (Trindade)—The natural monument—Surf five hundred feet high—Battle in the air between frigate bird and sailor lad—Capture of splendid ship *Constitution* loaded with coal and missionaries—*Georgia*, by mistake, fires into the *Constitution*— Capture of ship *City of Bath*—Despoiled of $16,000 of our hard-earned wealth by trick of shipper's wife—Learn of the death of "Stonewall Jackson"—The Cape of Good Hope.

On June 18, 1863, we sighted the barren island of Trinidad (Trindade) situated in the middle of the South Atlantic about twenty degrees south of the Equator. The island is some six miles in circumference, and its precipitous sides rise out of the ocean to a height of about eight hundred feet. A few hundred feet from the island, and towering several hundred feet above it, a natural monument about two hundred and fifty feet in circumference at the base, and perfectly round, rears its head skyward. It is a natural beacon, and very useful to navigators who wish to sight it after coming around the Horn, to see if their chronometers are correct before shaping their courses for Europe or North America. One of the most magnificent spectacles in the world can be seen here when a storm is raging. The huge waves, with the sweep of the whole Atlantic, strike this rock with their full force, bursting into spray that ascends four or five hundred feet before it comes tumbling down like a waterfall.

The island and the monument form a little cove where we anchored in deep water, although very near the land. We were so well

113

hid that, although we had a good view of the ocean from our mast-head, passing vessels would not be aware of our presence until they saw a shot skipping across their bows and heard the booming of a gun. From daylight until dark a cloud of sea-birds could be seen whirling round the top of the monument, where we supposed they had their nests. Great numbers of them also seemed to resent the presence of the ship and took no pains to conceal their feelings, flying very close to us while screaming their protest. One day a sixteen-year-old lad by the name of Cox was on the lookout on the foretopgallant yard when he was savagely attacked by a huge frigate or man-of-war bird. The ship was rolling slightly, and, to maintain his footing, the lad had to hold on to a backstay with one hand while with the other he defended himself with his jack-knife. Suddenly the bird got a hold with both beak and claws on the boy's clothes and was furiously beating him with his great, powerful wings. It looked for a moment as though the combatants would both fall from that lofty height, when a fortunate jab of Cox's knife disabled a wing and down came the leathered fighter to the deck, where he stood off the whole crew for some little time before they succeeded in killing him.

One day several of our officers in a small boat rowed around the island, but we could find only one spot where a landing could be made—just opposite to where our ship lay. After great effort a few of us climbed to the top. There were signs that at some previous time men had lived there,—probably some shipwrecked crew, but the only signs of animal life we saw were one or two wild hogs. How did they come there? Years after our visit to Trinidad(Trindade) an adventurous German baron, who had married an American heiress, went in his private yacht to Trinidad(Trindade), and, taking possession, declared himself king. On his return to civilization he advertised for subjects to people his new kingdom. This attracted attention, and Great Britain, under the impression that the island might be of use as a coaling-station, at once claimed it. Brazil at once contested this claim, and the dispute that followed was finally settled in her favor.[1]

We had lain at Trinidad(Trindade) for several days when one morning our lookout reported a sail on the horizon. Our fires were banked and it took but little time to get up steam, slip our cable, and start in pursuit. We did not want to waste coal, so we fired a blank cartridge as a signal for the stranger to heave to, but it had the effect only of making him crack on more sail. Getting nearer to him, we tried the effect of a solid shot across his bows, with no better result. We then sent one so close to him that his nerve failed, and, he hove to. The stranger proved to be the *Constitution*, a big, full-rigged ship, hailing from New York and bound from Philadelphia to Shanghai, with a cargo of coal and missionaries. She was forty-eight days out and carried a crew of twenty-six men. Half a dozen of us were put on board the prize, and, as there were several other sails in sight, the *Georgia* went off in chase, leaving us to work the big *Constitution* to the island where we expected our cruiser to rejoin us. The wind was very light and we made but slow progress. In the meanwhile the *Georgia* had disappeared below the horizon and we began to feel lonesome. For safety's sake we placed one half of the crew in irons and put them down below; the other half we kept on deck, making them work the ship for us until night came and then confined them all on the lower deck.

The *Georgia* had not returned by dark, and neither had we succeeded in making the island, so we stood "off and on" all through the night. The next morning was fair and clear, but still there was no sign of our ship.

The only restriction put upon the missionaries and passengers was that they were not allowed to communicate with the crew or go forward of the mainmast. The captain was confined in his cabin and the mates in their staterooms, but not in irons. Night had again fallen and the time for the extinguishing of all lights had arrived, when we noticed that there was a great deal of whispering going on in the staterooms. An order for silence was given to which very little attention was paid. A boatswain's mate came aft and reported that the prisoners forward seemed to be very uneasy and none of them were asleep. They were cautioned that if they did not keep quiet the hatches would be covered (which would have made it very uncomfortable for them), and by way of extra precaution an armed sentry stood at the hatchway with orders to shoot any man who showed his head above the combings.

The night was very dark, and the rising sea caused the ship to roll more than ever. Toward midnight a large vase became loosened from its fastenings and fell to the deck with a crash; then pandemonium broke loose. The women, screaming that the pirates were going to murder them, rushed out of their rooms in their night-clothes and prostrated themselves on the deck, begging for mercy. Just then—to add to the terrors of the situation—the cries of the women were drowned by the boom of a cannon and the shrieking of a rifle-shell as it passed over us. I rushed on deck and through the speaking-trumpet shouted to our unseen foe: "Ship ahoy! Don't fire, we surrender!"—A hail came out of the darkness, asking what ship we were. I was going to answer that it was the United States ship *Constitution*, a prize to the *Georgia*, but as the words "United States" came out of my mouth there was some more banging of the great guns. Things were too serious for further conversation, so hastily ordering a boat lowered I rowed over to the strange craft and found her to be the *Georgia*!

It seemed that after leaving us she chased first one vessel and then another until she had got a long way from us; then, as frequently happened, the wooden cogs of her engine had broken and injured several people, and it had taken some time to make repairs. As soon as possible she had returned in search of us and was nearing the anchorage in the darkness when the officer of the deck thought he heard cheers which sounded as if they were being given by a man-of-war's crew about to go into action. He also said that when he asked what ship it was, he was sure the answer he heard was: "The United States sloop-of-war *Niagara*." There was so much talk about the *Niagara* on board of the *Georgia* that she evidently had taken possession of his imagination. I have often wondered if those poor women on the *Constitution* ever realized the fact that they had given us a greater scare than we had them.

Several days were spent in coaling the *Georgia* from the *Constitution*,—a weary job, as our boats were small; then the passengers and crew of the prize were transferred to the *Georgia*, and our officers had to give up their staterooms to the ladies. They themselves slept in cots and hammocks crowded together and swung in the space between the rooms. We treated the women with the most respectful consideration, but nothing we could say or do seemed to allay their apprehensions. They were so very miserable that we felt sorry for them and prayed for a prize on board of which we could put them.

On June 27 we chased and boarded a neutral ship which gave us the sad news of the death of "Stonewall" Jackson, and in that lonely part of the ocean we paid his memory a last tribute of respect by lowering our flag to half mast.[2] After a few more days of great discomfort we captured the American ship *City of Bath*, and hastily made preparations to transfer our unhappy guests to her. We sent boatload after boatload of provisions, which we had taken out of the *Constitution*, to her, and exacted from her captain a promise that he would take our unwilling and unwelcome guests to an American port.

When the time came to transfer the women to the *City of Bath* the sea was so high that it would have been dangerous for them to have attempted to climb down the ladder to get into the boats. Both ships were hove to out on the open sea and were rolling heavily, so we rigged a "whip" on the main yardarm, and placing the poor, frightened creatures in a boatswain's chair, first hoisted them up and over the rail and then lowered them into the waiting boat.

We afterwards learned that the captain of the *City of Bath* had not kept the promise which had saved his ship from destruction, but had taken the unfortunate passengers and such of the crew who had not enlisted on the *Georgia* to Pernambuco, the nearest port, and left them stranded there while he went on to Boston with the provisions. The wife of the captain of the *Constitution* could not have suffered from want, as a few months afterwards we saw in a newspaper an interview in which she gave a very uncomplimentary account of her experiences with the pirates, but consoled herself by saying that she had saved from their clutches sixteen thousand dollars in gold of the ship's money by sewing the coins into her petticoats and safely left the corsair with her treasure. When we read this we felt that we had been robbed! Before leaving Trinidad(Trindade) we slipped the *Constitution's* cable, set her on fire, and turned her adrift; we then made a target of her and exercised our men at the guns—and mighty poor range-finders and gun-pointers they proved themselves to be.

On July 9 we overhauled a magnificent ship with towering masts and auxiliary steam power—the *Kent* from London bound to Australia. After perfunctorily looking at the ship's papers the captain offered me a glass of sherry, and when I went on the deck the passengers crowded around me, eagerly asking if my ship was the famous *Alabama*. Of course I told them yes, and answered a thousand other questions. One of the passengers made particular inquiries about my age, and when I was about to get into our boat he presented me with a brown paper bag full of most delicious cakes, a luxury I had not tasted for many a long day. I met this gentleman again twenty-odd years after the cake incident.

I lived the simple life on board the *Georgia* at this time owing to the fact that we had not entered a port where anything could be bought for so long a time. I only had my ship's ration of salt horse and hard tack to eat, but it must have been a healthful regimen as I had grown wonderfully in height and strength—and my sobriquet of "Little Morgan" had become a misnomer.

On the 15th of August we sighted Table Mountain at the entrance of Table Bay. Behind the mountain is the city of Cape Town, the capital of Cape Colony. We chased vessels right under the shadow of lofty Table Mountain with its flat top, and still kept well outside of the sacred marine league. Over the mountain, when the wind is from a particular direction, there hangs a white cloud formed by mist ascending which is called the "Tablecloth." Looking down on Table Mountain is the Lion, a much higher eminence, the crest of which from certain points at sea looks like a lion couchant. The whole coast scenery is very grand as viewed from the ocean.

The next morning we found ourselves very close to that awesome and forbidding-looking promontory called the Cape of Good Hope,—why so called is as mysterious as the ugly, ragged, and jutting rock itself looks to be. No wonder that the ancient Portuguese mariners believed that the demons who dwelt there dragged their ships back in the night and so prevented them from doubling the ugly headland. As we passed it under steam the sea was angrily lashing its base and the black rock was ugly enough to fill anyone with dread even though he had never heard any of the blood-curdling legends connected with it.

Seventeen

Simon's Town—The *Alabama* had just sailed from the port—Two of the *Georgia's* engineers, the boatswain, gunner, and several seamen get "cold feet" and leave us—Our first lieutenant, Mr. Chapman, ordered to Europe—Visit the city of Cape Town—Skippers of burned ships not friendly and posed to start a rough-house—H. M. troopship *Himalaya*—"Dixie"—Exciting experience with Malay fishermen—Albatross and Cape pigeons—Meet the tea fleet—Also the U.S.S. *Vanderbilt*—Myriads of fish follow the *Georgia* making the ocean at night appear to be in flames.

Passing into False Bay, which lies behind the Cape of Good Hope, on August 16, we dropped our anchor in front of Simon's Town, situated on Simon's Bay, a small indentation of the land, on the great False Bay. We had no sooner let go our anchor than a British official boarded us and ordered us to put to sea at the expiration of twenty-four hours. But we knew many a trick to get around international law, and showed him that our engine was broken down, omitting to add that the disaster had occurred just before we came to anchor. It was a habit of that engine to break down just as we entered port if we wanted to remain over the legal twenty-four hours. Besides, we wanted to caulk our decks which leaked badly, as the oakum, in the bad weather to which we had been subjected, had worked loose; besides we had been constantly at sea for four months in tropical waters and the iron bottom of the *Georgia* was covered with a growth of sea-grass from eight to twelve inches long which impeded her speed more than one half. The British authorities ordered their own officials to hold a survey on her and report on the absolutely necessary repairs.

The first news of interest to us was that the *Alabama* had sailed from Simon's Town a few hours before our arrival. It seemed that she had got into hot water with the authorities by capturing the bark *Conrad* too close to the line of the ubiquitous marine league, had changed her name to *Tuscaloosa*, and converted her into a Confederate cruiser.[1] This news that the *Alabama* had got herself disliked by the Colonial Government brought on an attack of "cold feet" which so seriously affected two of our engineers, the boatswain, and the gunner, all Englishmen whom we had brought from London with us, that they pleaded with the captain for their discharges. This he granted, although the loss of the engineers was a serious matter. Several of the British sailors who had joined us at Ushant Island, sailor-like, discharged themselves and left behind the pay due them. With three or four exceptions our ship's company was now composed entirely of Americans. But a much greater loss to us than these men was the detachment of our first lieutenant, Mr. Chapman. He had become dissatisfied with his position of executive officer of a little brig, knowing as he did that many men far beneath him in rank were in command of gunboats in the Confederacy and that others were aspiring to command the cruisers which were being fitted out in England and in France. Captain Maury sympathized with his ambition and allowed him to return to England—and a bad day it was, too, for the *Georgia* when he left, for he was a man of iron nerve, a strict disciplinarian with a kind heart, and absolutely just.[2]

Having been cooped up in very restricted quarters for more than four months, I longed once more to throw my leg over a horse and get a little congenial exercise. Having obtained leave, I mounted a livery-stable steed and started for a twenty-mile ride to Cape Town. The journey across country was a very uninteresting one. I only met one Dutch boy, who either could not or would not talk English, and a Kaffir Negro with whom I did not care to fraternize on account of his color. But I did see what interested me greatly—geraniums in profusion growing wild and called weeds, and "everlasting" flowers, which when plucked may be laid away in a drawer for months and when taken out and placed in water will regain their freshness in a very little while.

At the hotel where I stopped in Cape Town I found that eight or ten captains and mates of ships recently destroyed by the *Alabama* were guests. I was in uniform, and being in neutral territory I had no idea that they would attempt to molest me. But I was mistaken. I passed them in the lobby and on the piazzas without their taking any notice of me, but when I entered the dining-room where they were already seated, and where there were many other people, they arose *en masse* and swore worse than did the "army in Flanders," damning pirates in general and myself in particular. They were advancing on me in a most threatening manner when the proprietor of the place rushed into the room and commanded the peace. He begged me to go with him into his private dining-room, but I protested that it was the disturbers of the peace who should be made to leave. I was finally persuaded to accompany my host and at his private table found much more congenial society in the company of his charming wife, two lovely daughters, and two grown sons, especially as they told me that their sympathies were all with the South. They also gave me a glass of the sweet Constancia wine for which the colony is famous. The only thing that marred the pleasure of the meal happened at the end when my host unfortunately asked me what I would have done if the Yankee skippers had assaulted me. I naively answered that I was perfectly able to take care of myself, as I had a Colt's revolver strapped to me and very handy. I shall never forget the look of horror that passed over the faces of those English people. I could not understand it—coming as I did from a country where almost every man carried a weapon, and where it was considered the proper thing to resent an assault with a shot.

When I returned to my ship I found the caulkers still at work and the din they made interfered with our comfort for many a day. I also found that Her Majesty's troopship *Himalaya* had come into port with a regiment of Highlanders on board bound for India. One day, while returning from shore in one of our cutters, I steered her very close to the troopship. The band was playing on the quarter-deck, and as we approached the band struck up "Dixie," and I stood up in the boat and took off my cap. The *Himalaya's* crew and the soldiers raised a cheer which was quickly suppressed, and I afterwards heard that the bandmaster and the officers who had instigated him to play "Dixie" had been reprimanded. We afterwards met some of these officers on shore and they invited us to dine with them on their ship. The dinner was a very picturesque affair—the gay uniforms of the officers with their gold lace and the beautiful toilets of their wives and daughters: the scene was not one to be easily forgotten. The Highland pipers playing their bagpipes marched three times around the table and a more awful screeching noise than they made it had never before been my misfortune to hear. A Scot officer greatly embarrassed me by asking if I did not think it delightful music. When the table was cleared of all the good things, the colonel arose and said, "Gentlemen, will you fill your glasses?" This having been done, he again arose and solemnly proposed the toast which consisted of only two words, "The Queen!" The glasses were emptied, and the function was at an end.

The weather around the Cape of Good Hope is notoriously treacherous. One afternoon I asked permission to go on shore and it was granted me on my solemn promise that I would be back in time to keep the mid-watch. I had a most enjoyable time until about ten o'clock when I had to leave my companions so as to catch the *Georgia's* boat. I was disappointed to find that no boat had come for me, and that it was blowing "great guns." I wanted to keep my promise, but none of the native watermen would undertake to put me aboard, saying that the sea was too high. At last a man told me that some little distance up the beach there was a hut occupied by some Malay fishermen and that they would risk anything for money. I went to the shanty and had some little difficulty in routing them out of their slumbers. After a great deal of bargaining five of them agreed to go with me for two pounds, which I truthfully told them was all I had. At Simon's Town when the wind is from the southwest the huge rollers of the South Atlantic have a clean sweep into the open roadstead which answers for a harbor. The huge *Himalaya* could be plainly seen in the moonlight tugging at her anchors while rolling heavily, and the little *Georgia* was wallowing and plunging bows under and the spray in sheets passing over her. The curlers coming high on the beach did not look inviting, but it had to be done. Before embarking, the Malays insisted that in the presence of the witnesses gathered around the boat I should agree to take all the responsibility and steer the boat. The boat was high on the beach and was resting on wooden rollers. She was taken to the water's edge and we got into her—the Malays got out their oars, and their numerous friends seized hold of the gunwales and dragged us out until she was afloat, and then they let us go. It was an awful effort to get through the surf, but the feat was finally accomplished. Outside of the breakers the seas were still higher and we took a great deal of water into the boat which compelled two of the men to take in their oars and go to bailing. The water gained on us, and it began to look very dubious as to whether we would reach the ship or not. But by almost superhuman exertions the Malays succeeded and only just in time, for as a line was thrown from the *Georgia* the boat sank under us. The smart Malay at the bow oar the moment he caught the line had instantly taken a turn around the forward thwart and made it fast. The *Georgia* quickly sent down a "whip" from the main yard and we were safely hoisted on board. The officer who would have had to walk the mid-watch if I had failed to return seemed disposed to regard me somewhat in the light of a hero. The others said I was an idiot, and the captain gave me a good scolding for what he termed my foolhardiness. Somehow or other I never could make a success of that hero business.

We had received information that H. B. M. cruiser *Narcissus* was coming from Table Bay to investigate our long stay in a British port and to see that we did not longer infringe upon the rules set forth in Her Majesty's neutrality proclamation, so like the sensible dog which "got up and walked out when he saw preparations being made to kick him," we bade good-bye to Simon's Town. As we were leaving who should come into port but the *Narcissus*, and that policeman of the seas not only did not attempt to arrest us, but dipped her colors to us as her enthusiastic crew manned the rigging and gave us three lusty cheers—needless to say that we returned the compliment with interest.

Passing out of False Bay into the South Atlantic we steered a south-easterly course, followed by many graceful albatross and thousands of Cape pigeons, a pretty little speckled sea-bird strongly resembling in size and appearance its domestic namesake.

The sailors threw out a line with a hook baited with a small piece of fat pork which was almost instantly gobbled by a huge albatross measuring almost twelve feet from tip to tip. The poor bird was hauled aboard, the hook unfastened from its bill, and it was turned loose on the deck when it became fearfully seasick, causing much amusement for the men. It is a singular fact that all sea-birds, despite the fact that they will alight on the water and ride over the highest waves without discomfort, become ill the moment they touch a ship's deck. Besides his size, our albatross was remarkable for a brass bracelet he wore on one of his legs on which was engraved, "Condor 1854." His appetite had evidently got him into trouble on a previous occasion.

The morning after we lost sight of the Cape of Good Hope we saw on the horizon a large-number of sail. We knew at once that they were the quarry we were looking for. The wind was very light and fortunately they were coming toward us, for the *Georgia's* chasing days were over. The mass of long sea-grass on her hull had reduced her boasted speed of nine knots an hour under steam to less than five.

As the fleet of Indiamen loaded with silks and tea from the Orient approached us, we picked out those ships which we suspected might be American and ran up alongside of them, sending an officer on board to examine their papers without putting them to the inconvenience of having to heave to, as we knew how anxious they all were to get to the northward of the Cape before bad weather came on again. We went from ship to ship, but had no luck, as all we boarded were either neutral vessels or else American ships which had changed their nationality and had neutral cargoes aboard. We had changed our course and accompanied them until the evening of the next day when we found ourselves under the shadow of Table Mountain. The sun was setting when suddenly we saw a great paddlewheel steamer, her double walking-beam engines making her nationality unmistakable. She was headed for Table Bay, her course taking her across our bow and she soon was only about five miles away.

Captain Maury ordered all hands to assemble at the mast and said to them, "Men, that steamer is the *Vanderbilt*; she can outrun us and she can whip us after she catches us. I am going to lay you alongside of her and you had far better follow me aboard her and die like men fighting for your lives than to tamely allow yourselves to be hung from her yardarms. Go to quarters!"

We held our course and the *Vanderbilt* kept on without taking any notice of us and entered Table Bay, into which she had hardly poked her nose before we captured the American ship *John Watt* in plain view of the lights of the city of Cape Town which by this time were beginning to twinkle in the distance. I fear that we were perilously near, that sacred limit called the "marine league" within which captures were unlawful, but we saw no fence demarking private property and gave ourselves the benefit of the doubt.

The *Vanderbilt* carried twelve eleven-inch guns and she had come thousands of miles to capture the *Alabama*. She lay for some time at Cape Town and if her captain did not know where the *Alabama* was at that time, he must have been the only man in Cape Colony who was unaware of the fact that the Confederate cruiser was only a few miles away to the southward.[3]

We had not proceeded very far when we discovered that innumerable fish, albacore and bonito, seemed to be following the ship, many of them swimming so close to her sides that they almost touched her. As we were under sail alone and going very slowly, there was nothing to disturb them except the occasional throwing of a grange (a three-pronged harpoon) by the men. The fish were so close together that it was impossible to miss and we had quantities of fresh fish for all hands for ten or twelve days before they left us. The nights were dark and we witnessed a singular phenomenon caused by these myriads of fish rushing through the phosphorescent water, causing the ocean to be streaked, as though by flames, from horizon to horizon. In the daytime great schools of small fish could be seen flapping on the surface in mortal fright and giving one the idea of a huge silver salver as their shiny sides contrasted with the ocean's blue and shimmered in the sunlight. They had cause to be alarmed, as from under them hundreds of albacore would pop up, leaping fifteen or twenty feet in the air, each one of them having a victim in his mouth. Flying fish in efforts to escape were sailing in every direction through the air.

It was useless for us to chase any vessels so long as we were in the southeast trades, as they would run away from us in the fresh breeze, but when we neared the equator and got into the doldrums, that region of calms and squalls, waterspouts, and rains which fell in sheets instead of drops, we had no trouble in running up to any sailing vessel that we selected to examine. One moment a squall would strike them and they would be rushing through the water like ocean greyhounds and the next minute they would be becalmed with their sails idly flapping against their masts. One minute we would be scorched by the tropical sun and the next we would be drenched by a cloudburst. Our rubber raincoats were useless, as nothing but the yellow oilskins of the sailors could shed that torrent of water.

Eighteen

The prize *Bold Hunter*, abandoned and on fire, runs down and seriously damages the *Georgia*—Mirage at night—Peak of Teneriffe—Santa Cruz—Battle with a Frenchman—Rescue French brig *Diligente*—Captain Maury ill—Sailors get at the spirit-room—Mutiny.

On October 9, 1863, in a light breeze and after a lively chase we brought to, with our guns, the splendid American full-rigged ship *Bold Hunter*, of Boston, from Dundee, bound to Calcutta with a heavy cargo of coal. We hove to to leeward of her and brought her captain and crew over to our ship, where as usual the crew were placed in irons and below decks. Being short of coal and provisions we proceeded to supply our wants from the prize. This was easy so far as the provisions were concerned, but when it came to carrying the coal from one ship to the other in our small boats, in something of a seaway, that was another matter. After half a dozen trips one of our boats came very near being swamped, and the wind and sea rapidly rising, we gave it up as a bad job. This was about two bells (1 p.m.) in the afternoon watch. We signaled our prize master to set fire to the *Bold Hunter* and also to come aboard the *Georgia* at once, which he did.

We had hardly finished hoisting our boats to the davits when a great cloud of smoke burst from the hatches of the *Bold Hunter* coming from the thousands of tons of burning coal in her hold. The wind had by this time increased to a gale and the sea was running very high. As before mentioned, the wind was very light when we captured the ship and she had hove to with all sail set, even to her royals. The flames leaped from her deck to her tarry rigging and raced up the shrouds and backstays and burned away her braces—her yards swung around, her sails filled, and the floating inferno, like a mad bull, bore down on us at full speed, rushing through the water as though she was bent on having her revenge. To avoid a collision, the order was given on the *Georgia* to go ahead at full speed. The gong in the engine room sounded, the engine turned the screw, and the screw began to churn the water under our stern. The engine made two or three revolutions—then there was a crash—followed by yells as the engineers and oilers rushed on to the deck accompanied by a shower of lignum-vitae cogs and broken glass from the engine-room windows. The order to make sail was instantly given, but before the gaskets which confined the furled sails to the yardarms could be cast off, the burning ship was upon us. She had come for us with such directness that one could easily have imagined that she was being steered by some demon who had come out of the inferno which was raging in her hold. We stood with bated breath awaiting the catastrophe which seemingly was about to overtake us. The *Bold Hunter* was rated at over three thousand tons and had inside her a burning cargo of coal of even greater weight—the *Georgia* was scarcely one sixth her size. Onward rushed the blazing ship, presenting an awesome spectacle with the flames leaping about her sails and rigging while a huge mass of black smoke rolled out of her hatches. High above our heads her long, flying jibboom passed over our poop deck as she rose on a great wave and came down on our port quarter, her cutwater cleaving through the *Georgia's* fragile plates as cleanly as though they had been made out of cheese. The force of the impact pushed the *Georgia* ahead and for a moment we congratulated ourselves that we had escaped from the fiery demon whose breath was scorching us. But the *Bold Hunter* was not yet satisfied with the injuries she had inflicted. Recovering from the recoil, she again gathered way and struck us near the place she had previously damaged, but fortunately this was a glancing blow which had the effect only of wrenching off our port quarter davits and reducing the boat which was slung to them to kindling wood. Not yet satisfied, the apparently infuriated inanimate object made a third attempt to destroy the *Georgia*, this time, fortunately, missing her mark and passing a few yards to leeward of us. Her sails having burned, she soon lost headway and helplessly lay wallowing in the trough of the sea while the fire ate through her sides, and her tail masts, one after the other, fell with a great splash into the sea. Before she went down surrounded by a cloud of steam we had a good view through the great holes burned in her sides of the fire raging inside her. I imagine it was a very realistic imitation of what hell looks like when the forced drafts are turned on in honor of the arrival of a distinguished sinner.

The *Georgia* needed a port, and needed one sorely, to repair her injuries, as she was leaking badly despite the work of the carpenter's gang in stopping up the hole made by the *Bold Hunter's* stem. We were making all possible speed for some place—I did not know where—when on the night of October 13–14 we were the victims of a most singular false alarm. The night was starlit and the sea was smooth—the only air stirring being that made by the slow progress of the steamer. I was keeping the mid-watch on the forecastle. Four bells (2 a.m.) had just struck, when the stillness of the night was broken by a frightened yell from the lookout—"Land ho!" Instantly the officer of the deck asked, "Where away?" and the lookout answered, "Dead ahead, sir!"— and added in what was a frightened wail, "For God's sake, stop her, sir!" By this time the officer of the deck had seen the cause of alarm and had signaled the engineer to stop and then to go astern at full speed. A sailor, although asleep, instantly knows if anything has gone wrong on his ship. A sail taken aback—or the engines stopping,—yes, even the cessation of the regular tramp of the officer as he walks his watch, will awaken Jack instantly. In this instance the watch below were out of their bunks and hammocks in a jiffy and scampered up the hatchway to find out what had happened. One look was enough— there, not a ship's length ahead, was land which towered up into the darkness. It looked as though it would be impossible to stop our head-way before we should be dashed to pieces on it. Captain Maury and all his officers were gathered on the poop deck. It was the only time I ever saw the captain show any excitability. He rather peremptorily demanded an explanation from the navigator, who insisted that his calculations were right and that the nearest land to us was the Canary Islands, distant more than one hundred miles. The captain pointed to the land, a cable's length or less away, an unanswerable argument. The navigator could only shake his head doubtfully and reiterate that despite all appearances being against him he was sure his work was correct. The captain went into his room and together they went over the calculations, but no error could be discovered. Then the captain came forward and looked long and intently at the obstacle which barred our further progress, apparently. Suddenly I was surprised to hear him laugh in his usual gentle way, and then I almost jumped out of my boots as I heard him give the order to go ahead at full speed. As he passed me on his way back to his cabin he simply said, "Mirage!" I afterwards heard him say that it was the only time in his life that he had ever seen a mirage at night. Through the rest of my watch it seemed to me that the next revolution of the engine must necessarily plunge our flying jibboom into those phantom rocks. The mirage faded away before daylight, and that morning at a distance of a hundred and ten miles we plainly saw the Peak of Teneriffe towering above the clouds.

The morning after our mirage scare we dropped our anchor in front of the picturesque little town of Santa Cruz which nestles at the foot of the gigantic peak. The little fort which guards the harbor looked comical with its little popguns pointing seaward, but this fort will always live in history, for it was a projectile from one of its toy guns which removed the great Admiral Lord Nelson's arm.

The vicinity of the Canary Islands is a favorite hunting ground for American whalers, and United States men-of-war were constantly on guard to protect them; one had just left Santa Cruz the day before we arrived. Had she remained twenty-four hours longer it would have been the end of the *Georgia's* cruise.

We put our prisoners on shore, and as the authorities were as anxious to get rid of us as we were to get out of that neighborhood, our absolutely necessary repairs were hurried. During our short stay a native merchant who had supplied us with some necessities invited me to take lunch at his pretty villa in the suburbs and there I first saw a gazelle, a gentle, affectionate little creature who followed the owner of the establishment all over the house and through the gardens—I also learned for the first time that canary birds in the Canary Islands are green instead of yellow like the birds of commerce which are bred in cages.

After a two days' stay at Santa Cruz we got under way and on the 20th of October we had a rather amusing adventure with a bellicose Frenchman. The wind was so light that the sailing ships in sight had barely steerage way. Under steam we bore down on a bark which showed French colors, but looked like an American. As we ranged alongside of him my captain ordered me to hail him in French and I did so by bawling out through the speaking trumpet (called in these days a megaphone): "Mettez votre grand voile au mat!"—which is French for "Heave to!"—to which the excitable Gaul replied: "Je suis francais, et je ne m'arrete pas pour un canaille de corsair!"—which is French for "I am a Frenchman, and I don't stop for a low bred pirate!" We lowered a boat and I was ordered to go aboard the rude fellow's ship and tell him that he must show his papers. But when I got alongside of him I found a nice reception awaiting me. The furious Frenchman was standing in the gangway of his ship frantically waving a rusty old sword, while two men stood behind him armed with muskets and the rest of his crew were brandishing hand and marlin spikes, ugly weapons in the hands of sailors. Neither my boat's crew nor myself were armed, as we only intended to make a friendly visit, and I had no authority to use force in boarding him, so I returned to the *Georgia* for further orders. Captain Maury was provoked at the fellow's stubbornness and ordered us to cast loose our guns. We first fired a blank cartridge which produced no effect. We then fired a solid shot across his bow, with no better result. The *Georgia* was being turned around all this time so that the little Whitworth guns on the poop deck (stern chasers) could be fired, but the order was given to fire before they could clear the Frenchman and a projectile went screaming over his forecastle. I never before saw a mainyard swing so quickly, and the bark was hove to as though by magic. I got into our boat again, this time accompanied by Lieutenant Evans and an armed crew. As we passed under the stern of the bark we saw that her name was *La Patrie*. At the gangway we were received by the captain, unarmed this time, and I assured him that we only wanted to see his papers, and explained to him that any American ship could have a Frenchman on deck to forbid our coming aboard; hence the necessity of our seeing the proof of nationality for ourselves, and that as a man-of-war we intended to exert that right. To our surprise the Frenchman replied that he refused to let us see his ship's papers unless we used force! The lieutenant told me to ask him what kind of force he wished to have used, and whether the presence of an armed boat's crew was not sufficient, and getting angry he told me to ask the Frenchman if he wanted to be hocked down as evidence that force was being used. The captain replied that he only wanted one of us to touch his coat-sleeve with a single finger, and taking my hand in one of his with the other he took hold of my first finger and gently pressing it against the sleeve of a sailor who was beside me, showed us how he wanted it done. The lieutenant obliged him. He then showed the way into his cabin, and as Mr. Evans and I entered the room, with a graceful bow he said, "Ici nous sommes des messieurs" ("Here we are gentlemen"); and not only showed his papers, which were absolutely correct, but also opened a bottle of champagne for us. We thought that we had parted on the most friendly terms, but some days afterwards the Frenchman met and boarded a French steamer and sent a report of the outrage (?), as he termed it, to his Government, which would have caused us a great deal of trouble if it had not been for a good piece of luck which befell us in falling in with the French brig *Diligente*, which had been knocked over by a squall and was lying on her beam ends, out of food, and helpless, while every wave washed over her and her exhausted crew. Her cargo had shifted and her wearied men had been unable to right her. We sent a number of our crew on board who soon replaced the cargo in its proper place and we spontaneously burst into a hearty cheer as she regained an upright position. Her captain was very grateful, especially for the provisions we gave him, and he gave us several bottles of eau-de-vie de Danzig with gold dust floating in it. This was the only thing in the brig which was not saturated with salt water. The *Diligente* hailed from Cherbourg, France, and her captain gave us a letter to his owners telling them of his misfortune and speaking in very complimentary terms of the assistance we had given him, and begged us to mail it from the first port we entered.

A few days after we had rescued the Frenchman we experienced quite a little uneasiness on our own account. A smoke was seen on the horizon and shortly afterwards a steamer appeared coming straight for us. We soon decided that she was a merchantman, but that proved nothing, as the United States Government had converted so many merchant steamers into men-of-war. Owing to our foul bottom the stranger gained rapidly on us. We went to our guns and waited to see what was going to happen. On coming abeam she proved to be the Portuguese steamer *Braganza*, who wanted a comparison of longitude, as something had gone wrong with her chronometer. We were very glad that that was all she wanted, for things were not going well on board of the *Georgia*.

Captain Maury had been ill ever since we had left the Cape of Good Hope. While there he had received letters from home telling him that, owing to the maneuvers of the Northern and Southern armies, his wife and children had become refugees, and he did not know what had become of them. He became very melancholy and rarely appeared on deck. Dr. Wheeden spent most of his time in the cabin with him. The discipline of the ship also missed the iron hand of Lieutenant Chapman. Lieutenant Evans, who had succeeded Chapman as executive officer, was a most charming and accomplished gentleman, but he was not a strict disciplinarian. Things had gone from bad to worse than bad, until one day some of the stokers discovered that a coal bunker was only separated from the spirit-room, where their grog rations were stored, by a thin bulkhead; this they bored through. They must have known the location of a particular barrel of whiskey, for they bored through the head of that also, and inserting a piece of lead pipe into the hole they got all the liquor they (temporarily) wanted. This they distributed among the crew and soon there was a battle royal going on on the berth deck which the master-at-arms was unable to stop. The first lieutenant went below and his presence had the effect of causing a pause in the turmoil. He persuaded the ringleaders to go on deck and appear at the mainmast, which was the court-house on the old-time men-of-war. Several of the men were sentenced to be placed in irons and confined in the "brig" (ship's jail) on a diet of bread and water. But the biggest bully in the ship swore that the master-at-arms was not man enough to put him in irons. The latter official was the chief policeman of the ship; he was undoubtedly a scientific boxer and boasted that he had once been a prize-fighter, but if that was so he must have had a yellow streak in him, for it was evident that the men had cowed him and that he did not dare make a move. Here was a pretty kettle of fish!—the authority of the executive officer defied to his face. Instantly appreciating the danger of such a state of affairs on such a ship as the *Georgia*, I suddenly leaped upon the man and bore him to the deck, where, in a jiffy, the master-at-arms placed the bracelets on his wrists. The other mutineers, quietly extending their arms in sign of submission, were placed in irons, and confined below. The discipline of the ship needed as much repairing as the vessel did herself. It was time the *Georgia* sought a civilized port for more reasons than one.

Nineteen

Cherbourg—Letters from home tell of the deaths of my two brothers, captains in Stonewall Jackson's corps—French fleet arrives to keep us in order—Great storm and loss of flagship's launch and crew—Impressive military pageant at funeral—Captain Maury relieved from the command of the *Georgia*—The C.S.S. *Rappahannock*—*Kearsarge* and *Tuscarora* waiting for us outside.

We slowly dragged our heavy grass crop along and entered the English Channel where we knew Federal cruisers were on the watch, but we were fortunate enough not to be seen by them, and in the middle of the night of October 28–29, 1863, we quietly stole into the harbor of Cherbourg, France, and dropped anchor.

We had been at sea for eight long months, and with the exception of our captain, not an officer on board had heard from home. The news of our arrival at Cherbourg, however, quickly spread and the U.S.S. *Kearsarge* quickly appeared cruising up and down beyond the three-mile limit. But more welcome than the sight of our would-be captor was a package of letters which had run through the blockade and had been forwarded to us by the Confederate agents, Messrs. Fraser, Trenholm & Co., of Liverpool. There was great rejoicing for all save me—I received two saddening missives: one informed me of the death of my brother George, a captain in the First Louisiana Infantry, in "Stonewall" Jackson's division; and when I opened the other it told me of the death of my brother Thomas Gibbes, a captain of the Seventh Louisiana, also with "Stonewall."

Gibbes had been badly wounded at Antietam, and before his wound was well healed had rejoined his regiment, with the survivors of which he had been captured at Kelly's Ford while covering the retreat of General Lee's army. He was taken to Johnson's Island, where he died a prisoner, leaving a charming young wife and two little baby boys to fight their own way in those troublesome times.[1]

The morning after our arrival I was sent ashore to deliver to the owners of the brig *Diligente* the letter of her captain. The owners published it, and it was well for us they did, for already the French authorities had demanded an explanation of our treatment of the bark *Patrie*. It evened things up, and the people of Cherbourg, while not at all gushing over us, treated us with courtesy.

We had not been at Cherbourg twenty-four hours when the French ironclad fleet, headed by the flagship *Couronne*, the vessel that afterwards umpired the fight between the *Alabama* and the *Kearsarge*, entered the port, and the next day a fleet of old-time three-deckers, line-of-battle ships, also anchored near us. These, with the hundreds of guns mounted in the forts and on the breakwater which formed the artificial harbor, were certainly enough to keep even the formidable (?) *Georgia* in order.

C.S. *Cruiser* Georgia,
Cherbourg, France,
December 5, 1863.

My Dear Mother:

I hope that you don't think your prodigal has forgotten you. I have written to you from every port, but directed my letters to Clinton, Louisiana, via the blockade, and would have continued to do so had it not been for a letter I received here from Lily (my sister Mrs. La Noue) dated from Macon, Georgia, telling me that you had returned to New Orleans and were within the Federal lines.

We have been in the drydock and the bottom of our ship is clean once more, but she does look so ridiculously small alongside of these French ironclads and the great wooden line-of-battle ships. There are about twenty of them in all.

There has been a great storm here. Night before last one of the line-of-battle ships, carrying eighty-four guns, dragged her anchors and only brought up when she was within twenty yards of our little cockleshell of a ship. I assure you we spent several hours on the anxious bench while expecting every moment to be crushed by the leviathan. The storm raged all the next day, the battleships, as well as our little craft, pitching bows under into every sea. Many of the fishing boats were wrecked on the coast and the breakwater, which is supposed to protect this harbor, which it doesn't, at least in weather like this. Many tried to make the harbor, but were pitilessly thrown on the rocks and ground into splinters among the boulders on the beach. One little fishing craft made such a noble struggle—she weathered the end of the breakwater, but despite her heroic efforts it was evident that she must be wrecked on the beach before reaching smooth water or shelter. Anticipating trouble, the French flagship, the ironclad Couronne, had a launch towing astern with twenty men and a sub-lieutenant in it. The Couronne cast her off, and the young officer made a gallant attempt to rescue the fisherman, but it was a hopeless errand. We stood in silence on our deck and watched the pitiful struggle against the elements, while our own ship was dragging her anchors at which she was savagely tugging as she plunged bows under at every dive and the huge seas would sweep over our deck. At last the fishing smack struck the bottom and was almost instantly lifted by a great wave which carried her amongst the boulders smashing her to pieces.

Seeing that he could be of no assistance the officer in the launch attempted to put her about—but she also was doomed. One moment she was in the trough of the sea and the next instant the crest of a great wave swept over her. Wave after wave followed in rapid succession, turning her over and rolling her up the beach as though she were a barrel, until she struck the boulders where she was literally torn to pieces. It was heartrending to watch those who had not been killed, or too badly crippled by the first shock, struggling to save themselves. As the surf would recede, they would stagger to their feet only to be knocked down by the next wave and thrown violently against the jagged rocks, and even after they were dead the pitiless sea continued to maim the helpless bodies by picking them up and slamming them down upon the stones.

When the storm abated, the remains of the dead were recovered and taken to the navy yard where they were prepared for burial. The funeral, the next day, was one of the most impressive sights I ever witnessed. Ten thousand soldiers stood at "Present arms!" on either side of the road leading to the cemetery as the procession passed between them. First came a large number of priests followed by a military band playing the Dead March. Then came the twenty-one caissons bearing the bodies, each drawn by six horses, the coffins being covered by the much loved "Tri-Couleur." These were followed by a number of admirals and naval officers according to rank. These in turn were followed by six thousand sailors from the fleet.

Captain Maury was invited to attend the ceremony, and took me with him as his aide. We were given a place in the procession next after the admirals.

Arriving at the cemetery, we stopped in front of a great trench where all of those gallant fellows were to be interred in one grave, except the young officer who had commanded the launch—he had a separate grave. His was the last coffin to be buried, and just as it was about to be lowered an aide-de-camp of the Emperor dashed up on horseback, and saluting Admiral La Rose, the ranking officer present, he presented him with an order from the Emperor and also a small package. Admiral La Rose read the order aloud. It commanded that the accompanying cross of the Legion of Honor should be pinned on the dead officer's breast. The lid of the coffin was unscrewed, and in death the young fellow was decorated with the bit of metal he had doubtless so much coveted in life. The coffin was then lowered into the grave and the earth covered these martyrs to duty.

The officers and men then withdrew to some little distance from the newly made graves and stood watching a most thrilling spectacle as battery after battery of horse artillery dashed up to the edge of the graves, wheeled, unlimbered, fired a salvo, limbered up again and disappeared at the gallop.

You may say what you please about Napoleonic tyranny (?), but it must be a great government for a soldier or sailor to die under. It may have been all a coup de théâtre, but it looked splendid and sent a thrill through me.

I can form no idea as to what our future movements will be. If I knew I would not tell you, as there is no knowing into whose hands this letter may fall, so I can only ask you to continue writing me in care of Messrs. Fraser, Trenholm & Co., 10 Rumford Place, Liverpool, England. They will know where we are going, even if we do not.

The Kearsarge is off the port waiting for us. She can wait. When the little Georgia's bottom is cleaned, we will slip by her in the night.

The last cartoon in the French comic papers, making fun of the American war, represents two newly made graves alongside each other. On the headstone of one is written "Nord," and on the other "Sud." A dilapidated old slouch hat with a rooster's feather in it rests on each grave, and underneath is written "Finis de la guerre dans l'Amerique."

And now I must say good-bye, my dearest mother. With love and kisses for you and my dear sisters, I am

Lovingly your son,
James Morris Morgan

Captain Maury was summoned to Paris to explain about our little fracas with the *Patrie*, and I accompanied him as interpreter. Commodore Barron, C.S.N., and some twenty-odd other Confederate naval officers were in Paris by this time, the juniors waiting for ships that were building. At Captain Maury's own request, on account of his health, Commodore Barron relieved him from the command of the *Georgia* and ordered him to return to the Confederacy—so I went back to my ship alone.[2]

Every officer on the *Georgia* who could get leave got it, and Lieutenant Ingraham and I had to keep watch and watch, that is, four hours on and four off—sounds easy, but is rather trying on a growing boy. There was no competition among the higher officers for the honor of commanding the *Georgia*, so the post was conferred on Lieutenant

Evans. As for the juniors in Paris, they showed no wild desire to serve on the little ship either. Two lieutenants who had a strong pull with the commodore came to us, but managed to secure their detachments after being on board only a couple of days.

The monotony of my existence was broken by my being granted a week's leave of absence, which I utilized by going to Paris, and from there to Calais to visit some midshipmen who were on board of the C.S.S. *Rappahannock*, with whom I spent a morning before continuing my journey to Liverpool. The *Rappahannock* is worthy of being mentioned, if only on account of the unusual way in which she escaped from the Thames to become a Confederate cruiser. She was a condemned little British sloop-of-war and had been sold at auction and bought by a Confederate agent. The British Government knew all about the transaction and was perfectly willing that the Confederates should spend all the money they wanted to on her, but had no intention whatever of allowing her to escape to sea. English engineers, riggers, carpenters, joiners, and painters were busily at work on her as she lay at the dock, when one day Lieutenant W. P. A. Campbell, C.S.N., attired in civilian clothes, appeared on board of her armed with authority from the supposed owner to make a thorough inspection. It also conveniently happened that the engineers had up steam and were testing the engines which they were slowly turning over. Mr. Campbell amiably expressed satisfaction with everything except the steering gear, and insisted that the only way of testing that was to take the vessel out into the stream and turn her around two or three times. This was amiably agreed to and the lines securing her to the dock were cast off. Mr. Campbell headed her down the river, and listening to no protests, hoisted the Confederate flag when he was beyond the marine league, and with his unwilling crew of artisans steered for Calais, which neutral port he entered claiming to be a Confederate States man-of-war. Of course the incident brought protests from the American Minister in London and in Paris and stirred up quite an international row.[3]

When I saw the *Rappahannock* at Calais, the French were allowing us to spend all the money we wanted to in fitting her for sea, but I do not believe they had the vaguest idea of ever letting her escape again.

Continuing my journey to Liverpool, I spent two or three delightful days visiting Mr. Prioleau at Allerton Hall, where I met an old friend from New Orleans, Mr. C. W. Miltenberger, and Alfred Trenholm (whose clothes I had worn while in Charleston). These young gentlemen, on account of failing health, had been discharged from the Confederate Army and were recuperating in Europe.

My leave expired, and I returned to the monotony of my existence on board of the *Georgia*. It seemed that we never should get to sea

MAJOR W. P. A. CAMPBELL
Formerly of the C.S. Navy. Taken in Cairo in 1870.

again. Drills, watches, and meals—meals, watches, and drills. I don't think the French cared how long we remained so long as we spent money liberally on imaginary repairs.

At last Lieutenant Kirby King and Sydney Smith Lee, the latter a younger brother of General Fitzhugh Lee,[4] were ordered to us, and that put an end to the discomfort of keeping watch and watch, much to my delight. I suppose that our weariness of remaining in an uninteresting port was only equaled by that of the crews of the *Kearsarge* and the *Tuscarora* who were tumbling about in the choppy seas of the Channel waiting impatiently for us to come out. They would take turns in coming in close enough to the breakwater every day or two to see if we were still there in the harbor, until I think we should have felt neglected if they had failed to take an interest in us and ceased their visits.

Twenty

Leave Cherbourg—Storm off Cape Trafalgar—Coast of Morocco—
Anchor in the open sea near the Great Desert—Caravans—Moors
bring fish—Ancient Moor swims to the ship—We return visits and
are kicked into the sea—We bombard the troglodytes—Give up hope
that the *Rappahannock* will meet us—Weigh anchor and have a narrow escape from ship wreck and falling into the hands of the Moors.

One dark night in the middle of February, 1864, we weighed our
anchor as quietly as possible, got under way, and slipped out of the
western entrance to the harbor without seeing anything of either the
Kearsarge or her consort, and with a clean bottom raced down the Channel and soon found ourselves on the broad Atlantic. We saw many
ships, but molested none. Strange conduct for the *Georgia*, at which we
wondered. But none knew, save our commander, whither we were
bound, or what was our mission. Day after day we raced at full speed
under steam.

Off Cape Trafalgar one night we ran into a fearful storm, the most
terrific in my seafaring experience. We put the ship's head into the
wind and barely kept steerageway on her. The high seas dashed over
the ship in such volumes of water that to keep from being washed
overboard, Lieutenant King, the quartermaster, and I lashed ourselves
in the rigging ten feet above the deck. At one time the wind was so
furious that it blew the tops off the enormous waves and the sea became one mass of seething foam in which the little *Georgia* floundered

and wallowed until we had but little hopes that she would live through it. But with daylight fortunately, for us, both sea and wind went down, and by eight o'clock in the morning the officers were able to come out of the wardroom and we were relieved. The door leading into the officers' quarters as well as the hatches had been battened down to keep the water out, and no one could get in or out while the storm raged. Mr. King and I, as well as the starboard watch, had been on deck since eight o'clock the previous evening, and more exhausted men than we were could hardly be imagined.

The first land we sighted was the coast of Morocco. We passed down the coast in plain sight of the minarets of the ancient city of Mogador. When we reached a place where a range of barren-looking mountains ended at the sea and the great Sahara Desert extended into the unknown to the east and south, we dropped our anchor in the open ocean about a mile or more from the shore and about forty miles south of Mogador. We could see no signs of vegetable or other life on the desolate-looking land, with the exception of some bushes at the foot of the mountains. Day after day we lay there lazily rolling on the swell of the sea, the monotony only being broken occasionally by watching camel caravans to or from Mogador come along the beach and wind their way around the mountains, disappearing in the apparently limitless and glaring desert waste.

When the sirocco came in our direction from across the burning desert, it carried with it fine particles of sand which got into our eyes, ears, nose, and mouth, causing much discomfort, and added to this was the almost intolerable heat thrown off in the night by the thin iron sides of the ship, which made sleep almost impossible.

Early one morning we were surprised by seeing an open rowboat near us with five or six Moors in it. They came alongside the ship and offered us some fresh fish which we gratefully accepted, giving in exchange some old hoop iron, two old rusty razors, and two or three dilapidated old sheets out of which turbans could be fashioned. These were much prized, and when they left us the last we saw of them as they proceeded parallel with the beach instead of pulling for the shore, they were evidently wrangling as to which of them should have the turban material.

With the exception of the fishermen we had seen no evidence of there being inhabitants living on the shore near us, although we had been at anchor for more than three weeks, until about four o'clock one afternoon a round object, looking somewhat like a white sponge, was seen floating on the sea about half a mile off and between the ship and the shore. The waves were some four or five feet high, and as the strange object bobbed up and down on them it was soon discovered that it was coming toward us, and as it came nearer we discovered that it was the head of an old man. Finally he reached our vessel and we lowered a Jacob's ladder over the taffrail for him. With great effort he dragged himself up it and fell exhausted on the deck. Dr. Wheeden revived him with a drink of brandy and would have repeated the dose, but the old Mohammedan—true to his religion now that he had recovered his senses—pointed a bony finger heavenward, shook his hoary head, and muttered the holy name of Allah! When the old man was sufficiently rested, as he was clothed by only a ragged piece of sacking which was wrapped around his loins, we gave him some Christian raiment and a lot of old trash, for which he seemed very grateful, and then we put him in one of our boats which I was ordered to take charge of, and put him on shore. Nearing the beach the water became so shoal that the boat grounded when more than twenty yards away from it, but the old man stepped over the side and waded ashore with his newly acquired treasures held high above his head. I saw no other human being in sight and left him to find his way home alone.

Several of us, seeing that the few natives we had met were apparently disposed to be friendly, asked permission to go ashore to stretch our legs with a little exercise. The captain granted our request, at the same time instructing us to go unarmed as evidence of our friendly intentions if by chance we met any of the inhabitants. We got into a boat, and like little boys going on a holiday laughed and joked with glee until the boat grounded, and the sailors, with the exception of two boat-keepers, stepped into the water, and we mounted on their backs and rode ashore, dry shod, in great style.

It was delightful to feel the solid ground, or sand as it happened to be, under our feet once more, and we began at once to run and skylark up and down the beach. At the foot of the cliffs, some forty yards from the water, there was a growth of dwarf bushes. Suddenly—I never did know how it happened—we were separated and surrounded by hundreds of Moors armed with spears and old-fashioned guns of extraordinary length whose barrels were banded with silver at intervals of a foot or two apart. The Moors were shaking their guns and brandishing their spears while yelling like fiends, and all the time a seemingly endless stream of the black demons poured out from the bushes. I tried to see what had become of my companions, but could only discern a surging, struggling mass of Moors in every direction. One gigantic fellow seized me from behind and whirled me around until I faced the sea, and while others struck me with their hands, my particular giant preferred to use his feet, and he kicked me until I was almost up to my neck in the water. From my sensations I should judge that the sole of that Moor's foot without further roughening would have served very well for a blacksmith's rasp. Our unarmed boat-keepers gamely waited for us, and when I climbed into the boat I found my companions, who had been similarly treated, already there—safe but very wet, and looking very foolish.

When we returned to the *Georgia* we were disposed to treat our experiences at the hands of the Moors as a good joke, but our young captain could not be induced to regard the matter in that light. In fact he was very indignant and ordered the drummer to beat to quarters without giving us time to take off our dripping clothes. The guns were cast loose and the order to fire given. The guns roared and the screeching shells sped away to burst over the heads of the astounded Moors, who stood not upon the order of their going but disappeared, not however so mysteriously as they had appeared on the scene. The puzzle was solved: they seemed to run right into the side of the cliff. Evidently they were troglodytes and the caves were their homes. Whether or not our shells had hurt any of them we never knew.[1]

Three weeks and more had passed and we were getting very wearied. Our mission was now no longer a secret. We were waiting for the *Rappahannock* for the purpose of giving her our battery, ammunition, and a part of our crew—she was supposed to bring her own officers.

The evening after our little fracas with the moody Moors, the hour at which the discipline of the ship was usually suspended and when the men, after their day's work, gathered on the forecastle and sang their sailor songs, while the officers, having dined, were seated around the waist guns enjoying their cigars and engaged in conversation or dreamily listening to the words of a favorite sailor ditty, the refrain of which was, "Eight bells began to go: I love to hear them ring, my dear, and so do you, I know"—at this hour, the most pleasant of the twenty-four, when even a lonesome midshipman could butt into the conversation without fear of being snubbed—the lonely captain, it seemed, also craved the society of his fellow men, and he joined the group around the gun where we were speculating on the causes which might have delayed the *Rappahannock*. I was the only person on board who had ever seen her, and I expressed the opinion that she had never left port, and that anyhow I believed the little *Georgia*, bad as she was, was the better ship of the two—that the *Rappahannock* was a bluffbowed old water-bruiser that did not have any speed under steam, and that my friends, the midshipmen, on board of her had told me she was "hogged" (strained) by lying on the uneven bottom at low tide. I wound up my remarks by saying that unless the French Government had changed its attitude toward the Confederacy, there was little chance of the *Rappahannock* ever joining us, as when I had seen her in the slip at Calais two big chain cables were stretched from pier to pier, one in front of her bow and the other behind her stern, and that they were made fast around stone posts, and on each post sat a gendarme to see that they were not meddled with. The captain said he would give her just forty-eight hours more to put in an appearance, and if by that time she failed to materialize he would go and look for her.

We did not wait the forty-eight hours of grace we had given the dilatory *Rappahannock*, as something exciting happened which changed our plans. A little before sundown the following day the wind came out from the southwest and blew a gale. The *Georgia* began to pitch bows under with every sea that struck her, and then to drag her anchor. We paid out more cable, but still she dragged. We let go our other anchor, but the force of the wind increasing, we continued our promenade toward the rocky shore on which by this time the Moors, having become aware of the straits we were in, had assembled in hundreds to give us a warm reception in return for the compliments our guns had hurled at them the day before.

Our fires were banked while we lay at anchor, and the stokers appreciating the imminent danger were working like mad to get up steam. We were now within some two hundred yards of the shore, and an ugly black rock some thirty feet away poked out its head between the angry-looking waves as they swept over it. The Moors, like so many demons, were dancing with delight on the shore while yelling curses at us. No matter how ignorant one is of a savage language, there is no need for an interpreter when the natives are swearing at a fellow. Night was fast closing in on us when at last the engineer reported that there was steam enough to start the engines. The order was given to go ahead and the engine was started. Slowly at first, but with increasing velocity it relieved the strain on our cables, when, just as we had begun to have hopes that we were saved, there was a crash in the engine room and we knew that the wooden cogs had broken again! For two hours the engineers worked to repair the damage, and fortunately during this time the anchors held so well that the ship's progress toward destruction was very little, if any. It was a long and anxious two hours, and above the roar of the wind we could hear the yells of triumph emanating from the throats of those black devils waiting for the catastrophe which was to put us in their power, to say nothing of the loot they expected to get out of the wreck of the ship. At last the engine began to revolve again—at first very slowly, and we anxiously followed each revolution in mortal dread that it would break down again, but as it increased in power and took the strain off of our anchors we commenced to breathe freely again. Then came the welcome order to weigh the port anchor, and after an interval the other was also catheaded; but the progress we made away from the shore was woefully slow in the teeth of that gale. When day at last came we were clear of the danger and well out at sea with a clear appreciation of Jack's sympathy in a storm for "the poor people ashore in danger of having their heads broken by falling tiles from the roofs." It was a most narrow and fortunate escape for us slaveholders, as had we not been drowned in the surf, we most assuredly should have been either murdered on the shore, or worse still, sold into slavery in accordance with the customer of the Moors in disposing of their prisoners. Even if our fate had ever become known to the outside world, there was no nation on earth that would have lifted a voice for our release, save the helpless and unrecognized "Confederate States" which were already doomed for extinction.

I have always called this episode "the Confederacy's only Foreign War," unless that unfortunate affair with the *Patrie* could be called a hostile event.

After a stormy voyage we arrived off the mouth of the Garonne River, up which stream we steamed and dropped anchor in front of the city of Bordeaux.

Twenty-one

Bordeaux—U.S.S. *Niagara* and *Sacramento* wait outside for us—Two fine sloops-of-war intended for the Confederacy lay near, but beyond our reach—Escape from the United States men-of-war—Liverpool—A hero at last—*Georgia* put out of commission—*Georgia* captured by U.S.S. *Niagara*—Last of the *Georgia*—Men-of-war, privateers, and pirates.

No sooner was it known that we had arrived at Bordeaux than we were informed that the *Georgia* must leave at the expiration of twenty-four hours—but what we did not know about dodging neutrality proclamations was not worth learning. So on one pretext or another we made ourselves comfortable and prepared for an extended visit to our unwilling hosts. The *Niagara* and the *Sacramento*, two formidable men-of-war, were waiting for us at the mouth of the river.

Day after day we gazed on two beautiful new and freshly painted sloops-of-war intended to carry ten guns each. They lay in the stream only about half a mile from us, and the sight was tantalizing, for they belonged to us and had been paid for with our money, and there they were, so very near, but far beyond our reach, and there we were cooped up in a little floating iron pot without speed enough to escape from an enemy or strength sufficient to fight one. With boilers and engines away above the water line it would have taken an expert marksman to hit the *Georgia* any place except in the magazines, boilers, or machinery. The French had allowed us to build these formidable ships knowing

146

what they were intended for. They had taken our money, and now that they were finished, the Government suddenly became very punctilious about its neutrality.[1]

An order had come through the blockade that the *Georgia*, on account of her deficiencies in speed and fighting ability, should be put out of commission, and we thought we were going to part with the little ship in Bordeaux, but we were mistaken. It was written that we should take one more chance in her. We knew that two United States men-of-war were lying off the mouth of the Garonne and that either of them, if they caught sight of us, would have us at their mercy, and we were somewhat surprised when the order reached us to proceed to Liverpool before dismantling the ship.[2] We got under way very quietly and proceeded down the river to a point just out of sight of its mouth and there waited for night to shield us from our enemies. It was very dark when we passed out of the Garonne and crept by the big ships which apparently did not even suspect our proximity. We crossed the Bay of Biscay without further adventure and entered St. George's Channel where it was very foggy. A pilot boat approached us and asked if we wanted a pilot. We told him "yes" and at the same time hoisted the Confederate flag. When the pilot, who had not yet left his boat, saw the colors, he rudely remarked that he "would be damned if he would pilot any damned pirate!"—and going about, he disappeared in the fog while expressing the very humane hope that we would pile up on the rock. Despite his kind wishes, however, we safely entered the Mersey and dropped anchor off Birkenhead, opposite Liverpool, about three o'clock in the afternoon. The anchor had barely time to reach the bottom when the captain sent for me and said he was going to allow me to go ashore at once, as I had friends in Liverpool, but stipulated that I should wear my uniform. We had heard that feeling toward us had changed and English sympathy, especially among the lower classes, was now very much in favor of the North. If that was so I did not see any exhibition of it—I have always suspected that my captain used me as a trial horse to ascertain what sort of a reception awaited us. If that was his object, he ought to have felt highly gratified with his experiment, for I went alone to a theatre that night, and as soon as my gray uniform was noticed a whisper went through the audience that the *Alabama* had arrived in the port. Someone proposed three cheers for the *Alabama*, and they were given with a will. The manager of the theatre elbowed his way to where I was sitting and asked me to accompany him. I thought he was going to put me out, but instead of that he escorted me to a box and kindly took a seat by me. Every time the curtain went down, the audience cheered, not the actors, but the *Alabama*—and every time they cheered the manager would insist that I should stand up and bow my acknowledgments of the compliment. After the show was over, perfect strangers introduced themselves and begged for the honor of my company at supper, but the manager, who had taken complete possession of me by this time, declined all invitations for me, and carried me off in triumph to sup with some of the leading actors and actresses of his company, who made much of me. If I was not a hero I was at least conspicuous on this occasion, and what does a hero go heroing for if it is not to be flattered by such receptions as this one was?

On the 10th of May, 1864, the little *Georgia* was warped into the Birkenhead dock. All hands were summoned to the quarter-deck for the last time. Our captain read his orders to put the ship out of commission. At the word of command, the Confederate flag, proudly flying at the peak the Union Jack on the bowsprit, and the commander's pennant at the masthead, all came fluttering down together—and the cruise of the *Georgia* had passed into history. She was a poor miserable little tin kettle of a craft, but I loved her. I too was poor, and nothing much to brag of, and despite the fact that my life, as the youngest of her officers, and the only one of my grade, had been very lonely, still she had been the only home I had known for thirteen months and had borne me safely through many dangers and over thirty-three thousand miles of water. We bade good-bye to our shipmates—many of us never to meet again, and now (1916) I believe myself to be the only survivor of the officers of the lucky little cruiser.

The *Georgia* was dismantled and sold to an Englishman by the name of Jones, who, in good faith, fitted her out as a merchantman and entered into a contract with the Portuguese Government to carry the mails between Lisbon and the Cape Verde Islands. When she arrived off the mouth of the Tagus intending to take on board the Lisbon mails, she was captured by the U.S.S. *Niagara*, her old pursuer, and sent to the United States as a prize. Her owner never again saw his ship or his money.[3]

Once again I saw the *Georgia*—in 1866. On this occasion she was lying at a wharf in Charleston Harbor being loaded with cotton. I don't believe she had been painted since I left her in Liverpool and she looked like any other dirty old tramp steamer. I asked her mate if the wooden cogs ever gave him any trouble, and he replied, "Only when she gets us in a tight place in bad weather, or we are trying to avoid a collision." In 1867 the *Georgia* was wrecked on the rocky coast of the Gulf of St. Lawrence where her iron bones slowly rusted away.

The damage done to the North by these little cruisers should not be estimated simply by the number of ships they captured, for it should be remembered that for every ship burned hundreds took shelter under neutral flags never to return to the American mercantile marine. No country ever erected so many monuments to its soldiers as can be seen in the Southern States, and yet there is not a single memorial to the Confederate Navy. If the object of war is to inflict damage on the enemy, how stands the account between the army and navy of the South? Twice the Southern armies invaded the territory of the North, and on each occasion were hurled back across the Potomac before they had had time to spy out the richness of their foe's land. It is true that they fought valiantly and killed many brave Northerners and more German mercenaries, but the loss of these men did not affect the conquerors in the least as they swept through the fair Southern land with fire and sword. But the Confederate Navy struck the North such a vital blow, by destroying their mercantile marine, that although half a century has elapsed since the scenes I have tried to describe took place, the United States has not yet, and will not for many years to come, recover her former lucrative carrying trade on the high seas.[4]

The Southern naval officer has never been able to understand why his compatriots always refer to the *Alabama* and her consorts as "privateers." Why privateers? A privateer is a vessel belonging to private parties, as its name implies. She is provided with a "letter of marque" authorizing her to prey on ships belonging to an enemy, and also to protect her against being treated as a pirate. A privateersman is a fellow with all the instincts of a pirate, but without the courage to hoist the "Jolly Roger."

A man-of-war is a national ship, a sort of floating fortress, belonging to a government. Her officers hold commissions under that government, and her crew are shipped regularly in exactly the same way soldiers are mustered into the army on land. Her officers take prizes or burn ships only in obedience to orders which they are sworn to obey and not for the object of enriching themselves.

In the North the Confederate cruisers are always spoken of as *damnpirates*, as though it was one word. Why? These ships were regularly commissioned by a *de facto* government to whom they belonged, and were officered by men who, with rare exceptions, were the product of the United States Naval Academy. The crews were regularly enlisted men. As a man-of-warsman is simply a soldier who fights on the water, how came it that I was a pirate on the *Georgia* and became a regular Confederate naval officer when attached to a naval battery on shore? Was it because of the boat and the water? If so, did the armies of Lee and Johnston become pirates and deserve the hangman's noose every time they crossed a river on a pontoon bridge or waded a creek? Why should a man who cannot restrain patriotic cheers whenever he hears a band play "Marching through Georgia," yell with rage and indignation when the destruction wrought by the Southern cruisers is mentioned? Is the use of the torch in war so much more reprehensible on the water than it is on land?[5]

Some day, it is to be hoped, an unbiased history will be written which will give full credit to the Confederate Navy, not only for the gallant manner in which it bore itself in action, but also for the wonderful resourcefulness displayed by its officers, who, when the "bonnie blue flag was hoisted on high," found that their navy consisted of one burned frigate, and what was left of her was sunk alongside of the navy yard dock at Norfolk. This wreck they, by original designs of their own, converted into the formidable ironclad ram *Virginia*. The only thing about her that never would stick was her name, as the people, North and South, never would call her by any other name than the *Merrimac*. History, when truly written, will also tell how those Southern naval officers went with their men into the forests with axes and cut down trees and hewed out timbers with which they built gunboats, and how these same men went through the country gathering old rails and scrap-iron with which they armored those boats and called them ironclads; and above all, how they fought these makeshift men-of-war after they built them. It will also tell how the C.S.S. *Manassas*, an old tugboat, was converted into an ironclad ram and was the first craft of that character used in war to ram an enemy. It will also tell how the Confederates were the first to use the torpedo boat, the submarine boat, and floating and stationary mines in actual war, and how they built and nearly finished the ironclad *Mississippi* at New Orleans, certainly the first warship with three screws ever built in America.

After Norfolk was evacuated, the South had no navy yard. The *Albemarle* and *Arkansas*, ironclads, were built in cornfields, and other formidable ironclads were built between wharves at Charleston and elsewhere. For artillery they had only obsolete guns that had been left at the Norfolk navy yard at the commencement of the war. Lieutenant Brook (Brooke), C.S.N., made a gun which was regarded by both sides as the most formidable weapon in use at that time. It was the irony of fate that the United States Government, which had branded the Confederate cruisers as "pirates on the high seas," should have built among the first ships of its new navy (after the war) two "commerce destroyers," the *Columbia* and the *Minneapolis*, ships of great speed and cruising radius, and with little or no fighting power.

*T**wenty-two*

Paris—*Alabama* sunk by *Kearsarge*—Harve—Southampton—Ordered to return to the Confederacy—Halifax—Sail for Bermuda and passengers mistake us for pirates—St. George, Bermuda—Take passage in the blockade-runner *Lillian*—Chased by U.S.S. *Shenandoah* and have narrow escape running through blockading fleet off Wilmington.

While dawdling in Paris in the month of June, 1864, waiting for ships that were never to materialize, at least for our purposes, we were startled one day by the news that the *Alabama* had arrived in the port of Cherbourg, and that the U.S. sloop-of-war *Kearsarge* was waiting outside for her. We knew at once that there was going to be a fight, and so confident were we that the *Alabama* would win that among ourselves we decided that the *Kearsarge* must not be crippled too severely, but that the *Alabama* with her superior speed was to run alongside of her antagonist and carry her by boarding, and then turn her into a Confederate cruiser. So confident were we that we selected the officers for the new addition to our navy. But we had not taken into account the fact that the *Alabama* had not been in a drydock in more than two years and that her copper hung to her bottom in elbows, which greatly retarded her speed. Well, the fight came off and the *Kearsarge*, which was not a fast ship, proved that she could run two knots to the *Alabama*'s one, in her then condition. She took up her own position at a distance which suited her and the world knows the result.[1]

151

As soon as the unpalatable news of the result of the battle reached Paris, we were ordered to get out of the city at once and to scatter. I went to Havre, where I received orders to proceed to Southampton, and report to Commander Kell, the former executive officer of the *Alabama*, who would give me further instructions.[2]

At Southampton I found, among other officers who had been saved from a watery grave by the English yacht *Deerhound* when the *Alabama* went down, Becket Howell, a brother of Mrs. Jefferson Davis, who was a lieutenant of marines, and Midshipmen Anderson and Maffitt,[3] and I spent several days with them wandering around the curious old English town, the observed of all the observers, who seemed to take great delight in calling attention to the "pirates."

With Commander Kell I went from Southampton to Liverpool, where we were joined by several other officers who were going to make the attempt to run the blockade. Among them was Lieutenant R. T. Chapman, who had been executive officer of the *Georgia* when she was first placed in commission. Mr. Chapman was now entrusted with a special mission to take the great seal of the Confederate States, which had recently been completed in London, to Richmond. Lieutenant Evans, who had been the last commander of the *Georgia*, Lieutenant Campbell, who had taken the *Rappahannock* out of the Thames, Lieutenants Ingraham and King, and Passed Midshipman Walker were also in the party.[4]

We took passage in the *Cunarder Africa* plying between Liverpool and Boston, stopping at Halifax, Nova Scotia, on her way. Naturally it was more conducive to the health and longevity of our party to get off at Halifax. The voyage was a rough one, and the old paddlewheel tub was crowded with Yanks who scowled at us in a very unfriendly way.

As we entered the harbor of Halifax, Commander Kell said that, as I had been there before and knew the town, I must jump ashore the instant the ship touched the dock and run to the hotel and engage rooms for the party. It was twilight when I reached the hostelry, and there was standing behind the counter a man in a dress suit reading a letter. I asked him whether or not we could get accommodations, but he took no notice of me. I am afraid I repeated my inquiry in rather a peremptory manner, for he turned and left the office, saying as he departed, "Young man, I am not a waiter in this establishment!" At that moment the clerk arrived with a horrified expression on his face and told me that I had made a dreadful mistake, that the gentleman was Mr. Cyrus W. Field (who had laid the first Atlantic cable) and that he was waiting for his carriage to go to the Government House where Lord Mulgrave, the governor-general, was giving a dinner in his honor that evening!

After a couple of days' stay in Halifax we took passage on a small British steamer called the *Alpha* which plied on the line between Halifax, Bermuda, and St. Thomas, West Indies. She was crowded with passengers, but they were not disposed to be friendly with us. Doubtless they had become prejudiced by reading about "pirates" in yellowback novels. We kept entirely to ourselves.

In the early mornings we would gather on the little poop deck and pass away the time until the gong sounded for breakfast, when we would fall in behind Commander Kell, according to rank, and in Indian file walk into the saloon and take our seats. Commander Kell was a most commanding figure, being six feet three or four inches in height. When he sailed from New Orleans in the *Sumter* three years previously, he had determined to let his beard grow until he saw his wife again. It now reached to his waist and flowed over his breast like a waterfall—it was very red. He allowed only his intimates to see it, however, as he kept it plaited and stuck down his shirt collar. Ordinarily his beard looked to be about three inches long with the ends all turned in under his chin. One morning we were seated as usual on the poop when Commander Kell produced from the inner recesses of his shirt front the wonderful beard and proceeded to comb it out. Before he had finished the intricate operation the gong sounded, and with his habitual consideration for others, he said that he would not keep us from our breakfasts while he put up his extraordinary hirsute adornment, and he led the way to the saloon with his great red beard flowing over his manly chest. As he entered the door the passengers were all seated at the breakfast tables, and to our great consternation some idiot screamed out, "The pirates are going to take us!" Then followed a scene I shall never forget. Men dove under the tables and the women fell on their knees and begged for mercy. As for us—we were simply scared into speechlessness. It was Commander Kell's beard that had caused the fright—the passengers jumping to the conclusion that there were other pirates secreted on the ship, and that the time to take her and make them walk the plank had arrived. The captain of the *Alpha* rushed aft to find out what had happened, and even he did not recognize Commander Kell at first. Of course there was a hearty laugh when the mystery of the beard was explained, and we were all much better friends for the rest of the voyage.

At St. George, Bermuda, our party was divided and took passage on several of the blockade-runners then lying in the harbor. Lieutenants Campbell, Ingraham, King, and myself (the midshipman) went on board the *Lillian* commanded by as big a braggart and blowhard as ever commanded a ship.[5]

It was in the month of July, 1864, and by this time the blockade of the Southern coast was so complete that to get into a Southern port it was necessary to elude the United States war-vessels three separate times on each trip. Around the Bermuda Islands cruisers hovered to catch their prey when the blockade-runner was only a few miles from the neutral port, either coming or going. About fifty miles off the Southern coast other cruisers awaited them, and of course the channels leading into the Southern harbors were closely guarded. We passed out of the narrow and tortuous channel, which connects the harbor of St. George and the sea, in daylight, and then lingered near the shore until night shrouded our movements when we started at full speed for Wilmington, North Carolina, and soon ran into some very foul weather. The *Lillian* was a very small paddlewheel steamer whose deck was not more than three or four feet above the waterline, and she drew only between seven and eight feet of water. In heavy seas she labored so that she spent about as much time under the water as she did on top of it—reminding one of the sailor's commentary on the verse of the Bible about "Those who go down to the sea in ships see the wonders of the Lord." "That may be true about full-rigged ships," said the sailor, "but I can tell the fellow who wrote it that them as go to sea in barks, brigs, schooners, or other small craft, they see hell!"

We floundered across the Gulf Stream, and on the afternoon of the night we expected to make our dash through the blockading fleet, and while we were still distant some fifty miles from the Cape Fear River, a big, bark-rigged, steam sloop-of-war, which we afterwards learned was the U.S.S. *Shenandoah*, caught sight of us and gave chase.

The captain, when in his cups, would swear by all the gods of the sea that the little *Lillian* could run seventeen knots an hour, but we were to witness the phenomenon of a heavy man-of-war, that could not make more than nine or ten knots at most, gain rapidly on us, as our fool captain persisted in steering a course which permitted of the warship, carrying all of her immense spread of sail. Our captain went below and stowed several big drinks of brandy under his vest, and then, coming on deck, in a spirit of braggadocio, hoisted the Confederate flag. Mr. Campbell ordered us to go below and put on our uniforms and side arms, as we wished to be captured, if captured we had to be, as officers of the Confederate Navy.

Returning to the quarter-deck we awaited developments. The warship still steadily gained. Within an hour from the time she sighted us she fired a shot. We naval officers knew that she was only trying to get the range, as we saw the projectile fall short several hundred yards from us, but our captain thought that was the best she could do, and with his habitual swagger he mounted to the little bridge which reached from one little paddlebox to the other, and from that point of vantage he looked down on us and in the most dramatic manner said, "I want you naval officers to know that I am captain of her as long as a plank will float !" Just then the *Shenandoah*, having got the range, sent a screaming rifled projectile through both paddleboxes, the shot passing only a foot or two under the bridge on which the captain was standing. With a yell of dismay he threw up his hands and came scampering down the ladder, screaming, "Haul that flag down. I will not have any more lives sacrificed!" Nothing besides the paddleboxes had as yet been touched unless we except the captain's yellow streak. Lieutenant Campbell walked to the taffrail, a distance of some ten feet from where he had been standing, and took up a position alongside the little flagstaff from which the Confederate colors were fluttering. Laying his hand on the flag halyards he quietly said: "Captain, if you want to give up this boat, turn her over to me. I will not allow you to surrender her. These officers are branded as pirates, and according to President Lincoln's proclamation may be hung if captured." Just then the man-of-war yawed and let fly her whole broadside, cutting the *Lillian* up considerably. The captain looked dazed for a moment, but was brought out of his mental stupor by a shot from a rifled gun which grazed the top of one of the boilers letting the steam out with a roar. The engine-room force rushed on deck and gathered around us. The captain bolted for the booby hatch leading down into the cabin, stopping only long enough to say: "I told the agent in Bermuda how it would be if he forced me to take a lot of pirates on board. If you are going to take my ship away from me, take her!"—and disappeared below. Mr. Campbell, as cool as though nothing extraordinary was taking place, turned to us and said, "Kill the first-man who touches those flag halyards."

The chief engineer, a game little fellow, informed Mr. Campbell that the boilers could be disconnected from each other, a precaution against just such an accident as had happened, and that the boat, with the immense pressure of steam she was carrying, would run until the steam from the injured boiler cooled off sufficiently to allow the stokers to return to their duties. He added that he had been a prisoner once in Fort Lafayette and had no desire to return there. The crew gallantly cheered his remarks.

All this time the *Shenandoah* was yawing first to starboard and then to port, apparently so certain that she had us that she was amusing her crew at target practice. Mr. Campbell went into the pilothouse and took command of the *Lillian*. The first order he gave changed our course so that the man-of-war had to take in her sails, and after that we appeared to be holding our own in the contest of speed. Shots continued to fly over and around us, occasionally one striking the frail sides causing the splinters to fly as it passed through. The shells were bursting and their fragments whistling all around us. We were dripping wet from the spray thrown up by projectiles which hit the water alongside. In the midst of it all Mr. Campbell ordered me to go down into the cabin and report to him what the captain was doing. I reported: "Captain in his berth dead drunk with an empty bottle of brandy beside him."

All this time Lieutenant Campbell was edging the *Lillian* in toward the land which we sighted between sundown and dark, and how we did pray that night would come soon. With our light draft we continued the "edging-in" maneuver until the heavy man-of-war, drawing some eighteen or twenty feet of water, had to change her course for fear of striking the bottom. She hauled to the southward with the object of heading us off from Wilmington, from which port we were far to the northward by this time. We had to change our course to the southward, giving the broadside of the *Shenandoah* a fine target as we steamed in parallel lines down the coast, the *Lillian* being so close into the beach that she was rolling on the curlers of the outer line of surf. Night at last came to our relief,—or at least we thought it did,—when to our amazement two columns of flame about thirty feet high shot up out of our little smokestacks! This gave the warship a fine target to exercise her crew in night practice, of which she at once took advantage. Our engineer explained that to get more steam he had caused half a dozen bottles of turpentine to be thrown into the furnaces. The beacon soon expended its energy, however, and without further molestation we continued on our way to Wilmington.

We had hopes of reaching the bar before daylight, and thus elude the vigilance of the blockading fleet, but luck and the speed of the *Lillian* were against us. Day broke when we were still a couple of miles away and the fleet at once saw us and opened fire. We had no choice but to go on, as the last few shovelsful of coal on board were then being tossed into the furnaces. Fortunately none of the shots touched our remaining boiler or machinery. There was one small gunboat right in our path, inside of the bar, and very close to Fort Fisher. The people in the fort and on the gunboat must have been asleep. Lieutenant Campbell ordered the man at the wheel to steer for her, saying that she was so near the fort that she would not dare fire, as Fort Fisher would blow her out of the water if she did. He was right—for when she saw us coming she slipped her cable and scampered off without firing a shot, and a few minutes afterwards we dropped our anchor in safety under the sheltering guns of the famous fortress.[6]

The rattling of the chain cable, when the anchor was dropped, had awakened our captain from his drunken sleep, and he shortly appeared on deck looking very sheepish, but the arrival of several officers from the fort soon caused him to resume his swaggering air. Resuming his role as captain he received them at the gangway, and the first one who stepped on to the deck seized his hand and exclaimed, "Well done, captain! that was the most daring dash through the blockade we have yet witnessed!" The captain modestly replied, "Oh, it is nothing; we have to take some chances in our business, you know!" And Lieutenant Campbell, standing a few feet away, never said a word.

The captain invited the army officers (but none of us) into his cabin and opened champagne. Champagne at six o'clock in the morning had no terrors for a Confederate soldier. This same captain, after the damages to the *Lillian* had been repaired at Wilmington, loaded her with cotton, and started out again. He stopped and surrendered her when the first shot was fired and before any damage had been done. From a blockade-runner the *Lillian* was converted into a United States blockader.

As the *Lillian* was being made fast to the wharf at Wilmington, two men on the wharf became involved in a difficulty and, according to the custom of the country, drew their revolvers and began to shoot. One of them fell and floundered around on the planks like a chicken with its neck half wrung. Lieutenant Campbell patriotically exclaimed, "My own, my native land! Now I am sure that I am home again!"

In his report to the Navy Department concerning the chase of the *Lillian*, Captain Ridgely, U.S.N., commanding the Shenandoah, says:—

Sir:—

At 4 P.M. made another blockade-runner in latitude 36°34' N., Longitude 76°33' W., steering to the northward and westward. We made chase and overhauled her quite fast. She only escaped by darkness and running into shoal water. We fired 140 shots at her, and I think some of them took effect. He was a bold blockade-runner and flew the rebel flag as long as we could see him. . . . [1]

See *Rebellion Records, vol. 10.*

Abstract of log of U.S.S. *Shenandoah:*—

Saturday, July 30th, 1864—At 3:45 p.m. sighted a steamer burning black smoke to the eastward; made all sail in chase. At 4:30 p.m. made stranger out to be a double smokestack, sidewheel steamer, apparently a blockade-runner, standing to the northward and westward. At 5:45, he showed Rebel colors. Called the first division and powder division to quarters and began to fire at her with the 30 and 150 pounder rifled Parrott. At 6 p.m. beat to quarters and fired all the divisions. At 7 p.m. took in foretop gallantsail and foresail. At 7:30 took in foretop sail.

During the chase fired 70 rounds from 30 pounder Parrott, 53 rounds from 150 pounder Parrott, 18 rounds from XI inch guns, and one round from a 4 pounder howitzer. . . .[1]

After his capture the captain of the *Lillian* in answer to the questions of the examining officer gave the following version of the chase:—

My name is Daniel Martin, a native of Liverpool, England. Was three weeks at Wilmington repairing boiler injured in chase. The Confederate colors were hoisted by some of the passengers. . . .[2]

[1] See *Naval War Records.*   [2] See *Naval War Records.*

Twenty-three

Shells dropping in the grass-grown streets of Charleston, South Carolina—Mr. Trenholm is Secretary of the Confederate Treasury—Columbia—Mr. Trenholm's beautiful villa—Go to Richmond and ask the millionaire Secretary for the hand of his daughter—Mrs. Trenholm calls on Mrs. Stephens.

At Wilmington I went to a wretched little cottage which sheltered several naval officers who were stationed in the town. I thought our condition in the Confederacy was bad enough when I had left its shores two years before, but these officers had literally nothing in the way of clothing besides their shabby uniforms, threadbare and patched. I felt ashamed of my new uniform, made by a fashionable London tailor, and my well-laundered white shirt, so I moved my trunk into the center of the room and insisted on a divide of its contents. I had just come from a land of plenty and I had come in an empty ship, and these brave fellows were suffering for the simplest necessities. The foreign owners of blockade-runners no longer brought clothing or provisions into the stricken country, as they had found it more profitable to bring only a little gold with which they could buy all the depreciated Confederate currency they wanted to buy cotton with. Only the boats engaged in the risky business which belonged to the Confederate Government, and those belonging to Fraser, Trenholm & Co. and one or two other Southerners, ever brought cargoes into the blockaded ports any more. The foreigner wanted cotton, and if he could get that for his

gold the sufferings of our people did not interest him. I never could
understand why President Davis never issued a proclamation forbid-
ding an empty blockade-runner entering our ports.[1]

I had been only a few hours in Wilmington when I received the
usual order in such cases, to proceed to my home, notify the Secretary of
the Navy as to my address, and to there await orders. I had no home—
so I determined to go to Charleston and notify the Secretary from there.
Arriving in Charleston I stepped on to the platform and boldly asked
for a cab. My modest request was greeted with laughter by the few
loafers who were there assembled. If the Negro cabmen had not gone
to the front, their horses had. Knowing my way, however, I left my
baggage at the station and started on the long walk to Mr. Trenholm's
office which was located on one of the wharves. I soon found myself
in the deserted part of the city where the shells were falling.[2]

I passed through King Street to Wentworth and followed the latter street to Meeting. Ruin was on every side of me; the grass in the
street was above my knees; not a human being was to be seen. I turned
into the battered public market to take advantage of the shade afforded
by the roof of its dilapidated sheds and because no grass was growing
under them—not even a turkey buzzard disputed my right of way, as
they were in the habit of doing before and after the war, in that particular locality. My surroundings were not cheerful and my gloomy
thoughts were not dispelled by the bursting of a shell from the historic
"Swamp Angel" and the whirring of its fragments which passed unpleasantly close to me.

Arriving at the wharves, to my surprise I found a battery erected
within a few feet of the entrance to what once had been Mr. Trenholm's
counting-house. As I approached, a sentry appeared suddenly from
out of the ground and peremptorily ordered me to halt. I naively told
him I wanted to see Mr. Trenholm, which information seemed to arouse
his suspicions, and he called for the corporal of the guard, who informed me that he had never heard of Mr. Trenholm. But as I had
some official documents in my pocket I very soon convinced him that
I was harmless and he allowed me to retire. I passed up East Bay Street
to Broad and saw the old City Hall (used as a post-office). It was riddled
by shells. It was from the porch of this building that Washington had
addressed the people of Charleston when he visited that city. At the
corner of Broad and Meeting Streets I passed by the old colonial church
"St. Michael's," the rear wall of which had been smashed in and great
holes were to be seen in the standing walls, which had been and were
still being bombarded. About every ten minutes a shell was bursting
some place in the neighborhood. I passed on through the burned district, going uptown, and again found myself in the inhabited portion
of the city. Many Charlestonians who had taken refuge in the upper

part of the city, so as to be out of range of the shells, when the bombardment first began, returned to their residences near the battery when longer-range guns began to disturb them uptown, and in comparative comfort let the enemy shoot over their heads. In war times one can get accustomed to anything. At last I met a civilian who was very civil and gave me the information I wanted. He told me that Mr. Trenholm was no longer in Charleston, but was now Secretary of the Confederate Treasury and had gone to Richmond; but that he could show me where I would find his brother-in-law and partner, Mr. Theodore Wagner, and that the business office was in a residence on Rutledge Avenue.[3] When I found Mr. Wagner he was very kind to me, but he seemed to be in an awful hurry, and hustled me into a buggy, saying it was the only vehicle of the kind in the city. I asked where we were going, and after we started he told me we were going to the railway station as fast as possible, as I barely had time to catch the train; that Mr. Trenholm had instructed him to send me at once to his home in the suburbs of Columbia, if I got through the blockade safely.

I had brought a trunk with me that Midshipman Anderson had asked me to forward to his family in Savannah, and Mr. Wagner kindly attended to the matter for me. I was afterwards informed that when Anderson's family received it, and an accompanying letter, they had been mourning for him for some weeks. It happened that in the fight with the *Kearsarge* a man on the deck of the *Alabama* was cut completely in two by a shell, and the upper half of his body was hurled through the air striking Anderson on the head. Some of the crew of the *Alabama*, who were saved by either the *Kearsarge* or the French pilot boat, had reported that Midshipman Anderson had had his head blown off, and this story reached the Confederacy before I did.

It took me fifteen hours to reach Columbia, as trains in the Confederacy were not allowed to run faster than ten miles an hour and rarely attempted a disobedience of the law where the speed limit was concerned, and their interminable waits on the sidings were enough to try the patience of a saint, to say nothing of that of a midshipman.

Arriving at Columbia I was met at the station by Colonel Trenholm, his beautiful young wife, and his sister, the young lady I had two years previously presumptuously made up my mind to marry. Colonel Trenholm apologized for not alighting to meet me when the train arrived, giving as an excuse the fact that he could not walk, as he had been shot through the hips in one of the battles near Richmond. I was invited to get into the handsomely appointed landau (the Government had not seized Mr. Trenholm's horses, I suppose because he was a member of the Cabinet), and we drove to a beautiful villa, situated a short distance outside of the city limits, where I was most hospitably welcomed by the rest of the family.

"De Greffin" was the name of the villa, and besides a most lovable and happy family it contained many paintings and objects of art. In front of the house was a garden some half-acre in extent enclosed by a handsome balustrade, and at each corner was a vine-clad summer house. Flowers were blooming in profusion in the garden and on a succession of terraces which reached down to a little stream. As Mr. Trenholm was one of the largest owners of blockade-runners, of course the house was provided with every luxury and a most lavish hospitality was dispensed. A continual stream of guests constantly came and went, and the young people gathered there in flocks. Of course we danced,—Southerners in that day always danced when two or three were gathered together,—if only three, one would play the piano and the other two would dance. When we tired of dancing there were always the terraces and the moonlight, and the grand old trees under which we could stroll or sit and rest. There were saddle horses to ride in the mornings and carriages to take us driving in the afternoons, and the numerous servants who wanted to wait on us were in one another's way. After a blissful week of this life I decided that I had to go to Richmond. But one other person knew the nature of the business which called me there, but the incidents attending my mission were so characteristic of the manner in which a midshipman of that day would act in a serious matter that I must tell the story.

It took three or four days to go from Columbia to Richmond, the exact time not being important so far as the railway officials were concerned. Mr. Trenholm was staying at the house of some friends while waiting until his own house should be prepared for the reception of his family. I arrived in Richmond after dark and went at once to the address which had been given me. I had grown nine inches since I had last seen Mr. Trenholm, and I feared he would not recognize me. Arriving at the house I found several ladies and gentlemen seated on the piazza. I asked for Mr. Trenholm, and a tall, stately gentleman arose and came forward to greet me. I said that I was afraid he did not remember me, but he assured me in his hearty manner that he recollected me perfectly, and asked me to be seated. I thanked him and told him that I wanted to speak with him very particularly in private, and he showed the way into the drawing-room (where we were alone) and then he asked what he could do for me. I promptly replied that I had come to ask his consent to my marriage with his daughter, Miss Helen. Mr. Trenholm seemed startled, and exclaimed, "My dear young gentleman, I have not the slightest idea who you are!" When I told him my name, he said that it was difficult for him to realize that I was "Little" Morgan, as I had grown so much. An amused expression passed over his countenance, which embarrassed me, for I was in deadly earnest and did not see anything funny in the interview then. It had never occurred to me that others would have smiled at the idea of a penniless little rebel "reefer" asking the Secretary of the Treasury, the man who owned steamships, railroads, hotels, city houses, cotton presses, wharves, plantations, and thousands of slaves, for the hand of his daughter! Mr. Trenholm was a most kindly and sympathetic gentleman, and seeing my embarrassment, at once proceeded to treat my proposition seriously. He first asked me if I did not think his daughter and myself both very young to enter into such a serious engagement; but I nipped that objection in the bud by saying that I might be killed before the end of the war, and asking him where I would be then. He frankly admitted that he did not know. With a twinkle in his eye he asked me what the pay of a midshipman was. I told him that just at that time it was forty dollars a month, but that as soon as I received my orders to a ship it would be forty-five (Confederate money was then at a discount of a hundred for one). After a pause he told me that his daughter's choice would be his. I think he was going to say something else, but I jumped to my feet and interrupted him by saying, "Goodbye." He asked where I was going, and I told him I had just time to catch the train for Columbia, and dashed out of the house.

When I arrived at "De Greffin" with my good news, I was welcomed and ever afterwards treated as one of the family. But my stay in that delightful atmosphere was of short duration, as a few days after my arrival I escorted Mrs. Trenholm and her daughters to Richmond, where they were to make their home for an indefinite period.

On arriving in Richmond, of course, it was incumbent on Mrs. Trenholm to call on the wife of the President and the ladies of the Cabinet, and one of her calls afforded us intense amusement. Mrs. Trenholm had not met any of these ladies previously and knew nothing of the domestic affairs of the members of the social circle of which she was now to be a member. After calling on Mrs. Davis she thought it proper to call at the residence of the Vice-President, the Honorable Alexander Stephens. She rang the bell and the door was opened by Mr. Stephens' old Negro body-servant, who had been with his master for many years and who accompanied him everywhere. Mrs. Trenholm asked the old darky if Mrs. Stephens was at home, and the old fellow's eyes fairly bulged out of his head. "Mam," he said, "Mr. Stephens ain't married. My God! did you ever see him?" Needless to add that Mr. Stephens was far from being a handsome man—he was very diminutive in size and it seemed marvelous that so frail a little body could bear the weight of so gigantic an intellect. Besides, he had always been an invalid and looked like an animated corpse.

*T*wenty-four

"Pride goeth before a fall"—Humiliated and sent to school—A realistic war college—Call a commander "My man," and order him forward—Assault on Fort Harrison—General Lee appears on the battlefield—Repulsed—I prove to be something of a sprinter.

"Pride goeth before a fall." I fear that the dignity of being an engaged man caused my chest to enlarge disproportionately to my rank. I received my orders, and instead of being sent to an ironclad I was ordered to report on board of the schoolship *Patrick Henry* to be examined for promotion.[1] Most of my classmates had been nominally taken out of active service and put to school while I was at sea, and they were now passed midshipmen. I had not opened a schoolbook since I had left Annapolis, and the result was that I failed to pass. But I was given another chance and had to begin school again. Although I did not know it, if there was one thing that I needed more than anything else, it was a little schooling.

The *Patrick Henry* was a small sidewheel seagoing steamer with a walking-beam engine and a brigantine rig. She had formerly belonged to the "Old Dominion" line running between New York and Norfolk. She had been converted into a man-of-war by having ten guns put on board of her and she had played quite a conspicuous part in the naval battles in Hampton Roads. She had now become the most realistic war college that ever existed. She was anchored in front of Drewry's Bluff, Richmond's principal defense on the James River, which is situated

164

seven miles below the city. The reason for her being located there was that the "school" was expected to sink itself in the channel between the obstructions in case the enemy's ironclads tried to force a passage by the land batteries. One always associates a collegiate institution with peace and quiet, but this naval college was located in the midst of the booming guns. Below Drewry's Bluff, on the south side of the river, were the naval land batteries of Wood, Brooke, Semmes, and Howlett, and on the other side of the river were the Federal batteries of Bohler, Signal Hill, Crow's Nest, and the Dutch Gap batteries; and when they all broke loose together the din they made was not conducive to that peaceful repose so prized by all students.

There were about sixty young midshipmen on the *Patrick Henry*, varying in age from fourteen to seventeen. Their jackets were made out of very coarse gray cloth and the food they had to eat was, at first, revolting to me. The menu offered little variety. If it was not a tiny lump of fat pork, it was a shaving of fresh meat as tough as the hide which had once covered it, with a piece of hardtack and a tin cup of hot water colored by chicory or grains of burned corn, ground up, and brevetted *coffee*. But no one kicked about the food, as it was as good if not better than that the poor soldiers in the trenches received. The James River furnished a capital article of chills and fever—not malaria, but the good old-fashioned kind with the shivers which made the teeth chatter and burning fever to follow. On an average about one-half of the midshipmen went through this disagreeable experience every other day. No one was allowed to go on the sick-list on account of chills and fever; one was, however, allowed to lie down on the bare deck while the chill was on, but had to return to duty as soon as the paroxysm was over.

Lieutenant William H. Parker, who had been a professor of seamanship at Annapolis, was the superintendent of this extraordinary naval academy, and he was assisted by two or three navy lieutenants and a like number of civilian professors.[2] There were on the hurricane deck and between the paddleboxes two little recitation rooms, and on top of these rooms were posted signalmen who from daylight to dark wigwagged to, and received messages from, the batteries. The scenes in the recitation rooms were frequently exciting and interesting. The guns on shore roared and the shells burst, and the professor would placidly give out the problem to the youngster at the blackboard, to be interrupted by the report of some gun which his practiced ear told him was a newcomer in the fray. He would begin by saying: "If x - y— One moment, Mr. Blank. Would you kindly step outside and find out for me which battery it is that has opened with that Brooke gun?" The information obtained the recitation would be resumed, only to be

CSS *PATRICK HENRY*, CONFEDERATE NAVAL SCHOOL SHIP
On the James River below Richmond, 1864

again interrupted, by a message from the captain that a certain battery was short of officers and a couple of midshipmen were wanted. It was useless to call for volunteers, as every midshipman clamored for permission to go, so these details were given as rewards. It was from among these midshipmen that the men came who steered the boats when the gunboat *Underwriter* was boarded and captured in the night, and it was in that fight that Midshipman Palmer Saunders had his head cloven to his shoulders by a cutlass in the hand of a big sailor. Saunders was only seventeen years of age.[3] It was in that same boarding expedition that Dan Lee, another midshipman from the *Patrick Henry*, called out to his would-be rescuer, when a sailor had him down and was trying to kill him, not to shoot, as the man on top of him was so thin! Lee and Saunders were of the same age. This *Patrick Henry* may have been a unique institution of learning, but the "Confederate States Naval Academy" turned out men who afterwards became United States Senators, members of Congress, judges, successful and prominent lawyers, doctors, civil engineers, bankers, and successful business men as well as sailors.

The *Patrick Henry*, besides being a naval academy and stopgap for the river obstructions, also served as a receiving ship. Steamboats under flags of truce, carrying Northern prisoners to Harrison's Landing for exchange, had to stop alongside of her to get permits to continue their trips, and returning frequently discharged their human freight of Confederate prisoners on board the school ship while they went again down the river for more. One day, while I was assisting the officer of the deck in receiving these poor, forlorn fellows, I was trying to hurry them forward so that they would not block the gangway; this was necessary, as with few exceptions they were so glad to be once more under their beloved Confederate flag that those who did not succeed in embracing the officer of the deck at least wanted to swap congratulations with the gray-coated midshipman. I was continually interrupting them by begging them not to block the gangway, but to pass forward, and that I would attend to their wants as soon as the rest could come aboard, etc. Suddenly the shabbiest, the raggedest, and most unkempt of the lot, with his matted hair reaching to his shoulders and looking as though it had never known the caress of a comb, shambled across the gangplank, and in rather a peremptory manner demanded the name of my captain. I replied with the usual advice, "Go forward, my man; go forward!"—when to my amazement the human wreck drew himself up and rather sternly said, "Little Morgan, I will apply for you as soon as I get a command and I will then show you, sir, who goes forward!" The man was Commander Beverly Kennon, who had rammed and sunk the U.S. sloop-of-war *Varuna* when Farragut passed the forts below New Orleans.[4] I thought I should faint when I became aware of his identity. Here was I, a poor devil of a midshipman, ordering forward a man who ranked me so far that I would hardly be able to see where he passed along! It was not fair. Kennon was last seen by his compatriots in the fight at the forts standing on the paddlebox of his ship while the *Hartford*, *Brooklyn*, and the frigate *Mississippi*, with their tremendous broadsides, were shooing him ashore, when suddenly they blew him up, set fire to him, and sunk him almost simultaneously. By all the rules of the game he was a dead man, and had no right to come back and scare a poor innocent midshipman out of several years' growth. Several years afterwards Kennon served in the Egyptian Army where he was a full colonel and I was again his junior. He seemed to take a delight in telling his brother officers how, as he described it, he had once been "ordered forward by a d—d midshipman!"

From the *Patrick Henry* we could see the constant movement of troops, both Union and Confederate, on the north side of the river, where they frequently clashed in skirmishes; but this sort of thing was so common that to break the monotony two of the midshipmen got permission to go ashore, and improved the time by fighting a duel with muskets.

One morning we saw our soldiers hastily constructing a pontoon bridge on the river a short distance above where we were anchored. We soon learned that the cause of their activity was that General Grant's troops had surprised and captured Fort Harrison during the night, and that Fort Harrison was the key to our advanced line of defenses on the north side of the stream.[5] The bridge was no sooner completed than Hoke's North Carolina division were rushed across it. These were the best-dressed and best-cared for troops in the Confederate Army, as the State, with commendable paternalism, owned its steamers and had gone into the blockade-running business on its own account.

Believing that the object of the sudden movement was to retake the fort, Midshipmen Carter, Hale, Wright, and myself asked and received permission to go ashore and see at close range the coming fight. Following the troops we saw them form their line of battle in front of the fort and its outlying breastworks, while the shells of the enemy were bursting over their heads as well as in front, behind, and among them. Soon we heard the rumble of the wheels of gun carriages and caissons, as our light batteries came, at the gallop, from the rear and dashed through the spaces between our brigades and regiments, and wheeling and unlimbering a short distance from our front, they opened a rapid fire. There was no wind stirring, and soon the enemy's position, as well as that of our light batteries, was obscured from view by

COLONEL BEVERLY KENNON
Coast Defense, Egyptian Army

the dense smoke. Then their firing ceased, and so did that of the enemy's heavy guns. All at once our artillery was seen to burst through the bank of smoke and rapidly come back to us, dashing through our infantry line again, wheeling and unlimbering just in their rear: this manoeuvre was followed by complete stillness, the most trying time in the life of a soldier, that two or three minutes, which seem unending, while waiting for the order to charge.

The infantry moved forward, at the double-quick, under cover of the smoke which lay close to the ground in the heavy atmosphere. Nothing could be heard save the tramp of hurrying feet. Fort Harrison maintained an ominous silence. As our men neared the fortifications suddenly from twenty thousand throats burst forth the famous rebel yell which fairly rent the air. When within about a hundred yards from the coveted works there arose a long line of blue-coated soldiers, seemingly from out of the ground, who poured a deadly volley into the oncoming ranks of the North Carolinians and at the same time the heavy guns of the fort sprinkled them with shrapnel, grape, and canister. The fight was fast and furious for a time, and then we saw some slightly wounded men going to the rear; these were followed by the more seriously injured, each accompanied and assisted by two or three unhurt men, who, moved by compassion, assisted them. We then knew what was coming, and soon saw the whole line fall back, but not in any great disorder. We had been repulsed, but the enemy was not following us.

When we reached the line, from which we had started to make our unsuccessful assault, the troops re-formed and waited. Suddenly from the left of the line we heard cheering and wondered what it was for. It was not the rebel yell, which once heard could never be mistaken for any other sound; the sound we now heard was evidently a burst of enthusiasm, which was taken up by regiment after regiment until the whole line was adding to its volume. It was not long before we discovered the cause of the manifestation—for there, with his silvery head uncovered, hat in hand, was seen riding down the line— General Robert E. Lee. He was a picture of dignity as, mounted on his famous gray charger "Traveler," he spoke seriously to his unsuccessful troops. As he passed in front of where we were standing, we could plainly hear what he was saying—he was telling the men how important Fort Harrison was to our line of defense, and that he was sure they could take it if they would make another earnest effort. Their answer was given in deafening cheers.

Again they went forward to the assault, and again were they repulsed, this time with worse slaughter than had been their lot on the first attempt. The second retreat was much more disorderly than the first, but again they re-formed and waited—and again General Lee rode down the line.

I had always thought General Lee was a very cold and unemotional man, but he showed lots of feeling and excitement on that occasion; even the staid and stately "Traveler" caught the spirit of his master, and was prancing and cavorting while the general was imploring his men to make one more effort to take the position for him.

Again they went forward and again they came back—this time in great disorder. In fact, it was a sprinting match on a big scale. I had heard a great deal about the marvelous marching powers of the Confederate infantryman, and I was only a poor "webfoot," temporarily off his element, but I do not recall having seen any infantrymen pass me on the way to our second line of defense.

When the troops re-formed, General Lee again rode down the line trying to comfort his men by telling them they had done all that men could do, and, that anyhow the place was not of as much importance as he had at first thought it was. This talk cheered the men, and they, although worn out with fatigue, replied by cheering their beloved general.

After the battle a surgeon pressed me into his service and made me hold a soldier's shattered leg while he amputated it. I would have preferred to be shot myself. Medicines were scarce in the South and that particular surgeon had neither chloroform nor ether in his medical kit.

Disgusted, tired, and weary, I returned to my school and my studies.

_T_wenty-five

I finally become a passed midshipman—Battery Semmes—The Dutch Gap Canal—Mortar pits and rifle pits—The lookout tower—Trading with the enemy—Pickett's famous division charges a rabbit—A shell from a monitor destroys my log hut—Good marksmanship—An unexploded shell—General Lee inspects battery—Costly result of order to "give him a shot in fifteen minutes"—Demonstration against City Point—Confederate ironclads badly hammered—"Savez" Read cuts boom across the river—A thunderous night.

Shortly after the fall of Fort Harrison I passed my examination for promotion and arrived at the dignity of being a passed midshipman. I was immediately ordered to the naval battery called Semmes, situated on a narrow tongue of land formed by the river. It was the most advanced of our defenses on the river, and was the nearest of any of our batteries to the Dutch Gap Canal which was then being dug by General B. F. Butler.

Our seven heavy guns, rifled and smooth-bore, were mounted in pits dug on the brow of a gently sloping hill—the battery was only thirty feet above the river. Between each of the guns was a bomb-proof which protected our ammunition. The guns were mounted on naval carriages so that our sailors could handle their accustomed blocks and tackles.

On the opposite side of the river, and forming a semicircle around the peninsula on which Semmes was located, were the heavy Union batteries called Bohler's, Signal Hill, Crow's Nest, the Dutch

Gap batteries, and the Howlett House batteries, and when they all opened fire at once they made a perfect inferno out of Battery Semmes. It surely was a hot spot.

Some six hundred yards in front of Battery Semmes, on the land side, we had four little Cohorn mortars in a pit, and with these we tossed shells constantly into the canal to interfere with its construction. General Butler put a number of Confederate prisoners to work in his canal, and very thoughtfully sent us word that we were only killing our own men with our mortar shells. About the same time that we received this considerate message, Jeff Phelps, a midshipman who had been one of the "Brood of the Constitution," and who was one of the prisoners compelled to dig in the canal, in some way managed to get a note to us telling us that we "were doing fine" and to "keep it up." We only kept some eight or ten men at a time in the mortar pit and between the pit and our battery were a number of rifle pits. When the mortars aggravated General Butler too much, he would send a force across the river to charge the mortars. Seeing them coming, our men would hastily beat a retreat, and like prairie dogs tumbling into their holes, they would disappear. The Union soldiers would, of course, capture the mortars and spike them, but when we thought that as many of them as the pit could hold were well in it, we would cut loose with the heavy guns of the big battery behind us which were trained on it. Then the Federal soldiers would hasten back to the river, and before they could get across, our men, who were provided with bows and drills, would have new vent holes bored and would be again tossing shells as though nothing had happened to interfere with their day's work. Why General Butler's men never carried off the mortars with them we could never understand—two strong men could have lifted any one of them, they were so small and light.

General Butler had built a lofty lookout tower out of timber. It was very open work, and on the top of it he placed a telescope. I met a member of his staff after the war who told me that they could see every movement we made, and that on one occasion he had distinctly seen a man in our battery cut off a chew of tobacco and put it into his mouth.

There was a mystery as to the way in which privates would come to a tacit agreement with the enemy about not doing any sniping on certain parts of the line. I knew of one stretch of breastworks where our men could expose themselves with perfect impunity up to a spot on which stood an empty barrel, and on the other side of that barrel, if a man showed an old hat on the end of a ramrod, it was instantly perforated with bullets.

The Union soldiers craved tobacco of which the Southerners had an abundance and the "grayback" longed for coffee or sugar. At some points on the line trading in these commodities went on briskly without the knowledge of the officers. Their dealings were strictly honorable. A man, say from the Southern side, would creep outside the works, and when he reached a certain stump he would place a couple of large plugs of tobacco on it and then return to his companions. After a time he would again creep to the stump to find that his tobacco was gone, but in its place was a small quantity of the longed-for coffee and sugar. We always carried one or two long plugs of tobacco in our inside breast pockets, as it was a common belief that if a man was captured and had tobacco it would insure him good treatment.

One foggy night I was on duty and had visited our outposts. While returning to the battery on a path close to the riverside, I distinctly heard oars slapping the water—the rowlocks were evidently muffled. Although I could not see the boat I felt that it must be very near the shore, and I hailed it with a "Boat ahoy! Keep farther out in the stream!" The answer came back: "We don't do any picket firing on this line." I told the spokesman that I knew that, but we didn't want him to bunk with us, and hardly were the words out of my mouth when the bow of the boat was rammed into the mud at my feet. I felt sure my time had come, and hastily jerked my pistol out of the holster intending to fire so as to give the alarm, when I heard a voice say, "For the love of Mike, Johnny, give me a chew of tobacco." The tone was so pleading and earnest that I could not resist it and handed the fellow my plug. In return he gave me a canteen full of whiskey. We entered into conversation, and I discovered that he was an old classmate of mine at Annapolis who had "bilged" and was now a master's mate in charge of a picket boat whose duty was to give warning if our ironclads descended the river. I warned him about the folly of his act, and he shoved out into the stream and disappeared forever out of my life. When I produced my canteen before my messmates they fairly went wild with joy, but nothing ever could induce me to tell how I had come into possession of the liquor.

Muskrats or rabbits, when caught, which was rarely, were a welcome addition to our menu. Pickett's division supported our battery and was encamped about half a mile from us. One day we thought that those thousands of men had gone crazy—there was the wildest commotion among them. Men rushed to and fro in the wildest confusion, falling over one another in every direction—it looked like a free fight. We sent over to find out the cause of the riot and were informed that one poor little "cotton-tail bunny" had jumped out of a bush in the centre of the camp and that some ten thousand men had given chase in hopes of having him for supper.

The winter of 1864–65 was an intensely cold one. Snow from three to six inches in depth lay constantly on the ground keeping the trenches wet and muddy, and the consequent discomfort was great. Lieutenant Bradford,[1] our commander, and Lieutenant Hilary Cenas and the surgeon had two log huts to live in. Becoming envious I got several of the men to assist me in building a cabin for myself, with the chinks all stuffed with mud and with a beautiful mud chimney of which I was very proud. I had had it located in a little gulch behind the battery and it did look so comfortable, but alas, work had gone on very rapidly in the construction of the canal despite our continual mortar fire, and on the afternoon of the day on which my house was finished a monitor fired several eleven-inch shells through the canal, and with the whole state of Virginia to select from, one these projectiles could find no other place to explode in but my little cabin, which it scattered to the four winds.

Some days there would be a lull in the artillery fire, and we could walk about exposing ourselves to the enemy's fire with perfect impunity, and on other days the most trifling movement on our part, such as the moving of an empty water barrel, or a few men chasing a frightened and bewildered "cotton-tail" would bring upon us a storm of projectiles from the enemy's guns. Constant practice had made the artillery firing very effective, so much so that it was not an uncommon thing for us to have one or more of our guns knocked off their carriages. Lieutenant Cenas seemed to have a tacit understanding with the gunner of a rifled piece in the Crow's Nest Battery whose marksmanship he admired very much. Cenas would go outside of the works and place an empty barrel or tobacco box on top of a stump, and then, stepping to one side, he would wave his arms as a signal to his favorite gun-pointer on the other side, and immediately we would see a puff of smoke and the projectile would always tear up the ground very close to the stump and frequently both stump and barrel would be knocked into smithereens.

One afternoon a monitor fired a shell through the canal which landed a few yards in front of our battery. A sailor, in pure dare-deviltry, went outside to pick it up. Just as he got to it I saw a thread of smoke arising from the fuse, and I yelled to him to jump back—but too late. The sailor gave it a push with his foot and it bounded into the air taking off the man's leg; the shell then landed in one of our gun pits and exploded killing and wounding several men. It must have been spinning with great rapidity on its axis and only needed the touch of the sailor's foot to start it again on its mission of destruction.

We flew no flag, as it was useless to hoist one; the enemy would shoot it away as fast we would put it up. A wonderfully accurate gun was a light field piece, a Parrott gun, which would come out from behind the Bohler Battery, take up a position in the bushes, and shoot at any man bringing water from a near-by spring, and he was frequently successful in hitting him. One day General Lee was inspecting the line and stopped for a few moments at our battery. He ordered us to drive this fellow away, and then looking at his watch added, "Give him a shot in fifteen minutes." Then the general on his gray horse rode away. At the expiration of the fifteen minutes we let go our seven heavy guns into the bushes where we supposed the fellow to be with the result that he limbered up and hastily took refuge behind his works, and from fifty to seventy-five guns in the batteries which enfiladed Semmes cut loose into us and kept it up for three days and nights, dismounting three of our guns, killing and wounding a number of our men.

We could shoot just as well at night as we could in the daytime, as from constant practice we had the ranges of all of the enemy's batteries, and had marked the trunnions of our guns for range and the traverses for direction. Such firing was accurate, as was proved on several occasions by our discovering at daylight that we had dismounted some of the guns of our antagonists.

In the latter part of January, 1865, our supply of ammunition was running short, and as a consequence we were ordered to be sparing with it, so we would only fire a gun when the enemy's fire would slacken up a bit to let them know that we were still there. This seemed to encourage our opponents and they hammered us all day with their big guns, and all through the nights they dropped mortar shells among us. These shells, with their burning fuses, resembled meteors flying through the air; they made an awful screeching noise as they tore the atmosphere apart when coming down before we heard the thud of their striking the ground and the terrific explosion which would follow, and then would come the whistling of the fragments as they scattered in every direction. We were so accustomed to these sounds that we did not allow them to interfere with our slumbers, as wrapped in our one blanket we slept in the bomb-proofs or magazines.

The end of the Southern Confederacy was near at hand, although we at the front little realized the fact. The authorities in Richmond determined to make a daring attempt to capture or destroy General Grant's base of supplies at City Point on the James. Late on the afternoon of January 23, 1865, we received notice to be ready, as our three ironclads, the *Virginia Number 2*, the *Richmond*, and the *Fredericksburg*, would come down that night, run the gantlet of the Federal batteries, and try to force their way through the boom the enemy had placed across the river (at Howlett's) in anticipation of just such an attempt.[2] I happened to be officer of the day. The night was very dark, and suddenly I heard a sentry challenge something in the river. I ran down to the edge of the water and arrived there just in time to see a rowboat stick her nose into the mud at my very feet, and was much surprised to see my old shipmate,

"Savez" Read, step ashore. He was in a jolly mood, as he told me that our ironclads would follow him in a couple of hours, and that he was going ahead to cut the boom so that they could pass on and destroy City Point. "And now, youngster," he said "you fellows make those guns of yours hum when the 'Yanks' open, and mind that you don't shoot too low, for I will be down there in the middle of the river." And then he put his hand affectionately on my shoulder and added: "Jimmie, it's going to be a great night; I only wish you could go with me: a sailor has no business on shore, anyway." And laughing he stepped back into his boat and shoved out into the stream.

The enemy must have had some information as to our plans, for Read had not proceeded very far before the bank of the river looked as though it was infested by innumerable fireflies, as the sharpshooters rained bullets on his boat which was proceeding with muffled oars. They completely riddled it, but Read kept on while bailing the water out of her, and strange to say he reached the boom and successfully cut it.

About two hours after Read left, our so-called ironclads noiselessly glided by the battery. The stillness was unbroken for so long a time that we began to congratulate outselves that they had safely got by the enemy's batteries without being discovered. But our exultation was premature—they did get by the Bohler and Signal Hill batteries unobserved, but unfortunately the furnaces of the leading boat were stirred, and a flame shot out of her smokestack which instantly brought upon her a shower of shot and shell, and instantly the big guns on both sides were in an uproar. My! but that was a thunderous night; the very ground quivered under the constant explosions.

The next morning we learned that our demonstration against City Point had resulted in a most mortifying failure. The smallest of our ironclads, the *Fredericksburg*, passed safely through the obstructions, but the *Virginia*, which steered very badly, ran aground, and blocked the passage to the *Richmond*. The wooden gunboat *Drewry* also missed the channel and ran ashore. The *Fredericksburg* was recalled and the big monitor USS *Onondaga* with her immense guns arrived on the scene shortly after daylight. With one shot she smashed in the *Virginia's* forward shield. The *Virginia* got afloat again and presented her broadside, which was also perforated as though it was made of paper. She then brought her after gun into action and a shot from the monitor also smashed her after shield. They all returned that night under a rain of projectiles from the shore batteries similar to that they had been exposed to the night before, and on that occasion our ironclads, on which we had based such high hopes, fired their last hostile shot. The end was near.[3]

Twenty-six

The Confederate "White House"—President Davis gives an impromptu lecture on bridle bits—Letter of Mrs. Jefferson Davis denying truth of anecdote relating to President Buchanan, Mrs. Joseph E. Johnston, and herself—The Southern soldiers and girls dance, flirt, and marry, oblivious of the signs that the "debacle" draws near.

Notwithstanding the hardships we were all necessarily subjected to at the front, my life at that time was not devoid of pleasures. Frequently I was allowed to go to Richmond where I had friends and where I was made welcome. Among these dear friends were President and Mrs. Jefferson Davis. I have mentioned that one of my brothers had married a cousin of Mrs. Davis's, and her youngest brother, Midshipman Jefferson Davis Howell, was one of my most intimate friends, so I was made to feel very much at home at the Confederate "White House." I remember being there one day with my fiancée sitting on a sofa in a parlor adjoining the room Mr. Davis used as his private office, when unexpectedly the door between the two rooms opened and the President entered. He apologized for intruding on us, saying that he expected to find Mrs. Davis there. In one hand he held a steel bridle bit and in the other a piece of chamois leather with which he was polishing it. He at once proceeded to tell us about the merits of that particular bit, and becoming interested in the subject he went on to give us quite a lecture on bridle bits, their uses and abuses; he told us how the cruel Mexican bit, with which a brutal man can break the jaw of a horse, had come down from the ancients and had been imported into Morocco by the Arabs and into Spain by the Moors, and by the Spanish into Mexico and South America. He was familiar also with the modern bits and was quite eloquent over his account of how Chifney, a famous English jockey, had invented the most merciful of all curb bits. He told us a lot more about bridle bits which I cannot remember, and as he told it, it made the simple subject much more interesting than I could ever have imagined it could be made.

Mrs. Davis was highly gifted intellectually, and in her home was an affectionate wife and mother; her devotion to her husband and children was beautiful to see. In society she was bright and witty, and on occasion could blight with sarcasm anyone who had the misfortune to displease her, and when she did turn loose her tongue in that vein, society in Richmond was usually kept in a state of hysterical laughter for weeks afterwards.

There were many stories concerning Mrs. Davis's enmity toward Mrs. General Joseph E. Johnston, but they were without any foundation in fact. Mrs. Davis often spoke to me about her affection for Mrs. Johnston and how intimate they had been in Washington prior to the war. One of the stories, which is still current at this day, was that when Mrs. Davis went to bid President Buchanan good-bye, she told him that she could forgive everything except his having turned Mrs. Joe Johnston's head by making her husband a brigadier-general. This story was revamped and published in many papers years afterwards. I sent Mrs. Davis a clipping containing the story, and this is the letter she wrote me in acknowledging its receipt. The letter, with some others which she was kind enough to write me, are now in the Congressional Library:—

"The Rockingham," Narragansett Pier, R.I.
August 19, 1898.

My Dear Jimmie:—
I should have answered your two kind letters and offered thanks for them and also for the good likeness of my beloved brother, but I have been so utterly wretched I could not do so. My Winnnie has now been critically ill for twenty-eight days, and is still quite ill and suffering so that I can think of nothing else. Our physician seems not to fear the outcome of her illness, but she is dreadfully reduced and very patient in her pain.
The anecdote of Mr. Buchanan and me is nonsense. Nothing of the kind or the least like it ever happened. I was unaffectedly, fond of him and went to bid him an affectionate farewell.

My brother's likeness is such a comfort to me. I enjoy looking at his boyish face more than I can express. Thank you from the bottom of my heart for your kind thought of me.

I am more than glad that you did not go to Cuba, since the war has been so short and decisive—you could only have lost your health, and could not have added much to your reputation by any notable achievement.

I hope that Mrs. Morgan continues well.

I do not know how long we shall be here, perhaps until the last of October before we return home.

> *Believe me cordially your friend,*
> *V. Jefferson Davis.*

At the house of Mr. Trenholm I was always received as one of the family. The beautiful house, which had been built originally by an English gentleman of wealth and artistic tastes, was the centre of a certain amount of gayety and frequented, especially on Saturday evenings, by many distinguished people, among them of course many foreigners, who visited Richmond for the excitement of the experience. Mr. Trenholm, the Secretary of the Treasury, was a man of great wealth and probably the largest owner of blockade-runners, and consequently almost every luxury in the way of food was most hospitably placed before guests.

Where two or three young Southerners were gathered together there was sure to be singing and dancing. It is true that there were not many handsome toilets to be seen at these receptions, but the young girls were so pretty no one took the trouble to look at their dresses of a style fashionable before the war. The foreigners, of course, appeared in the orthodox dress coats and white ties, but we poor fellows who belonged at the front shamelessly joined the gay throng in our rags and tatters. My uniform, which had once been gray, had turned a green yellowish brown owing to its exposure to the element and the mud in the trenches. I had had the misfortune to have one of my coat tails burned off while sleeping too close to a camp-fire; one of my trousers legs had raveled out to halfway up the calf of my leg, and the lower part of the other trousers leg was very ragged; I wore a boot on one foot and a shoe on the other—the boot on the bare leg. This Falstaffian costume was set off with a sword, and if there is anything that will make a ragged man look more ridiculous than another it is the wearing of a sword. But the girls in their four-year-old dresses did not mind our appearance, and it would have been a cold day when a man in civilian togs, no matter how well dressed, could have persuaded one of those Southern girls to dance with him when a man from the front wanted a turn.

Mr. Trenholm, as I have said before, was most hospitably inclined and was the possessor of some of the finest and oldest Madeira wine in the country; naturally his invitations to dinner were rarely declined. I used to meet at his table the most distinguished generals of our army and the members of the Cabinet. These gentlemen for the most part were taciturn and serious, but Mr. Judah P. Benjamin, the Secretary of State, and Mr. Trenholm were both gifted conversationalists and very witty, and they always enlivened the banquets with anecdotes. Mr. Pierre Soulé, of Louisiana, was also a frequent guest; he was a most interesting talker. It was Mr. Soulé, who when United States Minister to Spain, after the duel between his son and the Duke of Alba, brother-in-law of the French Emperor, shot and crippled for life the Marquis de Turgot, the French Ambassador to Spain.

Despite the sad state of affairs, both in the Capital and in the country, there were balls and parties, and "marrying and giving in marriage" going on in Richmond. Mr. McFarland, a wealthy banker, was to give a ball and social Richmond was all agog over the prospect. To attend this ball it was necessary for me to have a new uniform. With any amount of Confederate money at my disposal, the modern man might ask why I did not go to a tailor and order one, but that was not the way we did things in those days. In the first place, there were no stores and had there been there would not have been anything in them for sale. I had to search the town before I found a man who possessed a few yards of gray cloth and willing to part with it for several hundred dollars in Confederate money. I finally found such a man; and also bought from him a pair of boots made out of thick, half-tanned cowskin for which I paid three hundred dollars. I looked so nice in my new togs that I was immediately asked by an army surgeon to be one of the groomsmen at his wedding, and I also attended the wedding of the beautiful Miss Hetty Cary to General John Pegram which had so sad an ending a few days afterwards when General Pegram was killed.[1]

While the young people were laughing, dancing, and being killed, the black clouds of adversity were gathering over our beloved Confederacy. Bitter dissension had resulted from the removal of General Johnston from the command of the Western army—a step which President Davis took in response to popular clamor for a change. This demand did not come from Johnston's soldiers, but from the populace, who cried out that if Johnston continued his strategy, the Western army would soon be in the Gulf of Mexico: they wanted an aggressive man put in command, and Mr. Davis gave them General Hood. He was aggressive enough, Heaven knows! After Hood's bloody victory at Franklin, in which some seventeen Southern generals fell, Mr. Davis was heard to observe that "one more such victory and there would not be any Western army left." After the disastrous defeat at Nashville the very men who had clamored to have General Johnston superseded, clamored against Mr. Davis for having removed him.

The Confederate Congress was at open war with President Davis and missed no opportunity to thwart his policies. They refused point-blank to adopt any of his suggestions for the relief of the pitiable condition of the country, and in rejecting the financial schemes submitted by Mr. Trenholm, the Senate Finance Committee frankly told that gentleman that under no circumstances could they adopt his suggestions, as it would imply their sanction of a measure emanating from Mr. Davis's administration! Mr. Trenholm told them that when they had treated Mr. Memminger, his predecessor in the Treasury Department, in the same way, Mr. Memminger had consulted him as a friend as to the course he should pursue, and that he, Mr. Trenholm, had advised him to resign. Now that he himself was placed in a similar position it was necessary that he should do likewise. The Senate Committee protested that such a course would not do at all, as they had a financial proposition of their own which they wanted him to father on account of the popular belief in his ability as a financier. Mr. Trenholm, no less frank than they were, informed them, after glancing over their bill, that he had a reputation among business men to maintain, and that if he put his name and gave his approval to such a measure, financiers would laugh at him. He then went to Mr. Davis and tendered his resignation. Mr. Davis told him that it was his duty to remain in the Cabinet; that he, Mr. Davis, recognized that with a Congress at open war with the administration nothing could be done to relieve the Treasury. He declared he needed Mr. Trenholm's clear head and advice, and begged him to stand by him in his hour of need.

As an example of the demoralization of the Confederate Government at this time, I remember going into the Senate Chamber one day while that august body was in session. Heavy firing was going on at the front which could not only be plainly heard inside the building, but made the windows rattle when particularly heavy guns were discharged. To this ominous obligato the lawmakers were earnestly debating the question as to how many daily newspapers should be placed on the desk of each Senator every morning. While these petty quarrels were going on, the destiny of a whole people was being ruthlessly decided in blood and suffering; we men in the trenches fought, shivered, and starved outside the city, and danced and made merry whenever we were allowed to come within its limits, little dreaming that the end was so near.

The Southern soldier was a very determined fellow, and at the same time reckless and light-hearted; one moment he would be in deep distress over the loss of some dear comrade and the next he would be shouting with laughter over some senseless joke perpetrated by one of his companions. I went one day to a tobacco warehouse, then used as a hospital, to see my friend Captain F. W. Dawson, who was very seriously wounded. The ladies of Richmond were very kind to the wounded and out of their scanty means they managed to make dainties which they would carry to the hospitals and distribute themselves. The day was hot and I found my friend lying on a cot near the open front door, so weak that he could not speak above a whisper, and after greeting him and speaking some words of cheer I saw that he was anxious to tell me something. I leaned over him to hear what he had to say, and the poor fellow whispered in my ear, "Jimmie, for God's sake, make them move my cot to the back of the building."

I assured him that he had been placed in the choicest spot in the hospital, where he could get any little air that might be stirring; but he still insisted that he wanted to be moved, giving as a reason that every lady who entered the place washed his face and fed him with jelly. The result was that his face felt sore and he was stuffed so full of jelly that he was most uncomfortable, as he was so weak he could not defend himself, and the procession of women would not listen to his protests. Shaking with laughter, I delivered his request to the head surgeon, who pinned a notice on Dawson's sheet to the effect that "This man must only be washed and fed by the regular nurses." Dawson was a gallant soldier and served on the staffs of J. E. B. Stuart, Fitzhugh Lee, and Longstreet. He recovered from his wounds and in 1873 married my sister Sarah.

Twenty-seven

Ordered to accompany Mrs. Davis and party south—No Pullman cars in those days—President Davis bids his family good-bye—Insolent deserters insult Mrs. Davis at Charlotte, North Carolina—A Hebrew gentleman gives her shelter—Midshipmen guarding the Confederacy's gold escort her to Abbeville, South Carolina—President Davis and his Cabinet at Abbeville.

The spring of 1865 was fast approaching and we expected soon to see great changes. One army or the other would surely attack; they could not stand still indefinitely. One morning things became very lively at Battery Semmes. A rifled gun in my division exploded and an eight-inch smooth-bore was dismounted by a well-directed shot from Signal Hill. About noon my commander sent for me and, to my amazement, ordered me to go up to Richmond and report in person to the Secretary of the Navy, adding that I had better take my belongings with me. I at once began to think of all my sins of commission and omission. What could a Secretary of the Navy want to see a passed midshipman for unless it was to give him a reprimand? Arriving in Richmond, I made my way to the Navy Department at once, and, to my surprise, I was shown into the Secretary's sanctum without delay. Mr. Mallory, instead of receiving me with a frown, was smiling, and if I had not been a midshipman I should really have thought he was glad to see me. To my surprise he told me that I was to accompany Mrs. Jefferson Davis south, and added, with a merry twinkle in his eyes, that the daughters

184

of the Secretary of the Treasury were to be of the party. I hurried to Mr. Trenholm's house with the news, but no one there seemed at all surprised. I then went to the President's mansion, which was only a block away, and had a few words with Mrs. Davis, who seemed to take it as a matter of course that I was to go south with her. There was not the slightest appearance of excitement or preparation for a long journey about the Confederate executive mansion, and no one would ever have dreamed that a flight from a doomed city was about to take place.

Returning to Mr. Trenholm's house, I dined with the family and we laughed and talked; but none of us spoke of the coming journey. In fact we young people were in blissful ignorance concerning the momentous events about to take place. After all, there was nothing extraordinary about Mrs. Davis's going south, for the President had frequently expressed a desire to have his family go to Charlotte, North Carolina, where they would be out of the turmoil and excitement of their surroundings in Richmond. So far as I was personally concerned, I took it for granted that I should return to the front after I had fulfilled my mission of accompanying the party to their destination.

It was then the Friday preceding the fall of Richmond, and about eight o'clock in the evening we received the expected word that it was time for us to start for the station. A few minutes after we arrived there we were joined by Mrs. Davis, her sister, and the children, escorted by Colonel Burton N. Harrison, the President's private secretary. The party arrived at the station in an overloaded carriage, Mrs. Davis being the fortunate possessor of about the only pair of carriage horses in Richmond. These animals had made some lucky escapes from being requisitioned for the army, as, owing to the necessities of the family, they had once been sold and had been bought by two or three gentlemen and presented again to Mrs. Davis, only to be seized shortly afterwards by a provost guard on the street while Mrs. Davis was seated in the vehicle. President Davis would not lift a finger to save them, saying that other people's horses had been pressed for service in the army, and he did not see any reason why his wife's should not be taken in the same way. But again influential friends persuaded the quartermaster to send them back, and their last service to their mistress was to start her on that memorable and eventful journey.

There were no Pullman sleeping-coaches in those days, and it was with great difficulty that an old creaky passenger car, long a stranger to paint and varnish, had been secured for the wife of the chief magistrate of a nation of some fifteen or twenty million of people. We at once entered the car and seated ourselves on the lumpy seats which were covered with dingy and threadbare brownish red plush, very suggestive of the vermin with which it afterwards proved to be infested. The sleepy little children were laid on the seats and made as comfortable as possible under the circumstances, but they had hardly closed their eyes before President Davis entered the car. He spoke to us all pleasantly and cheerfully, then took a seat beside his wife and entered into conversation with her. They talked earnestly until the signal for our departure was sounded, but in those days the trains were not run by schedule. You started when the train moved and you arrived when you got to your destination; that was all anybody knew about it. Mr. Davis rose from his seat at the sound of the bell and went from one to the other of his children kissing them good-bye; then he bade farewell to his sister-in-law, Miss Maggie Howell, and affectionately embraced his wife. Passing the seats where sat the Misses Trenholm and myself, he gave us all a friendly handshake and wished us bon voyage. He then stepped on to the platform closely followed by Colonel Harrison. The signal to start was one of many false alarms, and the President and his secretary walked up and down on the platform outside, while engaged in what appeared to us onlookers very serious conversation.

It was ten o'clock before our wheezy and feeble locomotive gave a screech and a jerk which started us on our journey. Colonel Harrison precipitately left his chief and jumped on board the moving train while the President waved a second farewell to his loved ones.[1] We proceeded at a snail's pace for about twelve miles when suddenly we came to a standstill. Our ramshackle locomotive had balked; no amount of persuasion on the part of the engineer could induce it to haul us over a slight up-grade, and we remained where we were for the rest of the night. It was the afternoon of the next day when we arrived at Burkesville Junction, where Colonel Harrison received the news of the battle between Generals Pickett and Sheridan and telegraphed the information at once to President Davis.[2]

We did not reach Charlotte until Tuesday; a journey which today requires only six or seven hours, had taken us four days to accomplish! There was a delay of two or three hours at Charlotte and, while waiting, Colonel Harrison used the time to go into the city in search of shelter for Mrs. Davis and her helpless family. The inhabitants, however, did not rush forward to offer this lady in distress hospitality as they might have done a year or two before misfortune had overtaken her. They seemed to take it for granted that the end of the Confederacy was at hand, although the news of the fall of Richmond did not reach them until two days after our arrival. Mrs. Davis would have been in a sad plight if it had not been for the courage and chivalric courtesy of a Jewish gentleman, a Mr. Weil, who hospitably invited her to stay at his home until she could make other arrangements. May the God of

Abraham, Isaac, and Jacob bless him wherever he is! The news of Mrs. Davis's arrival in Charlotte quickly spread through the city, which by that time was thronged with stragglers and deserters—conscripts—the very scum of the army, and a mob of these wretches gathered round the car in which she sat. The wretches reviled her in most shocking language. Colonel Harrison, who had returned from his quest for lodgings, and I closed the open windows of the car so that the ladies could not hear what was being said. We two men were helpless to protect them from the epithets of a crowd of some seventy-five or a hundred blackguards, but we stationed ourselves at the only door which was not locked, determined that they should not enter the car. Colonel Harrison was unarmed, and I had only my sword, and a regulation revolver in the holster hanging from my belt. Several of the most daring of the brutes climbed up the steps, but when Colonel Harrison firmly told them that he would not permit them to enter that car the cowards slunk away. When the disturbance had quieted down Mrs. Davis, her sister, and her children left the train, and with the daughters of Mr. Trenholm I continued on to Abbeville, South Carolina, where the Trenholms had previously engaged a pleasant house. It took us two more days to reach Abbeville, and it was not until our arrival there that we learned of the fall of Richmond and that President Davis and his Cabinet were at Danville, Virginia.[3]

Mrs. Davis remained for a few days in Charlotte, and then it was reported that General Sherman's army was headed that way. It was necessary for her to seek some haven of safety. She was indeed in a forlorn position, as nobody wished to shelter her for fear that the Union troops would destroy their homes if they did. Every road through the country was infested by deserters who would have given her scant consideration if they had wanted anything she possessed, and the only human being she could look to for protection was Colonel Harrison, who would have stood small chance of defending her against the bands of undisciplined shirkers who were traversing the country and who never hesitated to take what they wanted from the weak and helpless. Just as things looked most hopeless to this unhappy lady, the midshipmen from the schoolship *Patrick Henry*, under the command of Lieutenant William H. Parker, arrived in Charlotte. When Richmond was ordered to be evacuated the authorities almost forgot the midshipmen, and it was only at the last moment that Lieutenant Parker received the order to blow up the "school" and make the best of his way to Charlotte, North Carolina. The midshipmen were landed on the river-bank and as they trudged toward Richmond they were saluted by the explosions of the magazines not only of their own ship, but also of those of the Confederate ironclads and wooden gunboats.

When they arrived at the railway station at Manchester, across the river from Richmond, they found not only that the soldiers had left, but also that no arrangements had been made for their transportation. Here a piece of good luck came their way. The Treasury officials, with some five hundred thousand dollars in gold and silver coin (all that the Confederacy possessed) packed in kegs, were standing helplessly on the platform alongside of a train on which they hoped to get away, while a drunken mob was fast gathering around them. Hundreds of barrels of whiskey had been stove in and their contents had filled the gutters in Richmond, and this crowd of swine, after filling themselves with the fiery liquor out of the ditches, became very brave, and determined to divide the assets of the Confederacy among themselves. The Treasury officials rather doubtfully asked Lieutenant Parker if he could protect the treasure, and when the little midshipmen were formed the mob commenced to jeer the children. But something happened!—and before those ruffians realized it, they were all on the outside. Those midshipmen were regulars, and the mob instantly appreciated the fact that the guns and bayonets in the hands of those youngsters were going to be used at the word of command, and the scoundrels were not so drunk that they did not appreciate the fact that "discretion was the better part of valor," and they fled.

The Treasury men were so impressed by the easy way in which the midshipmen had handled the situation that they begged Lieutenant Parker to accompany the specie with his command; the money was loaded on the train and the midshipmen piled in after it, and thus it was that they arrived at Charlotte.

The little command only had a short breathing spell at Charlotte, as the enemy were fast approaching and there was little time for them left in which to make a "get away." Lieutenant Parker persuaded Mrs. Davis to trust herself to the protection of the midshipmen, and they again started on their sad and painful journey. The railways by this time were completely disorganized and they could only proceed as far as Chester, South Carolina, in the cars. There Lieutenant Parker commandeered some wagons which he loaded with the gold and Mrs. Davis and her family. They then started over the rough country roads for Abbeville, South Carolina.

What a distressing spectacle this train of three or four wagons, hauled by broken-down and leg-weary mules, must have presented, and what must have been the apprehensions of that stately and serene woman, the wife of the President of a nation of Anglo-Saxons, as she sat, surrounded by her helpless children, on one of these primitive vehicles while the half-starved animals slowly dragged her over the weary miles. A platoon of the middies marched in front of the singular procession, acting as an advance guard. Another detachment followed the wagons, serving as a rear guard, and on either side of the train marched the rest of the youngsters. And not far away, on either flank and in their rear, hovered deserters waiting either for an opportunity or the necessary courage to pounce upon the, to them, untold wealth which those wagons contained.[4]

When night fell on the first day of their march, they stopped at a country roadside church which at least afforded shelter from the elements. Mrs. Davis, her sister, and the children slept on the bare floor, and Lieutenant Parker, as commanding officer, rested in the pulpit. The midshipmen who were not on guard duty lay down under the trees outside, in company with the mules.

While Mrs. Davis and her escort of ragged boys were slowly plodding on their way, things began to happen in the beautiful village of Abbeville, where every residence was surrounded by a garden and which impressed one as a more fitting setting for a May-day festival than for the scene of the disruption of a government. First, Senator Wigfall, the man who had received the surrender of Major Anderson's sword at Fort Sumter, arrived. He was the most malignant and unrelenting of all President Davis's political enemies. Before making Texas his home he had been a resident of Abbeville, and he at once went to the house of Mr. Armisted Burt, an old friend, to ask for hospitality. Now it so happened that Mr. Burt had found means to send a message to Mr. Davis asking him, if he passed through Abbeville, to make his, Mr. Burt's house, his home. In less than forty-eight hours after Mr. Wigfall's arrival, who should appear at the house but Mr. Davis! Mr. Burt was placed in a most embarrassing position for a few moments, but Mr. Wigfall relieved the tension of the situation by hastily taking his departure out of one door as Mr. Davis entered the other.

The next distinguished persons to arrive were President Davis's Cabinet, in an ambulance, with the exception of Mr. Trenholm, and the Secretary of War, General Breckinridge, who preferred to ride on horseback. He made a great impression on me with his superb figure mounted on a large and fat charger, a rare sight in those days. The Cabinet camped in and around their ambulance which had stopped in the suburbs. I visited their camp and was somewhat surprised to see among these serious and care-worn-looking gentlemen the beaming smile on the round face of the rotund Secretary of State, Mr. Judah P. Benjamin. He was the picture of amiability and contentment. Mr. Trenholm, who had been taken seriously ill on the journey from Danville, had been left at a house on the road. Mr. Trenholm afterwards told me that Mr. Benjamin, up to the time he had left them, had been the life of the party with his wonderful fund of anecdotes which continuously rippled from his mouth during the daytime, and when the shades of evening fell, and a more serious mood came over him, he would hold his small but distinguished audience spellbound by repeating poetry from the apparently exhaustless storehouse of his memory. Mr. Trenholm also told me that he felt certain that Mr. Benjamin had at the time secreted in his valise (which was a sort of Aladdin's lamp from which he could instantly produce anything that was needed) a complete disguise with which he intended to make his escape from his pursuers—and such indeed proved to be the fact.[5] Throughout this whole trying journey Mr. Benjamin smoked most fragrant Havana cigars, much to the astonishment of his companions who wondered where he could have obtained such an unlimited supply of such a rare luxury.

Then Mrs. Davis arrived with her ragged and mud-stained escort, most of whom by this time were walking on their "uppers," or the bare soles of their poor bruised feet. On arriving at Mr. Burt's house she expressed to her host a fear that his home would be destroyed by the Union troops when they learned that she had been sheltered there. The grand old Southern aristocrat made her a profound bow and replied, "Madam, I know of no better use my house could be put to than to be burned for such a cause."

One of Mrs. Davis's children was quite ill, and it was sent over to the Trenholms' house where it could be made more comfortable, as Mr. Burt's home was crowded with guests.

The midshipmen pushed on to Augusta, Georgia, some eighty miles away, seeking for a safe place to deposit the treasure, and on their arrival were told to get out of there as quickly as possible, as Sherman's men were expected at any moment; so back they trudged to Abbeville where the Secretary of the Navy ordered them to be disbanded. These boys, averaging between fourteen and eighteen years of age, some of them nearly a thousand miles from their homes, the railroads destroyed, and the country filled with lawless men, were turned loose to shift for themselves. The money was turned over to the care of the soldiers. They took such care of it that unto this day never a dollar of it has been traced! The lie that was circulated about Mr. Davis having got any of it was afterwards disproved by the poverty in which he and his wife lived and died.

While Mr. Davis was at Abbeville a very unpleasant incident took place which those who were present and afterwards wrote accounts of his flight from Richmond have avoided mentioning, I suppose because it was not to the credit of some of the Confederate soldiers. In the mountains of North and South Carolina near the Tennessee line there were bands of bandits who called themselves "guerrillas." A false report reached Mr. Davis to the effect that these brigands, learning that a large amount of gold was being taken through the country protected only by a few little boys, had made a sudden descent from their mountain fastnesses and were rapidly approaching Abbeville. On receiving this report Mr. Davis mounted his horse and rode out to a camp where some of the soldiers were bivouacked. The soldiers were drawn up to receive him and he made them a short address—very short. He told them of the report about the guerrillas, and also told them that both General Sherman and General Johnston attacked this band wherever they found them on account of the many atrocities they had been guilty of against both Union men and Confederates, and wound up his talk by asking the men if they would go out with him to attack those robbers and murderers. As he paused for a reply, a private pushed his horse to the front and said: "Our lives are just as precious to us as yours is to you. The war is over and we are going home!" And without the slightest semblance of order the gang—I can call them nothing else— dispersed, leaving those few gallant and loyal fellows who accompanied Mr. Davis until he was captured.

Twenty-eight

President Davis departs from Abbeville—I carry a communication to General Fry at Augusta, Georgia—United States troops occupy Abbeville—We bury the silver chests—Paroled at Washington, Georgia—Accompany Mr. Trenholm to Columbia, where he buys a home—Mr. Wagner, of Fraser, Trenholm & Co., pays to avoid arrest in Charleston, and Mr. Trenholm is arrested in Columbia—Placed in the common jail—Mr. King hides the gold under the Federal commander's nose—General Gillmore, U.S.A., treats Mr. Trenholm magnanimously.

Before Mr. Davis left Abbeville I begged him to allow me to accompany him, but he told me that it would be impossible, as I had no horse, and that it was not in his power to procure me one. He spoke to me in the most fatherly way, saying that as soon as things quieted down somewhat I must make my way to the trans-Mississippi, where we still had an army and two or three small gunboats on the Red River, and in the meantime he would give me a letter to General Fry, commanding at Augusta, asking him to attach me temporarily to his staff. He also gave me an official communication for General Fry and instructed me to try and get transportation by some wagon going in that direction.

I watched Mr. Davis as he mounted his horse, bade him good-bye, and stood looking after him as he took the road which led to Washington, Georgia. That was the last time I ever saw him.[1]

192

Hearing of a farmer who had an old broken-kneed, spavined white horse hid in the swamp, I soon made a deal with him by which I became the owner of the equine frame and he the possessor of several thousand dollars in Confederate money which he believed some day in the vague future would have a value. I then went to Augusta, and when I gave General Fry the document Mr. Davis had entrusted me with (the contents of which I never learned) I believe I delivered the last official communication President Davis ever sent to a general of the Confederate Army.

In Augusta I remained only two or three days. Everyone realized that the end of the Confederacy had come so far as they were concerned, and people were flying from the city not knowing where they were going—only anxious to escape from the place they were in.

General Fry advised me to return to Abbeville, as I had friends there, and being of no possible use where I was, I accepted his kindly counsel and returned.

The soldiers who had accompanied Mr. Davis had not surrendered at Appomattox, but now there was a stream of paroled men, and men who had deserted before the end came in Virginia, passing through the once peaceful town. While these men committed no outrages when they went into a private house to ask for food or shelter, they adopted a threatening attitude which was very offensive. Fortunately a younger brother of Mrs. William L. Trenholm, a lieutenant in the South Carolina regulars, arrived, and while we could not prevent the crowds of hungry men from swarming over the lower floors of the house, where although not invited, they made themselves very much at home, we could and did keep them from invading the upper portion of the home where the ladies secluded themselves.

When the danger from our own men had passed, owing to their hurried exit from the town, we had immediately to prepare for another. Sherman's men were very near and were fast approaching, and the inhabitants were in mortal terror of the lawless crew known as "Sherman's bummers," who rode on the flanks of his army, accounts of whose fiendish outrages were on every tongue.

While we noticed no change in the demeanor of the slaves, still we had no means of knowing what their attitude would be when the Union troops entered the place, and this uncertainty caused us some anxiety.

In the house were two large and very heavy chests of silver which Lieutenant Macbeth (Mrs. W. L. Trenholm's brother) and I determined to attempt to save by burying it. We were afraid to take any of the Negroes into our confidence, so we determined to do the work ourselves. We waited until midnight when everyone on the premises was supposed to be asleep, and then, carrying our spades, we stealthily stole into the garden and proceeded to dig two large graves. The night was well suited for our work, as there was a moon but it was somewhat obscured by clouds. When we had finished our task we entered the house and by great exertion managed to carry out the chests and bury them. As soon as they were covered with earth, it was evident, even in the dark, that the newly upturned ground would betray us. There was nothing left to do but to dig up the entire garden if our hiding-place was not to attract the attention of the first passer-by, and this we at once proceeded to do. It was no light job, as the garden must have comprised nearly an eighth of an acre, and daylight came while the task was still uncompleted. I suddenly looked up from my work and there, to my consternation, I saw "Nat," Mrs. Trenholm's butler, the slave whose loyalty to the family we had grave doubts about, leaning against the fence, on the top of which his arms were resting while he calmly watched what we were doing. I asked him how long he had been there, and he frankly replied: "I'se been here ever since you gentlemen started work." I then asked him why he had not offered to help us, and he said it was because he thought we did not want anyone to know what we were doing. Naturally it was too late to make any other disposition of the silver, and we felt sure that it would be lost. That morning the advance guard of the Federals entered the village. Two or three soldiers came to the house and I saw "Nat" (standing over the very spot where the silver was buried) talking to them. Of course we expected a demand would be made for spades, but, be it said to "Nat's" honor, he never betrayed us. A few years after this incident occurred, I met "Nat" in Columbia. He was then a member of the legislature and one of our lawmakers! The Union soldiers did not molest us in any way, and much to our astonishment who should drive up to the house but "Daddy" Peter, Mr. Trenholm's old Negro coachman, with the landau and its handsome pair of bays. "Daddy" Peter, on the approach of Sherman's army to Columbia, had fled to the swamp with his cherished horses and hidden them until the danger of their being seized had passed. Mr. and Mrs. George Trenholm next arrived, Mr. Trenholm being still quite ill. Nobody seemed disposed to molest him, although the Federal authorities knew of his presence in the town.

Major Julian Mitchel unexpectedly arrived at the house and informed us that all Confederate officers who had not been paroled were being arrested and treated with a great deal of harshness. As there was no officer of the United States Army authorized to parole us nearer than Washington, Georgia, forty miles away, Colonel Trenholm, Major Mitchel, and myself got into Mr. Trenholm's carriage at daylight the next morning and drove to Washington, Georgia, where we were most affably received by Captain Lott Abraham, U.S.A., who took our paroles and gave us each, for our own protection, a certificate that we had been paroled.

In the evening Major Mitchel went to call on friends who resided in the town, and Colonel Trenholm and I paid a visit at the house of Judge Andrews, one of the most prominent residents of the place, and a consistent Union man, although his whole family were ardent "rebs." One of the judge's daughters, Miss Eliza Frances Andrews, kept a diary in those days which was afterwards published in 1911 under the tide of "Wartime Journal of a Georgia Girl," and in it she makes the following mention of our visit:—

May 16, 1865—Two delightful visitors after tea, Colonel Trenholm (son of the Secretary of the Treasury) and Mr. Morgan, of the navy, who is to marry his sister.

The news this evening is that we have all got to take the oath of allegiance before getting married. This horrid law aroused much talk in our rebellious circle, and the gentlemen laughed very much when Cora said, "Talk about dying for your country, but what is that to being an old maid for it?"

The chief thought of our men is how to embroil the United States either in foreign or internal commotions, so that we can rebel again. They all say that if the Yankees had given us any sort of tolerable terms they would submit quietly, though unwillingly, to the inevitable; but if they carry out the abominable programme of which flying rumors reach us, extermination itself will be better than submission. Garnett says that if it comes to the worst, he can turn bushwhacker; and we all came to the conclusion that if this kind of peace continues, bushwhacking will be the most respectable occupation a man can engage in. Mr. Morgan said, with a lugubrious smile, that his "most ambitious hope now is to get himself hanged as quickly as possible."

Possibly, if Miss Andrews had ever read President Lincoln's Proclamation ordering all persons who had engaged in preying on American commerce, when captured, to be treated as pirates, she would not have thought that remark so amusing. It was fortunate for me that none of the Federal officers in the neighborhood knew that I had been engaged in that business. As it was, when the amnesty proclamation was issued, I found myself excepted under three separate headings, namely: Having been at the United States Military or Naval Academy— being worth more than twenty thousand dollars—and having preyed on American commerce.

In Abbeville provisions were very scarce, and the farmers who did have a few vegetables and chickens, of course would not part with them for worthless Confederate money. Probably the only gold in the place was in Mr. Trenholm's house, and there was not a coin in the lot of less value than a twenty-dollar gold-piece, and of course nobody could change such a sum as that. But fortunately the family owned stock in the Graniteville Mills, which manufactory declared dividends in cotton cloth. Mr. Alexander Macbeth and I would take a bolt of this cloth, and put it into the carriage and drive into the country away off the usual routes of travel, stopping at farmhouses, where we had no difficulty in exchanging a few yards of it for anything in the way of edibles the farmers possessed. Mr. Macbeth afterwards married Miss Eliza, one of Mr. Trenholm's daughters.

The United States Army officers stationed at Abbeville showed no disposition to molest Mr. Trenholm, and their ignoring of his presence there lulled us into a false feeling of security concerning the Government's intentions concerning him, from which we were later to have a rude awakening.

The house in Abbeville was small for such a large family, and with the idea of giving young Mrs. Trenholm and her little children more room, Mr. Trenholm decided to go to Columbia to see if he could not get a more commodious house. Mr. Trenholm's beautiful villa in the suburbs had been destroyed when Columbia was burned, but there were still left in the city a few residences forming a sort of fringe around the outskirts of the once beautiful little city.

With two portmanteaus, one of which contained a large sum of gold, Mr. Trenholm and I entered his carriage soon after dark and started on the long drive to Columbia. We were compelled to go by carriage, as the railroads had been destroyed, the fat-pine cross-ties burned to heat the rails, and the red-hot rails wrapped around the trees growing near the track. We used to call these iron rails "Sherman's neckties," and the solemn-looking chimneys standing guard over the former sites of once happy homes were called by the natives "Sherman's monuments."

Arriving at Columbia we were hospitably entertained by Mr. William Ford De Saussure, who was then living in the residence formerly occupied by the president of the South Carolina College and which stands to this day on the college campus. Mr. DeSaussure's home had shared the fate of most of the houses of the city during the conflagration.

It was found impossible to rent a house, but Mr. Trenholm was fortunate enough to find a gentleman who was anxious to sell his home, a large and comfortable one, for gold, as he wished to leave the State. The people had not as yet become accustomed to the greenback currency of their conquerors and looked askance at it. The house was bought, and the family moved to Columbia where they lived for some weeks in peace and comfort until an unfortunate episode occurred in Charleston.

Mr. Theodore Wagner, who was one of Mr. Trenholm's partners, and whose first wife was a sister of Mr. Trenholm, was a most generous man who wore his purse on his sleeve at the service of any who cared to use it. He was also a highly nervous and timid man. Learning of the reputation he had for wealth and timidity, the provost marshal of Charleston sent one of his employees with a message to the effect that he was going to arrest Mr. Wagner on the charge of treason, and the agent confidentially informed the unhappy gentleman that he, the agent, had great influence with the provost marshal and that for a trifling sum of ten thousand dollars judiciously used he thought he could save Mr. Wagner from the ignominy and discomfort incidental to a long sojourn in a dirty jail, as well as an expensive trial for treason, a crime the punishment for which was death. Badly frightened, Mr. Wagner hurriedly produced the money, and was left in peace.

Laughing in their sleeves, the officials decided that if a junior member of the firm of Fraser, Trenholm & Co. could be so easily separated from such a large sum of money, untold wealth might be obtained from the head of the house, especially as that head had been a member of Jefferson Davis's Cabinet. So one sad day the colonel in command at Columbia sent for Mr. Trenholm and told the old gentleman that he regretted to say that he had received orders from the commanding officer at Charleston to arrest him and send him forthwith to that city. The colonel was very courteous and told Mr. Trenholm that if he would give his word to report to the commanding general in Charleston without delay, he (the colonel) would not place him under restraint or send him there under guard. Mr. Trenholm thanked him for his consideration and of course gladly gave the required promise.

That night Mr. Trenholm and I, carrying two portmanteaus, in one of which he had placed a very large sum in twenty-dollar goldpieces, entered his carriage and we drove to Orangeburg, about forty miles away where we could take a train, as the railway between Orangeburg and Charleston had not been destroyed. When we arrived at the station in Charleston we were shocked at seeing a company of Negro soldiers drawn up on the platform waiting for Mr. Trenholm. As the train came to a stop the white captain of the colored company boarded the car and walking brusquely up to the old white-haired gentleman demanded to know if his name was Trenholm. On being answered in the affirmative, he ordered Mr. Trenholm to come with him. I followed Mr. Trenholm closely, and when we stepped on to the platform the officer demanded to know who I was, and Mr. Trenholm assured him I was only a young friend of his who had accompanied him on the journey from Columbia, but the satrap was taking no chances, and as the soldiers closed in around us, he ordered me to "fall in," telling me I could explain at the jail. This was indeed a shock, as I had thought that of course a man of Mr. Trenholm's position would first be taken before the commanding general. It was a long and rough march over the rough cobblestones on some streets and through the mud of those which were not paved. There were Negro soldiers in front of us and on either side, and behind us. One would have imagined that we were two desperate criminals from the way all possible escape was guarded against. Arriving at the jail, I of course followed, or attempted to follow, Mr. Trenholm through the door, as I took it for granted I was expected to do, but a gruff voice called out, "Stop that man!" and instantly a brutal Negro soldier reversed his musket and with the butt struck me a fearful blow in the pit of my stomach. I staggered across the sidewalk and sat down on the curb where in my agony I vomited blood. Had I been an injured dog less notice could not have been taken of me than was shown by the Negro soldiers. After sitting with my feet in the gutter for some time, with a great effort, I stood up, and as no one objected I staggered away from the accursed place. I had been warned not to go near Mr. Wagner's house for fear of complications; it was therefore necessary for me to find a place where I could stay, and after a long and weary walk I saw a sign in a window in Calhoun Street announcing "Rooms for Rent." I engaged a room on condition that I would produce my baggage before I occupied it, and having Mr. Trenholm's checks and keys for his baggage, after a short rest I started out again to walk to the station to get the two heavy portmanteaus. There were no cabs in the place, so I hired a man with a wheelbarrow, and placing the portmanteaus on it I trudged alongside until they were unloaded at my new place of abode. I did not know the people who lived in the house and I was afraid to leave the room while all that gold was in one of the frail pieces of luggage. I felt sick and weary and had no appetite, so I was well content to go supperless to bed.

The next morning I had to take chances and go out, for two reasons, first, because it was necessary for me to get some information as to how I could manage to see Mr. Trenholm, and secondly, on account of the fact that the people of the house declined to furnish me with meals. I started out with the intention of trying to find some officer of the regular army, as I felt assured that when I told such a one that I only wanted to talk to Mr. Trenholm about private family affairs he would assist me. But I was even more fortunate than I had dared to hope, I ran into the arms of a naval ensign who had been a classmate and captain of my gun's crew on the old frigate *Constitution* when I was a midshipman at Annapolis! He was a big fellow by the name of Dichman and he was then on the admiral's staff. As he threw his arms around me he exclaimed, "Well, Little Morgan, I have caught you at last! What can I do for you?" I told him of my trouble and how necessary it was for me to see my friend, who was in the jail, and he said he thought he could manage it for me, and he did.

When I entered the jail with my permit I found Mr. Trenholm confined in a felon's cell which had only lately been vacated by a convicted murderer who had been released when the general jail delivery took place on the fall of Charleston. The only thing Mr. Trenholm had to sleep on was the dirty straw this wretch had left behind him.

While I was in the cell the door was left open and the sentry paced up and down in the corridor. Mr. Trenholm found occasion to whisper to me quickly that he wanted me to find Mrs. Henry King and ask her to take charge of the gold and keep it safely for him. Mr. Trenholm was the trustee of Mrs. King's small estate; he had been a friend of her father, Mr. James L. Pettigrew, a lawyer of national reputation, and a famous wit. Mr. Pettigrew had been a consistent Union man. He had died during the war, and among his friends, when living, he had numbered Abraham Lincoln, President of the United States, and when Charleston was captured Mr. Lincoln had instructed the military and naval authorities in the city to afford Mr. Pettigrew's family every protection and to show them every attention.

Mrs. King was a young and beautiful widow; also an authoress of some local renown; but she was more famed for her powers of witty repartee than she was for either her beauty, which was great, or her literary efforts. It was of this lady that the story was told about the novelist Thackeray. When he visited America, and was presented to her, he boorishly said, "I am glad to meet you Mrs. King, for I have heard that you are the fastest lady received in society in Charleston," and Mrs. King replied, "I also heard that you were a gentleman—we have both been misinformed!"

It was nearly nine o'clock at night when I found Mrs. King's house and sent in my name, as I had no card. The servant left the front door open and I could plainly see in the brightly lighted parlor a number of army and navy officers in their blue uniforms. Suddenly there appeared in the hall a vision of loveliness in a white muslin dress who asked in a soft and musical voice what my business was. I told her, in almost a whisper, that I had come from Mr. Trenholm with a request, and she hastily put her forefinger to her pretty lips and made a sign to follow her. She led me to the end of the hall, and there I whispered to her what Mr. Trenholm wanted her to do, and she told me at once to go and get the gold and bring it to her. She seemed somewhat surprised when I told her it was heavy and that as it would not be safe for any one to walk through the streets at that hour with a valise, as there were no policemen and outrages were occurring every night, I would have to bring it in my pockets and make several trips before I could deliver it all into her keeping.

In about half an hour I returned to the house and the manservant who received me, chuckling with laughter for some reason, showed me the way to the back door where I waited for a moment while Mrs. King excused herself to her guests before coming to meet me. She led the way upstairs to her bedroom, and directing me to help her we pulled off the coverings of a bed that was dainty enough to be the resting-place of a fairy. We then rolled back the upper mattress and I began to unload the yellow double eagles. The breast and tail pockets of my coat were filled with the handsome coins, as also were my vest pockets, my trousers and hip-pockets, and while I was thus engaged the beautiful lady, standing on the opposite side of the bed, was engaged in spreading them over the lower mattress. We then replaced the upper mattress, and I could not help but laugh when I realized the extraordinary situation in which I found myself, assisting a strange lady in the making-up of her bed! Mrs. King was laughing, too, but for a different reason. Her cause of merriment was so good that she could not keep it to herself. Everybody knew that Mr. Wagner had paid ten thousand dollars to keep from being arrested when nobody had any intention of arresting him, and Mrs. King's joke was that the provost marshal, who had scared Mr. Wagner out of the money, and the commanding general, were both present among her guests downstairs.

It was late when I finished my last trip and had assisted Mrs. King in secreting the last coin, and her other guests had long since taken their departure. Mrs. King informed me that she had utilized one of my temporary absences by cajoling the commanding officer into giving her a permit to visit Mr. Trenholm in the jail, and she appeared there early the next morning.

The day after Mr. Trenholm was incarcerated, the commanding general sent a carriage to the jail, and Mr. Trenholm, accompanied this time by a white officer, was placed in it and driven to headquarters. The general received him in his private office, and at first was very courteous, but changed his attitude before the interview closed. Mr. Trenholm told me that the first thing the general said to him was, "Mr. Trenholm, I suppose that you know you were arrested by my orders and that I am the only man who can release you." Mr. Trenholm said that he replied, "I am very sorry to hear you say that." And on being asked by the general why he was sorry, Mr. Trenholm told him that it was because he now realized that it would be useless for him to hope to be set free, for he said to the general, "If you had any intention to free me without the payment of money, you would never have had me arrested and as I regard it as disgraceful to offer a bribe as to accept one, I do not propose to part with a cent for the purpose of obtaining my freedom!" The general touched a bell, the door was opened, an orderly saluted, and the general commanded that the guard appear, and Mr. Trenholm was returned to the jail—but not in a carriage. A corporal's guard of Negro soldiers marched him there.

My permit to visit Mr. Trenholm still held good and I went to the jail every day and several times saw Mrs. King there—the gay and *debonnaire* Mrs. King, sitting on the dirty straw softly crying while the courtly old prisoner tried to comfort her. One would have imagined that it was the woman who was held in durance vile instead of her tall and stately trustee with his handsome face and white hair. I was not allowed to take anything into the jail for my friend, but Mrs. King was "a duchess who could do as she chooses," and took him many little comforts.

After Mr. Trenholm had been in jail for several days I was informed that he was to be sent to Hilton Head on Port Royal, where there was a large garrison stationed at the time. One of my naval officer friends kindly interested himself and got me a permit to go to Hilton Head on the same boat that was to take Mr. Trenholm there. I did not trust myself to go to the jail on the day of his departure, but went on board of the boat and waited for him there. When he appeared he was as usual surrounded by his Negro guard. This was an intentional humiliation, as there were large numbers of white soldiers in Charleston, and in addition to the Negroes a company of whites was stationed at the jail. When the boat started, Mr. Trenholm was allowed to sit on a bench on the upper deck and I was permitted to take a seat beside him, and the moment I did so a Negro soldier seated himself on the other side of him.

Arriving at Hilton Head we waited on the boat for some little time while an officer went ashore, probably to find out what disposition was to be made of his prisoner, for as soon as he returned he ordered Mr. Trenholm to be brought ashore, and then accompanied by the guard we marched to a neat-looking cottage occupied by General Gillmore as his headquarters. As we halted in front of the cottage a splendid, soldierly-looking man, came out, and extending both hands to Mr. Trenholm, exclaimed, "My dear sir, I am distressed to see you in this position. What can have brought you here?" Mr. Trenholm explained and added that he regretted very much that their very pleasant acquaintance of some years past, when General Gillmore had been stationed at Charleston, should be renewed under, to him, such humiliating circumstances. General Gillmore ordered the guard dismissed and invited the prisoner into his house where he offered us refreshments.

As near as I can remember, General Gillmore said to Mr. Trenholm: "I can see no reason for your arrest at this time. You could not escape even if you wanted to. You had better go back to your home. The boat you came on returns within the hour. You had better, however, give me your written parole that you will come back whenever I send for you." In less than an hour we were on our way home, free men, and without a guard!

General Gillmore's courtesy and consideration for an antebellum friend cost him dear. The general in command at Charleston resented his action in freeing Mr. Trenholm, and reported the matter to Washington, with the result that General Gillmore was relieved of the command at Hilton Head, and the sequel of his kind action was hardly less serious for Mr. Trenholm, as he had hardly got home before an order came from Washington to rearrest him and imprison him in Fort Pulaski below Savannah, Georgia.[2]

Epilogue

Morgan continues to chronicle his life's story in the second half of his book, *Recollections of a Rebel Reefer.* By the time the manuscript was begun, Morgan was approaching seventy years of age. While recollections of his experiences during the War Between the States are clear and accurate, (Morgan may have kept a journal of his wartime experiences) his remembrance of events later in life are not as concise and factual. Morgan's family, even to this day, can remember stories of Jimmy's propensity for getting into trouble. While a gracious and kind-hearted soul, who was known as the "Grand Old Man" of the family, he was also a tough fellow who would take no guff from anyone.

He served his country well, however. Although Jimmy Morgan was not famous, he did his duty, and lived his life to the fullest. He and his family were extremely close, and the hardships that they endured during and after the war brought them only closer. By reading his "Recollections," we too can begin to feel that we know him. And it is through his words that one can gain a slight inkling of what it must have been like to have been a midshipman in gray during those memorable times.

In the October 1928 issue of the *Louisiana Historical Quarterly*, Milledge L. Bonham, Jr., recounted briefly in an article entitled, "The Rebel Reefer Furls His Last Sail," the life of the old gentleman that everyone had come to refer to as "Jimmy." An excerpt from this article describes the years following the end of the War Between the States:

After the Collapse of the Confederacy, "Jimmy" Morgan married the daughter of G. A. Trenholm, secretary of the Confederate Treasury, and went to New Orleans. Realizing the need of further education, he entered the office of his brother, Judge P. H. Morgan, and matriculated in the law school of the University of Louisiana (now Tulane University). In his words: "In that law class there was a young man by the name of Edward D. White, who afterwards became chief justice of the Supreme Court of the United States, and that was as near as I ever came to a great lawyer."

He abandoned the study of the law. Having become a father and a widower just before his twenty-first birthday, he turned to cotton planting in Louisiana, which experiment was a costly failure, due to the insect pests. In that year (1866) he received a commission as captain in the Egyptian army, being one of twenty American veterans (Union and Confederate) engaged to train the army of the Khedive Ismail. In 1872, Morgan now a lieutenant-colonel, returned to America. One of his first calls was upon a friend in New York. "While waiting for my friend to come down," he says, "I opened a Bible which was lying on a table and the first words that caught my eye was the commencement of the thirty-first chapter of Isaiah: 'Woe to them that go down in Egypt for help; and stay on horses.' This verse was so apt that I had no curiosity to read any further for fear that it might become even more personal."

Helen Trenholm, daughter of George Alfred Trenholm, was Morgan's first wife. Helen died of yellow fever less than a year after their marriage.

Courtesy of Ethel S. Nepveux

Again he tried farming, this time on a plantation of General Wade Hampton's in South Carolina. He thus witnessed the horrors of the "carpet-bag" regime in that state and saw its redemption by the Hamptonites. Contraction and engineering in Mexico next engaged his attention. Through the influence of his brother-in-law, Captain F. W. Dawson, editor of the Charleston "News and Courier," Morgan was appointed by President Cleveland as consul-general to Australia. Here he met again some of the passengers of ships he had boarded as a "Rebel Reefer."

Back in America he spent ten years farming and breeding stock in Maryland. In 1903, as the representative of a New York banking house, Morgan was sent to the Isthmus of Panama, just in time to be a witness of the birth of the Republic of Panama.

For several years before his death Colonel Morgan made his home in Washington, where he was in touch with many old friends from all over the world. From time to time he visited his relatives in Louisiana and the families of his three daughters, who lived, respectively, in South Carolina, Texas, and Pennsylvania. For some years his health had been poor, though his vitality under suffering was amazing. In January last he suffered a slight stroke, from which he seemed to be rallying nobly, so his friends were shocked at the news of his sudden death.[1]

Appendix A

James Morris Morgan - Chronology of Events from 1865 to 1927

- Morgan married Helen Trenholm, daughter of George Alfred Trenholm, in October 1865.
- Helen Morgan died of yellow fever in September 1866, 10 days after giving birth to a baby girl.
- 1869 - Devastated at the loss of his wife, Morgan tried his hand at growing cotton. Failing at this, he accepted an invitation from the Khedive, Ismail Pasha, to travel in company with 9 former Confederate and 10 former Union officers to Egypt. There he was given a commission as a lieutenant-colonel in the Egyptian Army.
- In the early 1870s, Morgan went to Paris to observe at close hand the Franco-Prussian War.
- 1872 - Resigning from the Egyptian Army, Morgan returned to America and took over the sprawling Hampton Plantation on the Congaree River, four miles below Columbia, South Carolina.
- Soon after taking over the Hampton Plantation, Morgan married Gabriella Burroughs.
- 1874 - Morgan sold the Hampton Plantation and moved to Charleston, South Carolina.
- Here he accepted a position with the Charleston *News and Courier*. Morgan's brother-in-law, Francis W. Dawson (Sarah's husband) was co-owner of the newspaper with B. R. Riordan.

- 1875 - Returned to Columbia. In this year he became active in South Carolina politics, helping to oust the Carpetbag state government. Later he became an attaché to the U.S. Senate from South Carolina.
- 1881 - Morgan left politics and joined a mining expedition to Batopilas, Mexico.
- 1883 - He returned to New York in an attempt to acquire financing for a silver mine in Mexico, which failed.
- 1884 - Employed by Charles P. Stone who was in charge of the construction of the Statue of Liberty on Bedloe's Island, New York.
- 1885 - Morgan was appointed consul-general to Australia by President Cleveland.
- 1885 - His second wife having passed away, Morgan married Frances A. Fincke, and they sailed for Australia.
- 1886 - In Australia.
- 1888 - After bringing his wife back to the states, Morgan returned to Australia alone.
- September of 1888, Morgan returned home to find his wife very ill.
- Because of his wife's illness, he resigned his position as consul-general.
- After his wife's health improved, Morgan moved his family to a Maryland farm and raised horses for the next ten years.
- 1897 - He visited Mrs. Jefferson Davis at the Girard Hotel in New York.
- Morgan accompanied her to Richmond for the dedication of the memorial window to President Davis at St. Paul's Church.
- 1898 - Morgan sold "Cedarcroft," the farm in Maryland, and moved to Washington, D.C., becoming assistant manager of the Washington branch of the International Banking Cooperation.
- 1903 - Morgan traveled to Panama to investigate investment opportunities for the bank.
- Shortly after his return from Panama, Morgan moved to Washington, D.C., where at the urging of his wife and children, he began writing his "Recollections of a Rebel Reefer."
- 1917 - Morgan's book, financed by his wife, was published.
- April 21, 1928 - James Morris Morgan, "Uncle Jimmy" to his family and all those who loved him, died in Washington, D.C.

Endnotes

INTRODUCTION

1. Charles East, *Sarah Morgan, the Civil War Diary of a Southern Women* (Athens: The University of Georgia Press, 1991), p. 37.
2. Ibid., p. 39.
3. A "reefer" is one who folds the sails of a sailing ship.

CHAPTER 3

1. Louisiana had seceded on January 26, 1861. Evidently Morgan did not resign until after the firing on Fort Sumter.

CHAPTER 6

1. Brigadier General Braxton Bragg commanded all Confederate forces from Pensacola to Mobile. Later, as a full general, he would assume command of the Army of Tennessee.
2. Captain Raphael Semmes commanded the CSS *Sumter*, in which he destroyed or bonded 18 enemy merchant vessels between July 3, 1861, and January 18, 1862.

CHAPTER 7

1. CSS *McRae*, 680-ton, single screw. Armament: one 9-inch smoothbore, six 32-pounder smoothbores, and one 6-pounder rifle.
2. Huger, who was from South Carolina, commanded the *McRae* until he was mortally wounded during the Battle of New Orleans, April 24, 1862.
3. George N. Hollins was from Maryland, and after his resignation from the U. S. Navy, he was appointed a captain in the Confederate Navy on June 22, 1861.
4. The CSS *Manassas* was constructed as a ram and intended to be a privateer. Her turtle-back shell, which acted as a deck, was covered with a one and a half-inch layer of railroad iron. She carried only one gun—an old 32-pounder mounted in the bow and designed to be fired at the moment of ramming.
5. Alexander F. Warley, from South Carolina, had resigned from the U. S. Navy on December 24, 1860, just four days after his home state had seceded from the Union.

6. The CSS *Ivy*, a former privateer, was a side-wheel steamer which had been purchased by the Confederate Navy and was armed with one 8-inch and one 32-pounder rifle. She was under the command of Lieutenant Joseph Fry. The CSS *Tuscarora*, also a side-wheeler, carried one 32-pounder and an 8-inch Columbiad. Her commander was Lieutenant Beverly Kennon. The CSS *Calhoun*, another former privateer, was a side-wheeler with a total of five light guns and commanded by Lieutenant Jonathan H. Carter. Lieutenant Washington Gwathmey commanded the side-wheel steamer CSS *Jackson* which carried two 32-pounders.

CHAPTER 8

1. Lieutenant Charles W. Read. He acquired the nickname "Savez" while at the U. S. Naval Academy at Annapolis, from which he was graduated in 1860. It was reportedly the only word of French he was able to learn.
2. Samuel P. Blanc, from Louisiana.
3. John R. Eggleston, from Virginia.
4. Henry H. Marmaduke, from Missouri.
5. John W. Dunnington, from Kentucky.
6. Sardine Graham Stone, later promoted to first lieutenant, was from Alabama.
7. John Henry Comstock killed August 5, 1864.
8. Morgan is probably confusing the name of the army commander with the fort east of the town at New Madrid, which was known as Fort Bankhead. The Confederate troops at New Madrid were commanded by Major General John P. McCown.
9. Confederate forces abandoned New Madrid on March 13, 1862.
10. Island No. 10 surrendered on April 7, 1862. Contrary to Morgan's assertion, approximately 7,000 Confederate soldiers were taken captive.
11. Brigadier General Johnson K. Duncan was from York, Pennsylvania, and commanded all Confederate land forces around New Orleans, including Forts Jackson and St. Philip.
12. The CSS *Louisiana* was never fully completed and was utilized as a floating battery at the time of Farragut's attack. As Morgan accurately describes, she had two paddlewheels, one in front of the other, mounted amidship. In addition, two propellers were mounted at the stern and driven by separate engines, but these could not be connected in time to provide the necessary motive power to enable her to attack the Union fleet.
13. Morgan is referring to the CSS *Mississippi*, a huge ironclad of 1,400 tons. She was 280 feet in length and was designed to carry 18 to 20 guns, four of which were to be 7-inch pivots. With her engines still awaiting installation, she was too heavy to be towed up the Mississippi River when the Federals attacked, and her captain, Commander Arthur Sinclair, destroyed her on April 25, 1862.
14. New Orleans surrendered on April 28, 1862.

CHAPTER 9

1. The CSS *Nashville*, a side-wheel steamer of 1,221 tons, had been fitted out as a cruiser in the summer of 1861, and on October 21, ran the blockade out of Charleston. Her commander, Lieutenant Robert B. Pegram, sailed her to England where she became the first warship to fly the Confederate flag in the English Channel. Pegram captured and burned two prizes before returning to Beaufort, North Carolina, on February 28, 1862.
2. Morgan, as well as many other writers of the era, refers to the *Virginia* by her former name while in United States service. On February 17, 1862, the former *Merrimac* was officially commissioned as the CSS *Virginia*.
3. The "two or three thousand Confederate infantrymen," referred to by Morgan, was a two-company battalion of Confederate Marines (Companies C and B) under the command of Captain John D. Simms, CSMC.
4. The Battle of Seven Pines was fought on Saturday, May 31, 1862.
5. The Confederacy led the way in the development of the marine mine, or torpedo, as it was then called. By the end of the conflict, forty-three Union ships, including four monitors,

were either sunk or severely damaged by Confederate torpedoes, and hundreds of Federal sailors had been killed. Only one Confederate warship, the ironclad CSS *Albemarle*, was sunk by a Federal torpedo.

6. The CSS *Beaufort* was actually 85 feet long and carried one 32-pounder rifle.
7. First Lieutenant William Sharp from Virginia.
8. Rocketts Landing was the steamboat landing located at the base of the bluff upon which sat the huge Chimborazo military hospital. Next to it was one of two Confederate Navy yards, the other being across the river on the Manchester side.

CHAPTER 10

1. Duncan N. Ingraham, born in Charleston, South Carolina, on December 2, 1802, he commanded the Confederate naval forces at Charleston from 1862 until the end of the war.
2. CSS *Chicora*, two 9-inch smooth-bores and four 6-inch Brooke rifles. Service Record: Defense of Charleston; attacked Federal blockading fleet, January 31, 1863; defense of Charleston forts, April 7, 1863; sunk to prevent capture prior to the fall of Charleston, February 18, 1865.
3. George Alfred Trenholm—Charleston merchant and destined to be the Confederacy's last Secretary of the Treasury. Trenholm was born in Charleston, on February 25, 1807. Following the death of his father in 1822, he was employed by John Fraser and Company, an exporting firm dealing in cotton. In 1836 he became director of the Bank of Charleston and in 1852, was elected to the South Carolina legislature. By the beginning of the war he had amassed a fortune in plantations, warehouses, ships, and investments.
4. The Le Mat revolver was the invention of Dr. Jean Alexandre Francois Le Mat, a Frenchman living in New Orleans at the outbreak of the war. The gun had a nine shot .41-caliber cylinder which revolved around a 20-gauge shotgun barrel. Unsuccessful in having the gun manufactured in the Confederacy, Le Mat traveled to Paris, where he eventually supplied approximately 3,000 revolvers for the South. The famous cavalryman, General J. E. B. Stuart, carried a Le Mat.
5. Matthew Fontaine Maury, famous scientist, and also known as the "Pathfinder of the Seas," for his many published works on wind and ocean currents.

CHAPTER 11

1. Louis M. Coxetter. As commander of the Confederate privateer *Jefferson Davis*, Coxetter captured nine prizes during seven weeks in June and July of 1861.
2. The blockade runner *Kate*, owned by the John Fraser and Company of Charleston, actually made forty trips through the Federal blockade (twenty round-trips.) She hit a snag inside the Cape Fear River bar on November 18, 1862, and was lost.
3. When 240 miles east of Havana, Confederate commissioners James Mason and John Slidell were illegally removed from the British Royal Mail steamer *Trent* on November 8, 1861, by Captain Charles Wilkes of the USS *San Jacinto*.

CHAPTER 12

1. James Dunwoody Bulloch was appointed a commander in the Confederate Navy and dispatched to Europe by Secretary Mallory early in the war to build and purchase warships for the Southern nation. Bulloch designed and arranged for the construction of two famous cruisers, the CSS *Florida* and the CSS *Alabama*. Other ships built or purchased included the CSS *Shenandoah*, the CSS *Stonewall*, and numerous blockade runners.
2. First Lieutenant John Randolph Hamilton. The CSS *Alexandra*, which was intended to be a cruiser, was completed, but she was seized by the British in April of 1863 under the Foreign Enlistment Act. After a celebrated trial, she was finally released, but was sold and modified into a blockade runner.
3. The *Phantom* would become a very successful blockade runner, making a total of nine trips through the Federal blockade before she was run aground and destroyed while trying to reach Wilmington, North Carolina, in September of 1863.

4. First Lieutenant Robert T. Chapman, First Lieutenant William E. Evans, and Second Lieutenant John H. Ingraham.
5. Maury, who would command the Confederate cruiser CSS *Georgia*, was a cousin of the famous oceanographer Matthew Fontaine Maury.

CHAPTER 13

1. John T. Walker had served on the cruiser CSS *Florida* and the ironclad CSS *Chicora* before being assigned to Europe.
2. Thomas J. Wheeden and R. W. Curtis.
3. The CSS *Georgia* was commissioned on April 9, 1863.

CHAPTER 14

1. The CSS *Florida* was illegally attacked and captured in the Brazilian port of Bahia on October 7, 1864. Towed to Hampton Roads, she was later deliberately sunk in the Chesapeake Bay to preclude having to return her to Brazil.
2. The Confederate Congress had authorized the new "second national" flag on May 1, 1863. The Confederate Navy officially adopted this design as the navy ensign on May 26, 1863.
3. On January 11, 1863, the 15 minute battle between the CSS *Alabama* and the USS *Hatteras* took place off Galveston, Texas. Although darkness had settled over the scene, and the *Hatteras* went down quickly, the entire Federal crew was rescued by the *Alabama*.

CHAPTER 15

1. The uncertainties of whether the North would be able to defeat the South and prevent her from gaining her independence, caused Northern merchants to count the bonding of their ships as a very real loss.
2. Morgan's account of the freeing of the *Good Hope* is the only known incidence where a Confederate cruiser allowed an American merchant vessel to proceed on her way. It was common throughout the war for crewmen of captured vessels to volunteer to serve on the ship that destroyed them. Merchant sailors, most of whom were foreigners, did not have a strong allegiance to any particular flag, and there was always the lure of prize money if the war should conclude successfully for the Confederacy.

CHAPTER 16

1. Morgan has confused the name of the island in the South Atlantic with that of the famous resort island in the West Indies.
2. "Stonewall" Jackson was wounded accidentally by some of his own men in the fading light of the evening on May 2, 1863, during the Battle of Chancellorsville. After having his left arm amputated, Jackson developed pneumonia and died on Sunday, May 10.

CHAPTER 17

1. On June 30, 1863, the *Alabama* captured the *Conrad* en route from Buenos Aires to New York. She was carrying a cargo of wool and goat skins which were owned by Northern merchants. Rather than destroy the speedy vessel, Semmes took possession of her and commissioned her the CSS *Tuscaloosa*. Three 12-pounders, a supply of rifles, pistols, and ammunition was transferred to the bark, and Lieutenant John Low was placed in command. Fifteen men from the *Alabama* went on board her as crew members.
2. Chapman found no command waiting for him in Europe, but instead was entrusted with the responsibility of delivering, through the blockade, the Great Seal of the Confederacy. Leaving the bulky press in the Bahamas, Chapman conveyed the seal safely to Richmond on October 4, 1864, where it now resides in the Museum of the Confederacy. Chapman later served at Battery Buchanan, Fort Fisher, North Carolina.

3. The *Vanderbilt* was built by Cornelius Vanderbilt for transatlantic passenger service. Vanderbilt donated the 3,360-ton vessel to the Federal navy, which converted her into a fast, heavily-armed cruiser.

CHAPTER 19

1. Johnson Island Prison was located on a three hundred acre island in Lake Erie, two-and-three-quarters of a mile off shore from Sandusky, Ohio. The first Confederate prisoners arrived in April of 1862, and the long Northern winters were exceedingly brutal for the Southern troops who were not accustomed to such harsh weather. Federal authorities purposely withheld food and clothing in retaliation for alleged Confederate brutality toward Federal prisoners, and as a result, many Southern soldiers perished.
2. Maury returned to the Confederacy and later commanded the ironclad CSS *North Carolina* at Wilmington.
3. The CSS *Rappahannock* was purchased in England by Commander Matthew Fontaine Maury on November 14, 1863. She was spirited out of Sheerness, England, as Morgan describes, on November 24, and received her officers on board in the English Channel. After experiencing engine trouble, she was towed to Calais, France. It was intended that she should receive her guns and equipment from the CSS *Georgia*, but French authorities, upon one pretext or another, managed to detain her until the end of the war. Consequently, the *Rappahannock* was utilized as a receiving ship, and provided quarters for the many officers assigned to Europe who were awaiting the completion of other Confederate vessels.
4. Lieutenant Charles K. King, Jr.—Lieutenant Lee's father, Commander Sidney Smith Lee (Senior), was the brother of General Robert E. Lee.

CHAPTER 20

1. Some have referred to this incident as the Confederacy's only "foreign war."

CHAPTER 21

1. The vessels Morgan describes were two French-built corvettes intended to be the CSS *Louisiana* and the CSS *Mississippi*. The builder, Lucien Arman of Bordeaux, was forced by Napoleon III to sell the vessels to Prussia in May of 1864.
2. Because of her low speed and unreliable engines, it was decided to sell the *Georgia* and Liverpool provided a better market than any port in France. In June 1864, Bulloch sold the Confederate cruiser to a group of British merchants for £15,000.
3. On August 15, 1864, in spite of her legitimate sale, the *Georgia* was captured as a prize in international waters.
4. Morgan was correct. It was not until W.W. II that the United States began to recover from the devastating destruction wrought by the Confederate cruisers.
5. An admission that the Confederate crusiers were a legitimate form of warfare would have implied a recognition of the Confederate government, and this the Lincoln administration was not willing to do.

CHAPTER 22

1. On June 19, 1864, in a battle that lasted a little over an hour, the CSS *Alabama* was sunk by the USS *Kearsarge* off Cherbourg, France.
2. Commander John McIntosh Kell, first officer on the *Alabama*, had been rescued by the English yacht *Deerhound* when the Confederate cruiser went down off Cherbourg. Kell would later command the CSS *Richmond* of the James River Squadron.
3. Edwin M. Anderson had been wounded during the engagement with the USS *Kearsarge*. Eugene Anderson Maffitt was the son of Commander John Newland Maffitt who became famous as the captain of the commerce raider CSS *Florida*. The younger Maffitt was captured on an English steamer on December 6, 1864, at Portland, Maine, and was

incarcerated at Fort Warren in Boston. It was not until January 10, 1866, months after hostilities had ended, that he was finally released.

4. First.Lieutenant Robert T. Chapman, First Lieutenant William E. Evans, First Lieutenant William P. A. Campbell, First Lieutenant John H. Ingraham, and First Lieutenant Charles K. King, Jr. Passed Midshipman John T. Walker was promoted to a second lieutenant on June 2, 1864.

5. The *Lillian* was a side-wheel steamer built in Scotland in 1864 for the Importing and Exporting Company of Georgia. Her commander on this trip , whom Morgan calls a "braggart" and a "blowhard," was a civilian captain by the name of Daniel H. Martin.

6. The *Lillian* arrived on July 30, 1864.

CHAPTER 23

1. Morgan's critical analysis of blockade running near the end of the war is incorrect. While it is possible that a few boats may have arrived without a cargo, records indicate that this was highly unlikely. It is a proven fact that the Army of Northern Virginia depended on its daily ration of beef, while pinned down in the trenches around Petersburg and Richmond, almost solely on the blockade runners arriving at Wilmington. Only a small percentage of these were government owned.

2. Frustrated with their inability to capture the South Carolina city, Federal authorities unleashed an indiscriminate bombardment of Charleston on August 22, 1863. The shelling of the beautiful Southern metropolis, along with its inhabitants, would continue for 587 days. During one nine day period in January 1864, 1,500 heavy explosive shells were fired into the city.

3. George Trenholm accepted the position of Secretary of the Treasury on July 18, 1864.

CHAPTER 24

1. The Confederate States Naval Academy was established in March of 1863, and began operations on board the CSS *Patrick Henry,* off Drewry's Bluff in the James River below Richmond, in October of that same year. Morgan's description of the school and its operation is one of the best.

2. Parker had commanded the CSS *Beaufort* during that vessel's historic engagements at Roanoke Island and in Hampton Roads, Virginia. After the war, he wrote an interesting account of his experiences entitled, *Recollections of a Naval Officer.*

3. On the night of February 1–2, 1864, the USS *Underwriter* was boarded, captured, and destroyed by a force of Confederate sailors and marines led by Commander John Taylor Wood off New Bern, North Carolina.

4. Kennon had been in command of the Louisiana State gunboat *Governor Moore* at the time of Farragut's attack on New Orleans on April 24, 1862. In cooperation with the *Stonewall Jackson*, Kennon managed to ram and sink the USS *Varuna*.

5. Fort Harrison was overrun in the early morning hours of September 29, 1864.

CHAPTER 25

1. First Lieutenant William L. Bradford.

2. The ironclad CSS *Richmond* was begun at Norfolk and launched in an unfinished state on May 6, 1862. Federal forces had forced the Confederates to evacuate Norfolk, and the *Richmond* was towed up the James River to the Richmond Navy Yard where she was completed. The *Richmond* was 172 feet in length, and her casemate was sheathed with four inches of iron plating over 22 inches of oak and pine. She mounted two 6.4-inch Brooke rifles, one 7-inch rifle, and a 10-inch smoothbore. Two other ironclads were completed at the navy yard at Richmond, the CSS *Virginia II*, and the CSS *Fredericksburg.* The 197-foot *Virginia II* was protected by six inches of iron forward and five inches aft. She carried one 11-inch smoothbore, one 8-inch rifle, and two 6.4-inch Brooke rifles. The smaller *Fredericksburg* was similarly armored and armed.

3. This heavy fighting was the last offensive action of the James River Squadron. Three months later, the vessels were blown up as Richmond was evacuated.

CHAPTER 26

1. General Pegram was killed in the fight at Hatcher's Run, on February 6, 1865. His funeral was conducted at St. Paul's Church in Richmond, where only three weeks before he had married Miss Cary.

CHAPTER 27

1. The Davis family left Richmond on Friday, March 31, 1865.
2. The Battle of Five Forks, Virginia.
3. Richmond was evacuated on the night of April 2, 1865, and the Army of Northern Virginia began its long and painful trek to Appomattox.
4. This magnificent display of courage and devotion to duty which was displayed by the midshipmen from the Naval Academy, constitutes a fitting final chapter in the history of the Confederate States Navy.
5. Benjamin did indeed make good his escape and journeyed to England where he became one of the queen's counsels, practicing law in the House of Lords. He never returned to the South.

CHAPTER 28

1. President Davis and his wife, Varina, were taken prisoner by Union cavalry at Irwinville, Georgia on May 11, 1865. Davis was trying to make it to the Trans-Mississippi Department in order to continue the struggle.
2. Trenholm was finally released on parole on October 11, 1865.

EPILOGUE

1. Millege L. Monham, Jr., "The Rebel Reefer Furls His Last Sail," *The Louisiana Historical Quarterly*, October, 1928. Courtesy of Morgan P. Goldbaith, Jimmy's great granddaughter.

Index

Vincennes, USS, 42, 43, 45
Virginia (Merrimac), CSS, 48, 61, 63, 68, 150
Virginia II, CSS, 19, 176, 177

W

Wachusett, USS, 100
Wagner, Theodore, 161, 197, 198
Walker, Midshipman John T., 89, 107, 152
Warley, 1st Lt. Alexander F., 42, 48, 71, 73; commands CSS *Manassas*, 43–46

Water Witch, USS, 42, 43, 45
Wheeden, Assistant Surgeon Thomas J., 89, 131, 142
White Haven, England, 89, 91
White, Lt. Charles, 85
Wigfall, Senator Louis T., 26, 27, 189
Wildes, Frank, 18
Wilmington, North Carolina, 153, 156, 157, 159
Wright, Midshipman Augustus G., 168